# CONVERSATIONS ON *Success*

Insight Publishing Company
Sevierville, Tennessee

CONVERSATIONS ON *Success*

Published by Insight Publishing Company
P.O. Box 4189
Sevierville, Tennessee 37864


Cover design and book layout by Russ Hollingsworth.
Interviews conducted by David E. Wright.


*Printed in the United States of America*


ISBN: 1-885640-12-9

# Table Of Contents

# A Message From The Publisher

Some of my most rewarding experiences in business, and for that matter in my personal life, have been at meetings, conventions, or gatherings after the formal events have concluded. Inevitably, small groups of ten to fifteen men and women gather together to rehash the happenings of the day and to exchange war stories, recently heard jokes, or the latest gossip from their industry. It is in these informal gatherings where some of the best lessons can be learned.

Usually, in informal groups of professionals, there are those who clearly have lived through more battles and learned more lessons than the others. These are the men and women who are really getting the job done and everyone around the room knows it. When they comment on the topic of the moment, they don't just spout the latest hot theory or trend, and they don't ramble on and on without a relevant point. These battle scarred warriors have lessons to share that everyone senses are just a little more real, more relevant, and therefore worthy of more attention.

These are the kind of people we have recruited to offer their insights and expertise for *Conversations On Success*. The book is filled with frank and powerful discussions with men and women who are making a significant impact on their culture, in their field, and on their colleagues and clients. It is ripe with "the good stuff," as an old friend of mine used to always say. Inside these pages you'll find ideas, insights, strategies, and philosophies that are working with real people, in real companies, and under real circumstances.

It is our hope that you keep this book with you until you've dog-eared every chapter and made so many notes in the margins that you have trouble seeing the original words on the pages. There is treasure here. Enjoy digging!

**Interviews conducted by:**

David E. Wright
President, International Speakers Network

# Chapter 1

## BRIAN CARDEN

THE INTERVIEW

**David Wright (Wright)**

Today we are talking to Brian Carden. After almost 20 years in financial services, Brian has a broad base of knowledge and experience in which to have a conversation with his audience. He uses an array of experiences, examples, quotes, and facts to keep his listeners involved. His focus is to make the concepts of investments, insurance, money, and planning as simple to understand as possible. Brian has published many articles on personal finance for local and industrial publications in which he writes on a variety of topics including insurance and investments. He is a graduate of the University of Tennessee at Knoxville (UTK), a member of the National Speakers Association—Tennessee Chapter, and International Speakers Network (ISN). Brian says, "If I can not explain it on a bar napkin, we're not going to talk about it." Brian Carden, welcome to *Conversations on Success*.

**Brian Carden (Carden)**
Hello David.

**Wright**
Brian, what possessed you to get into the financial services business?

**Carden**
I must have been out of my mind. If you had told me when I was a freshman in 1976, that in 2003, I would have celebrated 20 years in the financial services business, I would have said you were crazy. But knowing what I know now, I would not have taken the first business course. Instead, I would have hightailed it straight to psychology. Because what I find right now is that people's emotions are really controlling the decisions about spending money and managing investments.

**Wright**
That's strange. Psychology is usually what people take when they haven't declared a major. Here's a question for you. Why do use the analogy of explaining finances on a bar napkin?

**Carden**
David, I find that people in my profession are highly intelligent and very well trained, but a lot of the time they are trained in product knowledge. It's very easy to get caught up in the technical aspects of certain insurance contracts, the analysis of stock, bonds and other investment options as well as retirement plans, etc. I believe people want things simple and I use the bar napkin analysis because there will inevitably be a salesperson in a restaurant somewhere. If that salesperson is unprepared to share an idea or a thought—and you've probably done this yourself—they used a napkin to jot down an idea or an explanation. So in my presentations, I like to use the bar napkin analogy so that I can keep it as simple as possible so anyone can comprehend what we are talking about.

**Wright**
I was reading one of your personal finance articles called, *How to Boil A Frog*. Where does that come from?

**Carden**

Oh, women love that one! The visual of that turns them off very quickly. That analogy has been used by a lot of people in my business. I've seen it in print on several occasions. I'd like to say that I created it first but, unfortunately, great ideas aren't often created, they are stolen. But then again, David, if you steal more than three ideas it's not plagiarism it's research. That idea kind of came about in explaining how to emotionally manage a volatile stock market. The analogy of how to boil a frog is this: If you put a frog in boiling water, it will jump out, but if put a frog in lukewarm water, and gradually turn the heat up, it will stay in there. The end result is you get what you want. We don't need to get to the visual, but you get the idea. So many people got into the market in the 1990's because it seemed easy. They quickly realized after "the bubble burst" in early 2000 that they either didn't have the risk tolerance or the patience for the stock market. So as soon as the market turned, they jumped out. Those people that will be successful in the market will stay in it over a long period of time by matching their risk tolerance to their time frame. Risk tolerance is simply an assessment of your emotions, your time frame, and how aggressive or conservative you are. Also, this is where a competent financial advisor becomes a key part of this success.

**Wright**

When you talk to most people are they interested in making money for cash flow or are they interested in things like long-term health care, putting their children through college, or paying off a mortgage? I guess the question is, do people make investments for long-term or short-term gains?

**Carden**

First off you've got to have a plan because we do not live in a "one size fits all" world. People spend more time planning their vacation than they do their retirement. If you are going on a trip you probably do is some research on your own first. If you don't get the answers you want you'll get a travel agent, if you are wise. The travel agent is going to put everything together to help you manage your expectations. Then he or she may take care of some things ahead of time, book some reservations, and give you a comfort zone so that your trip is a lot more enjoyable and a lot more predictable.

I think a lot of people right now are looking for a competent advisor that can provide a plan, or better yet, a roadmap to investing.

This is because in the 90's people planned to put money in the market, watch it grow, and get rich. That did not always happen and the two groups I see most affected are people that are either approaching retirement or are in retirement and parents who are putting their children through college. Emotionally the retirees feel like they've lost the last five years of their money. And to be honest with you it's all about cash flow. As a firm we say, "Let's see what kind of cash flow we can generate with what you have that will make you comfortable." Once we get them to that point, they are generally comfortable.

The other group that is concerned about this is parents putting their children through college. It's never a fun conversation to tell Mom and Dad that college costs are inflating on average between 6 and 10 percent a year. It would be nice to think that every child of every client that I have will get a scholarship, but unfortunately it's just not going to happen. Once again, these people with young teenagers have experience a five-year financial setback for putting that child in school.

**Wright**

Brian, you say that people want financial direction just like some people want to become better golfers, can you tell me what you mean by that?

**Carden**

Sure! Let's say that you want to be a better golfer. Now you know that the golf pro at your Country Club is a close personal friend of Tiger Woods and he says to you, "David, I tell you what, the clubs that Tiger won the Masters with are sitting in my closet, would you like to use them? Or would you rather me work with you and teach you everything that Tiger has taught me about swinging a golf club? Which would you rather have, Tiger Woods' clubs or Tiger Woods' swing?"

**Wright**

I'd rather have his swing.

**Carden**

No question. You've often heard the term "practice makes perfect." Well we take it one step further and say, "Perfect practice makes permanent." With what we do it's not about the financial clubs, it's about the process in which we use them. We all know that we need

4

certain types of insurance, certain types of investments, we need bankers, we need mortgage people, etc. We know that we need all these people in our lives. Inevitably selling financial clubs earns a living for these professionals. However, their advice comes with those clubs. What we do is sit down and build a plan. We help you swing those clubs so that when you need to use a particular financial club, you not only have the club, but you know exactly what to do with it when the time comes.

**Wright**

I understand one of your favorite quotes is from Satchel Paige, the old Negro Baseball Leagues pitcher. "It's not what you know that hurts you, it's what you know that just ain't so." How does that apply to financial services?

**Carden**

It's not the information that's out there that is harmful but the misinformation. We live in the information age. I'm sitting in front of the computer right now and I could go into my Google search engine and find any information that I could possibly want. Have you ever had someone call you with a question and then when you call him or her back they say, "David, I got the answer I was looking for." My question is, "But was it the answer you needed to hear?" We live in the information age where there are so many TV and radio channels and magazines that do nothing but talk about money. But there is no cookie-cutter way of doing things. In a nutshell, when I teach my classes and seminars I say, "Let's talk about what you know and let's see if it's really what you need to know."

**Wright**

By the way, I received the copy of *What I've Learned* that you sent me prior to this interview I just read one of the greatest things in it. The quote is this, "It's time in the stock market that will grow your assets, not timing in the market." Boy isn't that true!

**Carden**

It gets back to the how to a boil frog thing. If you took the best 30 days out of the market over the last 15 to 20 years, you would lose an annual average return of about 5 to 6 percent. The market as a whole has only averaged 10 to 12 over its entire history.

**Wright**

That's kind of scary.

**Carden**

Well in the market, people got overanxious and greedy. It was amazing in the late 90's when a 20 percent return wasn't good enough for a lot of people. We were sitting here going, "over the long haul it's only averaged 10 to 12 percent," and that's with being 100 percent in pure equities, of which, as you know now, people are scared to death.

**Wright**

I understand you have a new book due out this fall called *Conducting Your Financial Symphony.* How did that title come about and could you tell me a little about the book?

**Carden**

I have been carrying that title around in my brain for several years. I tend to be a collector of analogies and sayings, hence the *All I've Learned* collection that I sent you.

Think about going to the symphony. If you get there before the conductor takes the stage, the musicians are all focused on their individual instruments and they don't care what anyone else is doing. When the conductor comes up to the stage and raises the baton he immediately has everyone's total, undivided, and complete attention.

Now consider an individual standing up there with his or her pen, which signs contracts and agreements, insurance policies, investment accounts, and all those other things. That individual can look at his or her banker, attorney, real estate agent, mortgage banker, stock broker, financial planner, life insurance agent, property and casualty agent, and all of the other varieties of financial people who are in his or her life. If that individual were to put all of those people in a conference room sit at the head of the table, how would their financial symphony sound?

**Wright**

Yes, I see your point.

**Carden**

The key thing about the conductor is that he or she is the only one that has the complete sheet of music. As advisors we like to fit in by helping you put together a complete piece of music that you not only understand but can emotionally embrace and logically follow.

**Wright**

Brian, you have said that owning a business is like a house of mirrors. Getting in is easy and a lot of fun for a while, but it's knowing when to get out and how to get out that is the hard part.

**Carden**

Exactly.

**Wright**

What do you mean by that?

**Carden**

I work with a lot of business owners the mantra of a lot of them right now is, "You know Brian, it is just not fun anymore." You've probably heard business owners say, "You know David, my retirement is my business." In a lot of ways, their business is like the goose that laid the golden eggs. Every year that business lays the golden egg in terms of cash flow to the owner and because of that he has been able to enjoy a great life. A lot of the people in Thomas Stanley's books *The Millionaire Next Door and The Millionaire Mind* fit into this scenario.

In order to get their retirement out of the business, in order to get those golden eggs, sometimes you've got to kill the goose. In a lot of situations the goose (or business) is not worth a whole lot without the owner being involved in the business. Another good point of reference is that 70 percent of all family owned businesses do not make it to the next generation and 90 percent don't make it to the third generation according to the Small Business Association's statistics issued in 2001.

What we try to provide and what business owners need to understand is what Stephen Covey says in his book *The Seven Habits of Highly Effective People*, "Begin with the end in mind." So many people get into business because it's easy, it's what they love to do, it's their passion, and they are good at it. Then they build up an entity and eventually need to create an exit strategy. Actually, if you do "begin with the end in mind," the planning for getting out of the business should be as important as the planning for starting it. Many of us know this as retirement. So we need to find a way to create that exit strategy so that we can continue the business, allow the owner to re-tire out of the business, and maintain the cash flow that he or she and the spouse enjoyed during their working years.

**Wright**

There are two things that I put together. One was from the copy that you sent me about what you had learned and the other from your, *How to Boil a Frog* article. It has to do with emotions. In *What I've Learned* you say, "When emotion and logic butt heads, emotion always wins." I've felt that through the years. Like you, I have taken too many psychology courses. More importantly, in your article *How To Boil A Frog*, one thing that really caught my eye said, "The key emotion is patience, and being patient when it comes to investing has typically been rewarding for long-term investors." Boy that's good news isn't it?

**Carden**

Yes and no. Yes because almost every article written on money and investing mentions that the longer one stays invested in the market, the lower the risk they create for themselves. No because we live in a "microwave society." I'm sure that when you were growing up your mother actually cooked dinner. Maybe she even made things from scratch. She probably added a dash of one ingredient and a smidgen of another. I think the only things they make from scratch anymore are biscuits from Hardee's. But your mother probably pre-pared a "sit down" meal for the family. Today, most households throw something in the microwave and four minutes later they've got din-ner. So I think we've kind of grown to become an "I want it all, I want it now" type of society. And that patience thing...well what's that say-ing, "Lord, give me patience, but give it to me quick."

**Wright**

You are exactly right, you never harvest in the same season that you plant.

**Carden**

Another thing we have seen is that consumers tend to get short-sighted with regards to their returns. Those that bought in the 90's supposedly did so with a "long term perspective." Those are the ones that are on the sidelines right now. As of this writing, only 30 percent of the dollars in the market are in stocks and equity mutual funds according to a study dated 11/30/02 by Strategic Insight. The remainder is equally split between bonds and money markets.

Remember that according to the benchmarks of the stock market, the average annual return of a 100 percent equity portfolio is only 10 to 12 percent. The word to remember here is "average." This includes some "go-go" periods like the 80's and 90's and it also includes some "low-low" times like the Great Depression. If I have my head in a hot oven and my feet in the freezer, is it a fair statement to say, "On average, my body temperature is okay?"

**Wright**

So, one of the most important factors in investing is patience?

**Carden**

No question, planning and patience are the keys.

**Wright**

You are also well known for saying "Cash is King." What does that mean?

**Carden**

Well a lot of people in the South still think Elvis is King. However, in any situation that happens in your life including the birth of your children, the loss of a loved one, a good opportunity, or a bad opportunity cash is king. For example you've been employed with one company for 20 or 25 years and your job is eliminated. What you do and how you react in that interim period between your eliminated job and your next job all boils down to how much cash and cash equivalents you have and how fast can you get your hands on them. So many people that we meet today have their cash in two places: their company 401(k) and their home equity. Both are two very illiquid places unless you have planned ahead.

A great example of a cash equivalent is a home equity loan. However, try qualifying for a home equity loan if you are unemployed or disabled. Try pulling money out of your 401(k) and getting minimal tax treatment at any point before age 59.5. I think oftentimes the reason people don't have appropriate savings accounts or money market accounts is because money market funds do not come with some type of compensation to the advisor that recommends them. Obviously there is an incentive for me to sell you a number of investment options because I get compensated. However, if I set up a money market for you to accumulate cash for emergency funds there is no compensation involved there. Where does the motivation lie?

You have to have discipline to have a savings account. You have to physically go to the bank, stand in front of a teller, and give them your money. The reason 401(k) plans are so successful, pure and simple, is that the dollars come right out of your check before you see it. So it's that "pay yourself first" attitude that you embrace for your savings just like your retirement assets. If you have to make a trip to the bank to put money in savings, inevitably you are paying yourself last and by the time you get ready to pay yourself, you probably don't have any money left. In the 50's and 60's, U.S. Savings Bonds were the preferred method of saving for a lot of families. They worked simply because they were payroll deducted right from your check and the money never hit the household account.

**Wright**

Brian, in the presentations that I've seen you do you talk about Nobel Prize winning studies. What are these studies based on?

**Carden**

Well, let's get back to the emotions for a second. There was a Nobel Prize winning study done in the mid-90's that analyzed 100 of the largest retirement plans in the United States and their outcome. This study is known in our industry as "Modern Portfolio Theory." What the study said was that only 2 to 3 percent of the success in the market can be specifically attributed to what particular stock, bond, or other investment vehicle you actually purchase. Only 3 to 4 percent would be due to when you bought that particular security. 94 percent of your success, which is pretty good odds, is due to how your money is diversified over different classes of assets, which include large companies, small companies, growth companies, value companies, some international, and maybe some fixed income. That money would be diversified based on your time frame and your emotion or your risk tolerance. So if I'm going to Vegas, I've got a 94 percent chance of being successful and I ask you to give me $1,000.00. David, would you give it to me?

**Wright**

94 percent? I believe I would.

**Carden**

Okay, if you take the 6 to 7 percent that we talked about, which is investment selection and market timing, that's pretty much why the day traders are no longer around. Once again it gets back to emotions and it gets back to patience. The asset allocation model has traditionally worked, but only over a reasonable period of time.

I think a lot of people right now are feeling that maybe they were over allocated in equities and basically just too aggressive. In reality, now that they physically lost that amount of money, or they've lost the last five years, they are recognizing that maybe they shouldn't have been that aggressive to start with. That's the hard part right now. We have to be a coach and say we can do what you want to do; we just want you to step back up to the plate.

Let's back up real quick to the Nobel Prize, because it is something that will help tie this interview all together. A man that's never had an economics class won the 2002 Nobel Prize in Economics. Guess what he does for a living David?

**Wright**

What?

**Carden**

He is a Psychologist.

**Wright**

You're kidding? I'd like to ask you a question that you may not want to get into it but it has really caught my eye. You said, "Before doing business with someone, do not be afraid to ask him or her how do you get paid." What do you mean by that?

**Carden**

That's a great question. Based on the amount of damage control our firm finds itself doing with prospective clients, it is something that is not asked nearly enough. We have touched on it briefly earlier in this conversation, but it bears repeating. I think it's a fair question to ask how someone gets paid. Let's say for example you came to me seven years ago, in 1996, and you had a sizeable amount of money to roll over from a 401(k) plan. So I met with you, shared my philosophies with you, and we agreed to work together. With a commission-based compensation arrangement, many advisors will tend to take it all up front. You give me money, I invest your money, I get paid, and then there might not be a whole lot of accountability because obviously I have to go find more David Wrights to work with to get paid again. But if I sit down and say David, I will help you with this investment and I will work with you using a fee-based compensation arrangement. This means I'm going to charge you a very small percentage of your account balance, but I'm going to charge you that every year. If you lose money, does my compensation go down?

**Wright**

Absolutely, it goes to zero if I lose money.

**Carden**

Exactly. Well it's highly improbable based on past performances that you're going to lose 100 percent, but if you lose 15 percent of your account balance in a year, does my compensation go down 15 percent?

**Wright**

I say yes.

**Carden**

If you make money, does my compensation go up?

**Wright**

Absolutely.

**Carden**

If you know that I'm getting paid as we go, is our relationship going to be important to me, the advisor?

**Wright**

It's going to be a partnership.

**Carden**

Exactly. Am I going to pay attention to the David Wright's of the world in which I am working on a daily basis for them?

**Wright**

I see what you are talking about now. You say that financial institutions make the greatest amount of profit on the products for which consumers feel that they get the best deal. Can you explain to me what you mean?

**Carden**

Sure, that's simple. A great example that is often written in print and said in the media is that the only type of life insurance to own is term insurance. And I use term insurance as an example because you can buy a lot of coverage for not a lot of money. However, it has become a commodity product. Every time you flip on your computer and every time you watch a television show, someone is trying to sell you some type of term insurance.

We sell a lot of term insurance in our firm, but we do it as part of a client's plan and we do it only when the plan calls for insurance. A 1993 study done by Penn State University says, "Of 100 term insurance contracts issued, only one percent of those contracts issued resulted in a check in the form of death benefits being paid to the beneficiary."

So here are consumers thinking I'm buying this life insurance for a very inexpensive price. However 99 percent of those contracts issued are not going to help the family. So if you think about the transfer of wealth involved the insurance company gets to keep the premium, they get to invest the premium, and then they get to keep the death benefit that was set aside in their reserves when the client cancels the insurance.

It's one thing if you actually have enough money set aside and you've invested the difference so that you don't need that death benefit. However, this strategy takes a lot of discipline from not only a financial and budgeting standpoint, but from an emotional (patience) standpoint as well. Add to that if you've lost the last 5 years of accumulation, that you may find yourself in a deficit going, "Wow, I need that insurance." If something happens to me, what happens to my family and loved ones?

**Wright**

Brian, I really appreciate the time you've taken to talk to me today. It has been really, really informative as far as I'm concerned.

**Carden**

I appreciate it, sir.

**Wright**

We have been talking today to Brian Carden who is a financial advisor with Securities America Advisors, Inc. Brian started in the financial services industry in 1983. His mission is to help his clients reach their financial and personal objectives by applying ethical strategies of wealth accumulation and distribution, and to provide the highest level of professionalism, honesty, and integrity. That's a lot of benefits for your clients. Thank you so much for talking to me today.

**Carden**
Thank you, David.

---

## About The Author

Brian Carden brings 20 years of experience in investments, insurance and fringe benefit planning to business owners and entrepreneurs. Through his affiliations with accountants, attorneys, bankers, management consultants and other business associates, Brian brings a wealth of knowledge and financial strategies to the podium. Brian has spoken to such groups as the Society of Chartered Life Underwriters, the Association of Insurance & Financial Advisors, the Women's Society of Realtors, the Association for Education for Young Children and several chapters of the Tennessee Society of CPA's. He is a member of NSA Tennessee Chapter and International Speakers Network.

**Brian Carden**
Carden Solutions
370 Mallory Station Road, Suite 511
Franklin, TN 37067
Phone: 615.221.1294
www.cardensolutions.com

# Chapter 2

## BRIAN TRACY

## THE INTERVIEW

### David E. Wright (Wright)

Brian Tracy is one of America's leading authorities on the development of human potential and personal effectiveness. He is a dynamic and entertaining speaker with a wonderful ability to inform and inspire audiences towards peak performance and high levels of achievement. He addresses more than 400 thousand men and women each year on the subjects of personal and professional development including the executives and staff of IBM, Arthur Anderson, McDonald-Douglas, and the Million Dollar Round Table. His exciting talks and seminars on leadership, sales management, and personal effectiveness bring about immediate changes and long-term results. Brian has a Bachelors Degree in communication and a Masters Degree and is a chairman of Brian Tracy International, a human resource company based in San Diego, California, with affiliates throughout America and in 31 countries worldwide. Brian Tracy, thank you for being with us today.

**Brian Tracy (Tracy)**

It's a pleasure to be with you.

**Wright**

In a recent article, you write that life is a continuous succession of both large and small problems. When you become a success, you simply exchange one type of problem for another. Can you tell our listeners and readers what you mean?

**Tracy**

Well, the bottom line is that everything in life is a series of problems and your success in life is totally determined by your ability to solve the problems that you meet on your level. What we have found is that problems with a solution orientation are the hallmark of the most successful people. The successful people think about solutions all the time and unsuccessful people think and talk about problems. The most wonderful thing is that everybody desires to be effective. Being effective means you can deal with the difficulties of your life. In fact, Colin Powell said, "Leadership is the ability to solve problems and success is the ability to solve problems." The only thing that stands between you and your goals are problems and obstacles. And the wonderful thing is the more you focus on solutions; the more solutions you will come up with, the smarter and more effective you become. So you find that all successful people are good at solving the problems that they meet at their particular level. Once you solve a problem, all you get is the right to solve even bigger and more difficult problems, which of course pay more and offer more opportunities for success.

**Wright**

So it's like exercise throughout life. The more you do, the better at it you get.

**Tracy**

Absolutely.

**Wright**

You know most people define success in a general way that almost always includes setting goals, but you seem to go a step beyond by asking questions such as "What are you made of? When the chips are down, what lies at the very core of your character?" Are character issues involved in success?

**Tracy**

More than anything you can imagine. You see, in order to be successful, you have got to be motivated. But in order to be motivated, to overcome all the obstacles and difficulties and persist to the challenges that you face, what you are striving for has to be consistent with who you are inside. And so the starting point that we do in our long-term seminars is values clarification. We have people sit down, think out, and analyze: Who am I? What do I really care about? What's important to me? What do I love? What am I excited about? What am I fascinated by? We can only be motivated to achieve great success when what you're doing on the outside is in harmony with who you are on the inside.

**Wright**

You know, I don't know how far I am behind in reading your books, but I read about a 90 page hardback—that I read last year or maybe seven or eight months ago— having to do with how to get a job and make more money.

**Tracy**

Yes.

**Wright**

Do you remember that one?

**Tracy**

Yes, absolutely. It's called *How to Get Paid More and Promoted Faster*.

**Wright**

That's it. That's it. You talked a lot about character and that was a great, great book. You talked a lot about becoming a better employee. It was just great stuff.

**Tracy**

Absolutely, well, thank you. What it basically says is if you really want to get ahead in life, the secret to success is to look for a way to contribute at a higher level. Look for a way to serve other people at a higher level. Whatever your job is, you can find a way to do it better, so that you are putting in more than you are taking out. The great majority of people don't understand this. They think that we are all lazy. They think that if they want me to do more, they should pay be more. No, no, that's not the way it works. First, you do more, you contribute more value, and then they'll line up to pay you more.

**Wright**

Yeah, I was getting a lot of college people and young people, asking me about making important decisions. I told them I didn't know and then gave them your website and told them to find the book, because it was a great book.

**Tracy**

Well, thank you.

**Wright**

How important is creating wealth to personal achievement; and is achievement and success always tied together?

**Tracy**

You know there's a whole bunch of definitions. I think success is being happy with what you have. Achievement is getting what you want. In life, human beings have no limit to what they want. Human beings want so many things. Their favorite word is "more", we want more. The only limit on the *more* that we can get is either the limit that we impose on ourselves with our own thinking, or the limits that we perceive are in the world around us. The fact of the matter is that virtually all of our limits are within ourselves. So what we encourage people to do is to decide how much you want to earn and then increase it by ten. All right, if you can decide what you want to accomplish in life and then dramatically increase it. I was listening to a really neat discussion just yesterday with Vic Conan and he was saying some people set a goal on a 15-foot boat and they get it. Some people set a goal on a 150-foot boat, and they get it as well. We see nature as an equal opportunity employer, because nature doesn't care what you want. If you want a big boat, you get a big boat. If you want a little boat, you get a little boat. So you can accomplish vastly more than you had ever accomplished before simply by setting bigger, bigger goals for yourself.

**Wright**

I've seen people in goal setting workshops stare at a blank sheet of paper, and I've also seen people write goals such as, "Establish more relationships", or "Help make the world more peaceful." Are these nebulous thoughts really goal setting that leads to success?

**Tracy**

You know there's a little gremlin deep inside our subconscious mind that sabotages us if we are not careful. The whole point of this little gremlin is to keep our actions on the outside consistent with what we have fed into ourselves or believed in the past. So if we don't believe that we are very worthy, we're not very capable, other people are better than we are, or we lack discipline or something else, when it comes to goal setting, this little gremlin will sabotage us by setting goals for us that aren't really goals at all. They are just fantasies. I'll give you an example. I had a woman come up to me in a seminar and she said, "Well, I've decided on my major goal." I said, "Well, what is it?" She said, "World peace." I said, "Well, that's not a goal at all, that's a fantasy. Everybody wants world peace; even the heads of the super powers want world peace. That's not a goal, that's just a fantasy." She said, "Well, that's my goal. I'm going to set that as my big goal and work toward it." I said, "No, no, by setting that as a goal you end up setting no goals at all." I said, "Because just between you and I, if you are the head of a major super power, then you can have very little effect on world peace. And unless you feel that you have the ability to become the head of a major super power, then I would suggest that you set a goal that is within your reach. You can work on world peace, that's fine. But it's not a goal. It's sort of like brushing your teeth in the morning. It's something that you do but it's not a goal that you set for your life."

**Wright**

Right. When you talk about success and achievement, you advise your listeners or readers to analyze their beliefs. Can you tell us how this exercise might help?

**Tracy**

This is the most important single part of it. In fact, I'm working on a new book now called *Change Your Thinking, Change Your Life.* What it basically says is that your beliefs lie at the core. The values and beliefs lie at the core of your personality. And that you don't believe what you see, but you see what you already believe. Especially about yourself. One of the most important things that a parent can do is to raise a child so they have very, very strong positive beliefs about themselves and their abilities. One of the most dangerous things that can happen is that we can accept beliefs that aren't true. You know the old saying, "It ain't what a man knows that hurts him. It's what he knows that ain't true." Sometimes we know things that ain't true. We say, "Well, you know, I'll never be financially independent because I didn't go to college and nobody in my family has ever been wealthy." That's nonsense. Almost every single person is financially independent today.

What you need to do is test your beliefs. What I encourage people to do is imagine that your beliefs are not true at all. The worst of all beliefs are your self-limiting beliefs. These are beliefs that hold you back. These are self-limiting beliefs where you sell yourself short and you say, "Well, I couldn't do this", or "I couldn't do that." Or you might say, "I'm not good enough for this", or "I'm not good enough for that." The fact of the matter is that you are as good as anybody you'll ever meet. There are virtually no limits to what you can accomplish, except the limits that you have set for yourself. We encourage people to throw them all out and imagine that you didn't have these beliefs. Imagine that you have all the time, all the money, all the intelligence, all the experience, all the ability, and all the contacts, that you could do, be, or have anything you would want in life. If you had no limitations at all, what goal would you set for yourself? That's where you begin.

**Wright**

I have often heard repeat exactly what you just said. "I can't do it; "I don't have a college degree", or whatever. I remember many years ago hearing a man—before I started listening to every tape I could get my hands on—telling me that the smartest person in the whole world is a man standing in the Library of Congress with the knowledge of how to use the card catalogue system. I mean, it's all there.

**Tracy**

Yes, absolutely. I was just reading an article about Dewey who developed the Dewey Decimal System for cataloging books. It transformed the entire world of reading.

**Wright**

Right. There are two suggestions that you make that seem to stop or perhaps slow down most people who try to implement goal setting, you know their success strategy. One is to visualize your goals continually. The other is to unlock unborn creativity. I've heard many people say, "I'm not creative at all." Can you give us some suggestions that will help us visualize and be creative?

**Tracy**

First of all with regards to visualization, everybody visualizes. When you daydream, when you're driving along, when you're thinking of what you are going to have for dinner, when you think about your problems, everybody is visualizing. The key is what is called control visualizing. Keep your visual images consistent with what you want, because the picture of what you see on the inside is what you'll experience on the outside. So therefore, keep visualizing and imagining what you want to have in life. Remember, winners think about what they want, talk about what they want, imagine what they want, and think about how they can get it. But non-winners—unsuccessful people think and talk about what they don't like. They think about the people they are mad at. They think about the problems they have. They think about their worries. They think about what might go wrong and surprise, surprise.

Henry Ford said that if you believe you can do a thing or you believe you cannot, in either case you are probably right. If you visualize something that you can do, you'll move toward doing that and being that. If you visualize something or a problem that you have, you will increase that. There's a law that says whatever you dwell upon grows in your life. Whatever you concentrate on, whatever you continually think about actually begins to expand in your life. It's almost like a flower or a weed and you're feeding it with your visual images. Here's one of the ways that you can unlock your creativity. Take your biggest goal or problem today and write it at the top of a page in the form of a question. Let us say your goal is to double your income in the next 24 months. It's a reasonable goal. So at the top of the page you write what can I do to double my income in the next 24 months. It is a very simple, specific question. Then force yourself to write 20 after it. I call this mind storming. I teach it all over the world. I teach it to executive groups. I walk people through it. I've taught it to entire roomfuls of IBM executives and staff. With this mind storming exercise, just write down 20 answers to the question about your biggest goal or problem. There must be a minimum of 20, and it's always very hard the first time you do it. But it starts to loosen up your creativity. It's like warming up your muscles. The more ideas you come up with, the more ideas you come up with. Your brain starts to work, your blood starts to pump into your brain, and your brain cells start to light up like lights being turned on in a darkened room. You start to become brighter, and you see more and more possibilities. The next thing you do is you take your list after you've got at least 20 answers, and I generate now 30 or 40 answers to every question I come up with. What you do is you pick one. You just pick one answer and say, "All right, which one of these am I going to activate immediately?" Remember the key to creativity is to come up with the idea and take action on it immediately and get feedback. Generate the idea, take action, and get feedback. All successful people are intentionally action oriented. And all unsuccessful people are not. If you take action on an idea, what happens is you get more ideas, you get more energy, and you get more feedback. Look for solutions which is another way of using this exercise, when you think about solutions all the time, you get more solutions.

**Wright**

I've noticed down through the last few years that people who have this ability to visualize and that are creative also have the ability, since that visualization is so crystal clear in their mind, to communicate it to me. And sometimes I just get jerked into their goal setting programs and I start helping them because I understand what they are trying to do. It would be almost impossible to follow someone who didn't know where they were going, I would think.

**Tracy**

You know, the mark of leadership in over 3300 studies of leaders done over the ages, they find that leaders have two qualities. The first quality that is common to all men and women who become leaders is vision. They have a vision of what they want to accomplish. They can see the future and then begin today to make it a reality. So vision, visualize is the mark of leadership, and the more of it you do the better you get at it. By the way, the second quality is courage. They have the courage to take action on the vision. They step forward and they give it a try, give it a shot. It's the most amazing thing. If you have the clear vision, people will follow you. If you take action, people will help you.

**Wright**

When we discuss success, it's difficult to leave out the United States Armed Forces. I mean, look what they are doing now, and look what they've done in the recent past. One of your latest books, *Victory,* is a great read by the way. Could you tell us a little bit about military principles of strategy practiced by our great leaders throughout the ages?

**Tracy**

Well, when I was a young man, I began to read about great leaders. It was very helpful to me, and I found later that many people who are successful later on in life read a lot of biographies of successful people when they are young. When you read a biography, a story about someone else, you cannot help but soak up some of their qualities. You absorb some of the qualities that you most admire. There's a rule just like the moth goes to the flame, we move in the direction of people and qualities that we admire as young people. If you study successful people, you become like them. So I began to study military leaders. I began all the way back with Cyrus the Great of Persia 600 years B.C. and all through the Peloponnesian Wars, the Punic Wars, and Hannibal and Caesar, and then the great generals like Napoleon. I even studied the modern world like Patton and Rommel and McArthur. And you find the more you study the great generals, the more you learn that they have certain practices that lead to victory. All the military colleges in the world, Annapolis, West Point, Sandhurst, all teach the 12 principles of military strategy which my book, *Victory*, is based on. This is basically the foundation training for officers, and the 12 principles lead to victory and the failure of one single principle can lead to defeat. So what I do is I show how these 12 principles that lead to great victory against overwhelming odds far from home are the same principles that lead to success in business, in selling, and in personal life. They are rules of thumb like two plus two is four. Stop at stop signs. They are just basic rules of thumb that all top people use over and over again to achieve extraordinary things.

**Wright**

I was glad that most of the people in Houston yesterday, after the catastrophe of the seven astronauts, the first thing that they said is, "We must go on."

**Tracy**

Yes, absolutely, a mark of courage, we must go on.

**Wright**

I seem to get the impression from your best selling cassette program, *The Power of Clarity*, that as we consider a success path, clarity seems to speed things up for us. Am I reading that right?

**Tracy**

Absolutely, I personally believe that success if 90 or 95 percent cloudy means you are clear about a whole variety of things. For the last two years, I have been teaching it and preaching it. I do an advance-coaching program for successful entrepreneurs who earn more than $100 thousand a year. In this program, the very first thing we start off with is a series of exercises. Even before they come to the program, they start to become very, very clear about two things: Who they are—going back to your discussion of values. Who are you really? What do you care about? What are you good at? What do you love to do? Where would you like to be in the future? What excites you? The second thing is priority above a goal that you will need to achieve to fulfill the kind of life that's possible for you. Then we talk about priority of skills. What skills will you need? What do you need to be absolutely excellent at doing in order the achieve the goals? What habits will you need? What behaviors every single day will you need? What priorities will you set on your time? What's the single most important thing you can do each minute that will help you to achieve the goals that fulfill your vision? The greater priority you have, I have found is that everybody who comes through my program first of all develops priority, second of all doubles and triples their income. One of my graduates after one year just told me last week he increased his income by 580 percent. His limit was 40. In one year he increased his income 580 percent simply by developing absolute clarity about who he was and what he wanted.

**Wright**

Brian, when you talk or write about achieving success, you use phrases such as, take charge of your life, reprogram your mind, unlock the powers of your subconscious mind, and release your brakes. Can achievement in success be reduced to a function of psychology?

**Tracy**

Oh yes, very much so. In fact, it's funny, just before I spoke to you, I was reading, studying in psychology this morning, and one of the things I came across was the almost routine that psychology has found. It's that people are clear about their goals. They are clear about their values. They see themselves as responsible agents. They take action in the direction of their goals. They solve the problems that are between them and their goals. They get the cooperation of others to move toward their goals. There's a simple series of things that all successful people do over and over again. The turning point in my life came when I was about 20 years old. I realized then because I was a high school dropout, I was working at a laboring job, I had no money, I was broke, I was cold, I was alone and I realized that I was responsible. I was responsible for my whole life that everything and anything that ever happened to me was going to be up to me. That changed my life at that time. I learned later that the turning point in every person's life is when they finally stop making excuses, stop blaming their problems on their past or their childhood or their boss or anything else. They start saying, "I am responsible. I am where I am and what I am because of myself, and by gum, I can do, be, have anything I want, but it's up to me." That is the turning point in life.

**Wright**

So you can trace it back to a time then?

**Tracy**

Yes, absolutely.

**Wright**

Lastly, if you could give advice to someone who has never thought about success in terms of their control over it, what would you say to them?

**Tracy**

The fact is that we are living in the very best time of all of human history today. We have never lived in a better country. We have never lived in a better time. The OECD, the Organization for Economic Co-operation Development, in Paris just announced that America is the most entrepreneurial country in the world. Their conclusion was that it is more possible to be successful in America today than it ever has been at any other time in any place in all of human history. I have many people, many friends who have come over from different countries, and they walk around like kids in a candy store at Christmas. They say, "You know, if you can't do it here, you can't do it anywhere. This is the best place in the world." I mean, they are just smiling. They say people here have no idea how hard it is to accomplish something somewhere else in the world. I was just in Moscow recently. They told me to start a business, to start the smallest business like a hair salon or a shoe shine stand takes six to eight months of applications, it takes hundreds of thousands of dollars of payoffs, approvals, bribes, and permits. It takes about 110, 120 different signatures from different bureaucrats to start any kind of a business. Here in America you can start a business right now. You can say, "By gum, I'm going to start a business, and you are in business." Legally you don't even have to register it if you name it after yourself. You can name the business after yourself and you're in business. You can say, "Well, I think I'm going to start a company. I'm going to call it, well let's see, David Wright Enterprises. Good, now I'm in business." You are now in business legally. You can now rent offices, open bank accounts, buy and sell things. I mean, you're in business. This is a dream. It's never been possible before. So I would say to everybody listening that there is no limit to what you can do, be, and have except the limits you place on yourself. When you stop placing those limits on yourself, then you have no limits.

**Wright**

I get the impression that on the bottom line, everything that you have been doing in the past few years that I have been listening to and reading is pointing towards people controlling their own destiny, which is really a gracious way to spend your time.

**Tracy**

Yes, that's all I've ever talked about is that you do control your own destiny. Now, here's an important thing to understand. Will it be easy? No. Will it be hard? Yes. Will it be continually hard? Yes, it will always be difficult. It always takes extra effort to rise above the ordinary, but the wonderful thing is when the going gets tough, the tough gets going. The stronger you become, the stronger you are. And there's a price that you have to pay for success, and it's overcoming adversity. It's picking yourself up, dusting yourself off and carrying on. The more of it you do, the better you get. All successful people you find have a particular set, they've got a particular way about them because they've had to overcome tremendous adversities to get to where they are. If you don't look for it to be easy, it will be much easier on you. If whenever you get knocked down, you say, "Well this goes with the territory. I want to be a big success so I'm going to have all kinds of setbacks and difficulties." So you just pick yourself up and carry on. You get stronger and stronger, and better and better. Your self-esteem and self-respect goes up and pretty soon you reach the point where you become unstoppable.

**Wright**

Well, Brian, you know it's always a privilege and a real pleasure for me just to talk to you. Every time I do talk to you, I've got this feeling that I want all my family members here on the speakerphone so everybody can get it. I wish you the greatest of success as you go about leading development and human potential in this country and other countries. You're just one of the best.

**Tracy**

Thank you, and you know if anybody wants my free newsletters, my free audio programs, free quotes and things like that, just come to **briantracy.com**. All my books and programs are on there. There are also free newsletters that we send you every week on personal success, financial success, business success, and sales success. There are all kinds of free things because we want to help you to be more successful. The key to that is to take in new ideas, continue to learn new ideas that will help you to be even more than what you are today.

**Wright**

The free quotes on there are worth the surfing. I really enjoy your newsletter too. By the way, one person I told to go to your website misspelled your name. They put an "e" in Tracy. The correct address is www.briantracy.com.

**Tracy**

That's right.

**Wright**

Brian, thank you so much for being with us today.

**Tracy**

Well, David, it has been a pleasure. Thank you.

One of the world's top success motivational speakers, Brian Tracy is the author of many books and audio tape seminars, including *The Psychology of Achievement, The Luck Factor, Breaking The Success Barrier, Thinking Big, and Success Is A Journey.*

**Brian Tracy**

*www.BrianTracy.com*

# Chapter 3

CYNTHIA HERNANDEZ KOLSKI

## THE INTERVIEW

**David E. Wright (Wright)**

Today we are talking to Cynthia Hernandez Kolski. Cynthia formed Communication Education, Inc., in 1999 after recovering from a life threatening accident. Cynthia began her career as a nurse where she discovered the essential link between mind, body, and spiritual health. With over 30 years in the field of human resource development, Cynthia has developed a wide breadth of knowledge and an energetic and hands-on training style. She has worked in partnership with police, judicial, and governmental agencies, and community organizations alike. Her past experiences include such diverse activities as conducting workshops for intercity gang members, caring for the terminally ill, and serving as a surrogate mother for abused children. Cynthia has presented to national and international groups. Some topics on which she presents include effective communication skills, parenting education, team building, diversity, and conflict resolution. She is committed to the personal and professional growth of her workshop participants, which is evident in her interactive and comprehensive program materials. Cynthia, welcome to *Conversations on Success*!

### Cynthia Hernandez Kolski (Hernadez Kolski)

Thank you, David. I'm honored to speak with you and be a part of this book.

### Wright

You know from your bio, I see your past experiences have led in many directions. Can you give us some highlights?

### Hernandez Kolski

It's my pleasure. Throughout the years I have had an opportunity to wear a variety of "hats" as they say. My favorite, of course, and most important is being called Mom. As you have noted, I've worked in the medical field for over 21 years as an office nurse. I worked for private doctors in pediatrics, obstetric, and gynecology. I also worked as a nursing supervisor. My children, Christina and Joseph, were very young when I realized that in spite of my nursing background and my husband's psych degree, I really needed and wanted more to prepare myself for raising them to their full potential.

So, I went out and became certified, and started teaching four different parenting education programs. One of the places that I taught parenting classes was at a Chicago Community College where I eventually became an Assistant Dean. Being a nurse in the academic arena, gave me the opportunity to be part of a team where I wrote the Alzheimer's CareGiver book for the State of Illinois, along with two certified nursing assistant programs for other community colleges. That developed into a whole medical-health care division at the college. While teaching at the college, I also had an opportunity to be part of a company that created and presented programs for our youth and for women in business. I think it was an excellent stepping-stone for my future in owning my own company. And when I turned fifty, I was participating in a conference in Washington, D.C., at the White House, and there was speaker talking about NAFTA. I thought what a great opportunity to begin an importing business. So, for a brief time, I was part of a company that imported from Mexico to the United States. It was challenging to see if I could build a whole company from scratch, which I did. Unfortunately, as you mentioned earlier, it was because of my serious accident that I was unable to work for a long while. During that recovery, I had to limit myself to how much work I could do. I then started working for a company that offered public speaking and training. It was a great opportunity for me to practice my own material at the same time. From there I started my own company.

**Wright**

You know as I am talking to you, it's September 1st, 2003. Yesterday was Sunday, and Parade Magazine goes through all over the country now in most large city newspapers. The feature on the Parade Magazine yesterday was the fact that there were so few nurses, and what a great field it was to get into.

**Hernandez Kolski**

Yes, I agree.

**Wright**

Of course, you got out of nursing. Why do most people get out of nursing, do you think?

**Hernandez Kolski**

Remember, I was a nurse in the 70's, and at that time it was a career that limited itself. As I was passing through the different paths in my life, other areas came open to me and I followed them. Opportunities came before me that I never anticipated and had no idea I could accomplish certain things until I faced them. I naively did not put limits on myself and found that I could achieve anything I put my mind to. I expanded myself without realizing it.

**Wright**

Did you find it difficult changing career fields?

**Hernandez Kolski**

I didn't find it difficult. I believe the opportunities, that were before me led me from one career to another. The path just seemed to naturally flow. The nursing prepared me for the parenting education classes, and that also helped me in writing the various programs when I was at the college, and that also led me into speaking and to training. When I approached those city colleges to do parenting education, I had no ambition to becoming the Assistant Dean. I was honored and I felt very privileged and I served in that position for over ten years. So teaching parenting education was the only thing I actually wanted to do because that helped me in raising my children. I still learn a great deal from the parents that participate, you know.

**Wright**

Raising children is a very challenging task. Do you believe you have succeeded well with your children?

**Hernandez Kolski**

That's an answer David, that would best be answered by my children. Joseph, who is now 30 and is a promising actor doing very well in his own career. And Christina, 25, a very beautiful young lady, who has a wonderful career herself as an MSW. David, I believe two things. I believe that the hardest task anyone is ever going to have in their life is staying happily married, and the second is successfully raising their children. I think it's unfortunate in our society people still have a tendency to look down on others who seek help to improve either of these techniques. If you look at it, it's necessary for us to have a driver's license in order to drive. You have to have a certificate or a degree if we want to teach publicly and often times we even have to have to pass a test in order to get a job. Yet we have no training or preparation mandated for becoming a parent. We can only teach what we have been taught. God has been very, very good to me. He gave me two beautiful children, two bright children, and two, that I believe, are outstanding children. You know, we are talking about my children and I sound like a proud mother, and I am. Joe and Chrissy have worked really hard to achieve everything that they've accomplished. When they were very young and I was doing parenting education classes, they would sit me down, and they would tell me, "This is what we want you to know that you need to know in order to do parenting education classes." At the same time I was also teaching self-esteem classes in grammar schools, and I was working with intercity kids, so I would bring Chrissy and Joey with me to assist and ask their input. I thought it was a good lesson for them to be exposed to different things in their lives and to see what was going on and what could be expected in the future and what events they may be faced with. But then, David, they've been very fortunate. They both attended very academically competitive universities, and they have had great opportunities. I, hopefully, have taught them to make positive choices in their life and to be responsible for those choices.

My children are loving. They're honest, and they care about their fellow man. If I had anything to do with that, I feel very honored. I think they've learned that the secret of success is to let success come from within. You know, if you are successful, chances are you are doing what you want to do. As I said earlier, raising kids isn't easy, and I believe what Jacqueline Kennedy said, which is 'if you bumble raising your children, I don't think whatever else you do matters very much.'

## Wright

Sometimes, unfortunately, I've felt that it's kind of the luck of the draw. I, like you were stating, I didn't have to pass any tests or take any classes or anything, but I did learn my parenting skills from a loving, dedicated, great parent—my mother. But I had a lot of friends who had terrible mothers and terrible fathers.

## Hernandez Kolski

Unfortunately, not everyone has that opportunity to be able to have parents who are open to sharing their loving and their caring. I have never met a parent who didn't love and want the best for their children. I have met too many parents who were unable to share that love with their children, and I think that's unfortunate.

## Wright

Did you find yourself in danger when you were working with the gang at-risk youths?

## Hernandez Kolski

I loved working with gang-at-risk kids. I will tell you that there were a few times which were pretty intense situations and I found myself saying, "Oh please, God, just let me get out of here alive." On the whole, I really never felt unsafe. I also had someone else training with me. Being that I'm a short Latina female, I felt a good counterpart was appropriate. I would bring in a male to balance off the team. Most of my participants, you know, were male and they were all active members of various gangs, and I would talk to them, David, about changing the choices that they had been making in their life. So I found that having male influence, and opinion, helped. Having also that extra testosterone on my side couldn't hurt either. I don't think gang kids are any different from any other kid. As you know, gangs have been around since time began, since this country began. In earlier years, gangs were called clubs, and these were the people who protected the neighborhoods, and they protected the people who lived in these neighborhoods. What I don't approve of, what I disapprove of are the changes that have occurred with the gangs in recent years. Some people have asked me, "Why do you work with these kids? Aren't they hopeless?" Many people are saying they are just hopeless. I don't believe anyone is hopeless, and I also believe that all kids are at risk. If you think about it, where can parents move and take their children where their children won't have to face the everyday challenges that our youth have to deal with today? It's much different than when we were growing up. Today, there is no safe place for our youth. What I believe is that you need to discover what the child finds to be worthwhile, what motivates them, what inspires them. The youth look and they see what their choices are, and it's up to us to show them that they can choose their own destiny.

I have a very dear friend and we talk about this, because when he was young, he had people who always said he would not amount to anything. As a youth, they said he was just hopeless. He was what people considered "not good", and wouldn't accomplish anything. He failed grammar school. He got kicked out of his first high school. He ended up going to college only because he said he was too lazy to go to work. Yet today, he is the mayor of a village. He's achieved almost all of the goals that he set for himself. Why? I think it's because he wouldn't accept what people said about him. He knew that it was his choice; that he held the destiny of his life in the choices that he made; and he made his own decisions. Sometimes I think he succeeded to prove these other people were wrong. I do believe that all people are basically the same. Gang kids are no different. They are just looking for someone to listen to them. At the end of the program that I have, David, that I was doing with the gang kids, there is a part where they participate and they write a letter of support to every member in the group. And I wish you could see all of the letters that have come back to me that say, "Cynthia, thank you for listening." "Mrs. Kolski, thank you for letting me talk." They just want to be heard. I'm a really big youth advocate, and I just love to talk to young kids and help them express their own ideas. This generation is our next generation of leaders. This is where my social security is going to come from, and I'm expecting a great deal from them. Therefore, I think we need to do our part and teach and give them the different tools they need.

**Wright**

Could you tell our readers a little bit about what you attribute your success too?

**Hernandez Kolski**

David, that's an easy question. I believe I owe my success, and everything that I am, to my God, to my family, and to my dear friends that God has brought into my life. Don't laugh, because that's not an ultraistic point of view. It honestly is the truth. If you look, in order to succeed in anything, I believe you have to take a risk, and that risk means facing your fears and the possible failure that you are going to experience. And the road to success—does have hurt, and rejection along the way. That comes with it. I believe we learn by our failures as well as our successes. That's maybe the humanistic part of us. We need to look, and we need to prepare ourselves for what lies ahead. I have been very fortunate that I have always had people who have helped me through these challenges, even as early as my childhood. We have what I call "war stories". These war stories happen throughout our lives. And these war stories, as I call them, are about the difficult times. Friends have helped me face these difficult times. The difficult times, can be as serious as sexual abuse or physical abuse, the death of a parent, or divorce. It doesn't matter what the war stories are what matters is the choice that we make and how we choose to survive and deal with it, and also learn from it. Are we going to become the victim, or are we going to become the survivor?

My friends have taught me that my war stories are like a cut that we have, or like the scar on a cut. If you look at the cut, when you initially have it, it hurts and it gives you great pain. However, if you take care of that cut, if you nurture that cut, it gets better and as it heals, the pain subsides. Though the scar remains, the scar is purposeful because it always will remind us of what we have been through. The scar becomes like part of us. It's to remind us of who we are and the experiences in our lives that influence us. It tells us how we got there. It helps to remind us that we can get through it, no matter how difficult it is, because it's not always easy. It's easy for me to sit here and talk about it now. It's not easy when you are going through that particular pain and that particular hurt. And I've had friends who, when I was feeling sorry for myself, when I was doubting myself, they literally hit me on the head and wouldn't let me feel sorry for myself. My philosophy has always been about making positive choices and finding a lesson in that experience. So, my tenacity would also be part of my success. I never give up. Sometimes, my friends say I'm like a dog with a bone! And I've been very lucky. God has been very good to me. He has entrusted me with a great deal of faith and trust. He brings wonderful people into my life. And no, my life has never been boring. My life has always been an adventure and sometimes a challenge.

**Wright**

When you consider all of your friends and the people that you've known all down through your life and the way they live their lives, do you believe your philosophy of live is different than the norm?

**Hernandez Kolski**

That's an interesting question because people are always telling me how different I am. There is one thing that I think I do that's a little different than a lot of people is that I've learned to compliment people whether I know them or not. What I mean by that is if I'm walking down the street, if I'm in a public place, even on an elevator, if I see someone that's nice looking, if I see something that they are wearing that I like, I have no difficulty saying, "Oh, what a pretty woman you are." Or "That's a nice shirt or what a handsome man," because I've learned to share my appreciation for people and things with them at the moment. Many times people are initially uncomfortable when accepting compliments. However, most people have looked at me and smiled and said, "Thank you!" or "You've made my day!"

**Wright**

I think I'm in trouble here. When I met you for the first time, I don't remember you telling me how handsome I was.

**Hernandez Kolski**

I did tell you how nice looking you are. Trust me. It's just whatever I focus on in regards to the person, and I think that our society is more open to that. Also part of my philosophy is about making choices. The choices that I make are about bringing more positivity to people and to looking at that more than the negativity in their life. If someone were to say five positive things about you and one negative thing, what will you remember the most? Because I do remember saying a lot of positive things to you and bringing you a beautiful gift, again to work on the positivity, and yet you remembered that I didn't say, "You were handsome!"

**Wright**

But I tell you, that was a beautiful gift. It's sitting on my desk even as we speak.

**Hernandez Kolski**

Well, I want people to enjoy the good things of life. There is much more positivity in this world than there is negativity. If we focus on the positivity, then it will multiply itself. It will triplify itself! That will bring us to more unity than division. It's all about choices. And I want to share with parents the importance of teaching their children the power of choice, and not just the power of choice, along with that comes accepting the responsibility of these choices. I believe, and I really do believe, that if we do, this children would learn to make more positive choices in their lives.

**Wright**

I understand you're presently in the process of publishing a book. Could you tell me a little bit about that?

**Hernandez Kolski**

Yes, I have discovered writing is different than speaking—much different than speaking. However, I have connected with a wonderful company called Insight Publishing, and I've been part of their books as I am here today. And I'm hoping by the end of the year I can talk to them about the book that I have been working on for more years than I care to think of, and it's titled, *I Should Try, But I Can't. I Should Try, But I Can't!*

**Wright**

That's interesting.

**Hernandez Kolski**

Well, the premise, David, is that if you take these four words out of your vocabulary: "should", "try", "but", and "can't", you will become the person you are meant to be. Look at your life, David. I believe that these words, and words like them, are the words that hold us hostage to what we think we can and cannot accomplish. By not using these words, we put ourselves into a new mindset. We find that we are no longer the victim. Again, it's about choice. "Should", "try", "but", and "can't", these are the words that paralyze us. By removing these words from our everyday speaking, we place ourselves in a mindset that allows us a new freedom. A freedom that allows us to remain focused on our goals. It becomes a win-win situation. Win-win results. And I know that some people may find this strange. They find it different and they find it new. Except I challenge anyone to take these words out of their vocabulary for just one month, and they will see changes occur in their life.

**Wright**

That's very interesting.

**Hernandez Kolski**

It is! It is amazing. It is how I live my life and it's the basis of the challenges that I give to my children and other people. Take these four words, four simple words, out of your vocabulary. It's like unlocking the chains on us.

**Wright**

You had a serious accident a few years ago. You alluded to it a few minutes ago. Is that what gave you your philosophy of life?

**Hernandez Kolski**

Well, the accident that you referred to is when I broke my neck. I was unaware that my neck was broken for six months.

**Wright**

Oh my! It's a wonder you didn't die.

**Hernandez Kolski**

It's a miracle! I am a miracle! And doctors said that, because now I have a six-inch plate in my neck. It was a really difficult time for me. They immobilized me for almost a year. I definitely found out who my friends were and who were not. It was more than physically painful. It was very mentally and emotionally draining as well. One of the side effects that I had from the surgery is that I had vertigo or dizziness for three months. Anytime anyone touched me or moved the bed that I was in, caused unbelievably excruciatingly pain. I was in recovery for a year, and I'm still in rehab, and I have one more year for rehab.

**Wright**

Goodness!

## Hernandez Kolski

The accident, though David, gave me a lot of time to think and to put things into a more concrete frame. And even though I've always had the philosophy of looking at the positive perspective, I think, David, it just gave me more of the framework that I needed. When I was young, my mom and I used to talk about my trust in people and my faith in people. She would get upset when I was a little girl. I would give my clothes away to people who were not as fortunate as I not that I had that many. It just seemed that I could share them. As a teenager I worked as a volunteer at the USO and I would always bring soldiers and sailors home to eat dinner. And she would say, "This is not the USO!" She said, "Cindy you just trust everybody and anybody." It's been in recent years that I have been able to verbalize my beliefs more clearly. It was always just the natural thing for me to do, I thought. I thought everybody did it!

## Wright

I understand your mother was the first Latina elected official in Chicago. What was that all about?

## Hernandez Kolski

I am really, really proud, very proud of my mom, David. Yes, she was the first elected Latina woman not only in Chicago, in the County of Cook, in the state of Illinois. She held the highest position as the first woman, the first Latina woman to hold those high positions. She was a Cook County Commissioner for over 21 years, and if you know anything about Chicago, she was hand picked by 'the' Mayor Daley.

## Wright

Goodness!

## Hernandez Kolski

She's also the person who taught me exactly what we are talking about—that I could accomplish anything that I wanted if I wanted it hard enough. In fact, I wrote a program in her honor called "La Voz de Nena". It's a program for Hispanic women that emphasizes the quotes and sayings that our mothers taught us as we were growing up. You know, I believe that those quotes, I'm sure your mother gave you similar little quotes, the same little quotes and sayings that you will remember while you were growing up. I believe those are become the foundation for our morals and our values. There is a saying in

Spanish 'Si Puedo', which means 'yes, I can.' And I've kind of adopted that in my life and I've taught it to my children, and my friends. I have a little pin that says 'Si Puedo'. I share it with my participants in the programs that I teach. I think if we believe we can, we will!

**Wright**

Obviously, you have accomplished a lot in your life, and of course, you've been involved in many things. What dreams are you looking to still fulfill?

**Hernandez Kolski**

God only knows, David. I'm sure there is much in store for me. You know with the accident, I knew that if I survived that, I was going to be around for a long time, and I believe my purpose on this earth is not through yet. God has something in store for me. When he tells me what it is, I'll be glad to go and do it. Until then, I'm just moving along. I'm a fifty-six year old woman. In the process of re-inventing herself once again. I'm recently divorced, and I'm living on my own for the first time in my life. I have never lived on my own before. So sometimes it's a little scary and quite challenging. My immediate goal, right now is to get settled, to clear my head, to move into my new home, to finish the book that I've been talking about, *I Should Try, But I Can't*, and to continue speaking and sharing my experiences in my seminars. I hope to do some more traveling again overseas, and someday, I hope to have a Center where people can come to and provide various types of training, and hopefully my daughter would also be involved in that. It's always interesting. Things are always constantly moving and growing. Wonderful opportunities open to me.

**Wright**

Has being alone for the first time been a liberating experience or a scary one?

**Hernandez Kolski**

It's always liberating. As I said, I think I wouldn't change anything in my life because I think everything that has been part of my life has made me what I am today. And if I left any of that out, I would be leaving out a part of me. Some of the things have been repetitive, because I believe that things occur in our lives over and over again until we learn our lesson. You know there are two ways of learning a lesson. God's way easy, or God's way hard. And sometimes the latter for some reason or another, maybe because of my stubbornness, has caused me to have repetitive lessons return into my life. So it can be a little scary though it's always positive, and it's always to give us something. What's that old saying, 'if it doesn't kill you, it makes you stronger'. Well, I've become a very strong and rather independent person, I think. And that's okay.

**Wright**

Well, success seems to breed success. A man told me many years ago that successful people had a success awareness attitude. And so the probability is that every time they get involved in something, it will also be a success. So I'm sure that's going to be the way with you.

**Hernandez Kolski**

I thank you for that confidence in me, and I hope so. I believe so. Si Puedo! Si Puedo! is what I always go by. Yes I can!

**Wright**

Well, Cynthia, I really appreciate you taking this much time to talk to me on *Conversations on Success* today, and I wish you the very, very best as you are changing once again.

**Hernandez Kolski**

Thank you. I appreciate that, David, and I thoroughly, thoroughly enjoyed this. Thank you for this opportunity.

**Wright**

Today we have been talking to Cynthia Hernandez Kolski. She is a teacher, a speaker. Some of the topics that she presents include effective communication skills, parenting education, diversity, conflict resolution, and as we have found today, she is very diverse and I'm sure holds great workshops and seminars. Thank you so much, Cynthia, for being with us on *Conversations on Success*!

**Hernandez Kolski**

Thank you, David. God bless.

## About The Author

Cynthia Hernandez Kolski is a dynamic innovative speaker. She wears many 'hats" and faces all challenges from a positive perspective. She believes success comes from within and all people are successful when they accept responsibility for their choices, stay committed to their goals and are persistent. She believes her strength comes from God, her family and friends, who are family to her. She is an inspiration for she touches the hearts & souls of many.

**Cynthia Hernandez Kolski**

Communication Education, Inc.

Phone: 773.294.0576

www.communicationeducation.com

# Chapter 4

## PAUL WILLIAM CLARKE

### THE INTERVIEW

**David Wright (Wright)**

Paul William Clarke is a powerful speaker and is rapidly becoming a recognized authority on personal and business success. Many believe that his unorthodox high-energy approach in the presentation of success-driving topics has propelled him into the keynote-speaking arena as a result generating guru. Paul was inducted into the National Speakers Association in 2001. Paul is the developer of the "Crucial Elements Of Success" (CEO'S) concept and program, which focuses on navigating the challenges of personal and professional success. Paul is also the innovator behind the "Sales Force" and the Discovery Sales Process, sales training process peppered with his real world sales experience.

While serving in management for an American top 10 Fortune 100 Company, Paul was recruited as a Senior Consultant within a prominent training and business-consulting firm with affiliate locations throughout the United States and Canada. His experience there was instrumental in his launch of Discovery Systems International, Inc.,

(DSI) an organizational and human development company. Today, in addition to professional speaking Paul remains highly involved with the DSI operation and despite his demanding travel schedule he continues to personally conduct training for some of his long-term local clients. Paul, his wife Anna and their three children make their home in Central New York State. Paul William Clarke, welcome to *Conversations on Success*.

### Paul William Clarke (Clarke)

Thank you. I'm happy to be here, David.

### Wright

Paul, can you tell us a little about your company Discovery Systems International?

### Clarke

Sure, I am happy to. DSI is an organizational and human development company. What we really do is help companies increase their effectiveness by elevating individual performance within the workforce. Individually, one person at a time and then certainly collectively. We focus in on three areas: Sales training and sales force development, leadership development and of course team building.

### Wright

In preparing for this interview, I had the pleasure of reviewing a section of manuscript for your book entitled, *The Crucial Elements of Success*. I was hoping you could summarize the message or meaning of this title.

### Clarke

Absolutely, if you think about the title *The Crucial Elements of Success*, the first letter of each of these primary words, Crucial Elements Of Success, you are left with an acronym CEO S. I like to refer to it as the CEO's book or the CEO's program because it is based on the premise that everyone is the CEO of themself incorporated. Now, I'm not suggesting that ones personal life needs to be operated as rigidly as a corporation, but like a successful business there are clearly defined mechanisms that over time ensure success and in the CEO'S program I talk about corporate structure and planning these principles combined with action can transform you and your personal business into a success-driving machine.

## Wright

You refer to a couple of simple formulas at various times through-out the reading. Where did they come from?

## Clarke

Both of those come from my teenage years. You see, I came from a small town and I had a good friend of mine who's stepfather happened to be a multi-millionaire. That was kind of the "hang out" house. We would always congregate and ultimately spend a lot of time there. The stepfather would often share thoughts and ideas with us over dinner. He told a couple of stories over and over again. And, It was always in about a three-hour seminar format. The first story he would tell was the *relevance of time*, as I call it. And basically, he would say, when you are a baby and you are one-year old, one year is a lifetime, but when your are ninety-nine, one year is not very long at all. He would explain to us that as you age and get older, it seems time will go faster and that actually, it's not that time is really going faster, it just seems that way because there is more time to compare the current period of time to thus making time itself seem shorter or move faster. He would always say, "you'd better start paying attention" and what he was really trying do in his own crude way was to get us thinking about our future and set some goals and visions for our futures.

The second seminar he would give us kids over and over had a major impact on me. He would say right up front, "Listen, most people are not successful if life," He was always careful to let us know this didn't mean you had to have money and businesses or own a lot of things like he did. He would say, "Just look around at people and do the opposite of what most people do and you will have that of which few people have and that is success." He would challenge us. He would tell us to go ask adults what they wanted to be when they were your age. And of course, as a foolish young kid, I did. I went to every adult and asked, when you were fifteen, thirteen, whatever it might have been, what did you want to be when you grew up? And I found out that none of these people were actually doing or living the life that they wanted when they were my age. Because of the type of person that I am I even probed a little further to find out that most of these people went to college; the field that they were currently working in had nothing to do with the studies that they had at college. This was interesting to me.

One of the things he would do was ask us what we wanted to be. I didn't know what I wanted to be. I guess I wanted to be a real-estate tycoon. I wasn't really sure what a real-estate tycoon did, but there was a guy on late night television in Hawaii with a panel of people who claimed to be a real-estate tycoon. He taught this panel of people how to make a lot of money. So, about this time in my life, I was working on a dairy farm. Yes, my first job, $2.25 per hour. I was working pretty hard at it as I recall and this guy kept coming up on late night television. His name was Dave Del Dotto and he sold real-estate courses for about $500.00 I guess, to teach people how to be successful in real estate. As it turns out, I ended up saving up the $500.00 and sent off for this real estate course. I still remember when I got it because the day that it came—it was a UPS package addressed to me. When you are fifteen or sixteen years old you don't get a lot of UPS packages. When I received the package, I rushed up to my bedroom and opened it upside down because I was in such a big hurry. I went through book, tapes and manual's and got to the bottom, which was actually the top, and found three pieces of paper. The first one was really a list of the tapes and manuals and so on of the things you should find enclosed.

The second one was a letter addressed directly to me signed by the millionaire on TV. So, I read down through it and as I did, the letter said something in it that was very important and stuck. To paraphrase it because I don't remember exactly what it said, it said: Now Paul, so many people are going to order my real estate course because they are interested in financial freedom and success and so on. Don't do what so many people are going to do. So many people are going to read, go through my manuals and books and tapes but they are not going to do anything, they are going to be afraid and let fear hold them back. That had a very powerful message to me. All I knew is from the millionaires story, was that if I just did the opposite of what most people are going to do, in other words, if most people are just going to read it and do nothing then all I had to do is the opposite which is something and I could have success with this real-estate wealth building course. As I tell this story around the country I like to close it out by saying, that while my friends were closing down the bars in college, I was out closing deals in real estate and I ended up buying my first apartment building when I was eighteen. I guess we are not here to talk about real estate but those two formulas, the first being from the millionaire story, do the opposite of what most people to and that third piece of paper from the real estate tycoon—which I didn't share with you yet. It was a piece of paper turned side ways and it said: A System plus sign (+) Discipline equal sign (=) Success.

## A System
## + Discipline
## = Success

I hung that on my bedroom wall for many, many years. What was so easy for me to grasp and understand was that this gentleman, Dave Del Dotto, had a system for buying real estate and generating additional income and wealth. And, if I followed it and disciplined myself to do it, I could have additional income and wealth. Most people won't follow it. Most people won't do the things they need to do. All I had to do was the opposite of what most people did or thought. And, despite what so many believed that I never could do at eighteen years old with no money or credit. I did it! But that's another whole story.

**Wright**

Unfortunately, things have not changed all that much have they?

**Clarke**

No, absolutely, they don't change much at all.

**Wright**

In the book you say, "Wealth does not equal success." Can you help our readers better understand this statement?

**Clarke**

I certainly can. I believe I was referring to financial wealth. That is simply because I know a lot of people who have a lot of money and are very unhappy. Despite having so many things like planes, trains, automobiles, homes, summer homes, and money in every pocket, these people are not happy. It is because many of them seek money in the hopes that it will make them happy. What they fail to realize is that money is an instrument. It's a tool. A tool without a purpose is no tool at all. Money cannot fix things. It can certainly make things easier don't get me wrong, but it cannot fix things. I guess if all I had was a toolbox full of tools that couldn't fix anything I wouldn't be happy either.

**Wright**

I had a brother that died at fifty who would have probably—not probably—he would have paid every cent he had to live another day.

**Clarke**

Certainly ...?

**Wright**

So, money didn't buy him anything.

**Clarke**

No, it never does in the end David, and it's interesting that in my profession I get asked how do I become a success in some form or another, more than anything else. I never tell people to chase money. My typical reply over the years has been, "Well how do you define success?" The response I've grown accustomed to, and almost anticipate, usually start with a puzzled look and ends with an "I don't know" in one form or another. I am astonished that so many people go through life day by day in pursuit of success with no clear understanding of what it is that they are actually pursuing. So many people in life just end up ending up. And many times those places don't seem too bad some are even quite desirable, but are these people living the life that they have created or are they living a life that has created them.

**Wright**

Could you explain the difference?

**Clarke**

Sure, Let me give you a real world example. A young couple gets married, all they can think about is how wonderful their lives together will be. Right off, three kids come out of no place. Life starts to get busy now. Both mom and dad go to work so they can provide the things they believe will supply their children with a happy life. As their lifestyle ratchets up, they have to work even harder. Along with all the work comes anxiety and stress. Over time they withdraw from one another and then eventually the children. This is not a recipe for a happy family. And as for their lives together, its non-existent. The problem is that the train is moving so fast now there isn't enough time to question where it is all going, let alone ask if they are even on the track. This is an all too common problem where peoples lives are controlling them as opposed to people controlling their lives. I have yet to meet a couple that walked down the isle thinking about how great it will be to have their lives spinning out of control in a few years. See, I believe that in life you are either the master of your own plan or the victim of not having one. And, this is what I mean when I talk about your life creating you instead of you creating your life. Its' all about control and who has it, you or your life. In the CEO'S program I talk about the development of a strategic plan, which in business is process of continuously and systematically evaluating and finally communicating the purpose of the business to the work force. It also involves defining your overall long-term objectives and breaking them down into quantifiable pieces. Then developing strategies and identifying avenues which will make it possible to meet those objectives. Successful companies continually update and reinforce their plan to give their workforce a sense of purpose.

**Wright**

Why exactly do companies do this Paul?

**Clarke**

There is a basic theory in business that says, show your workforce where you want to go and you enable them to take you there. What this really means is that if your workforce knows where you want it to go, they will be able to recognize and seize opportunities as well as avoid pitfalls. The human brain works similarly in that once it has been provided clear destination or purpose; it immediately and continually works toward it, even when you're not thinking about it. There is always a sense of that purpose present and this is what makes the difference between people who get what they want and those who do not.

**Wright**

This is very interesting Paul, could you give me an example of how you have used this in your own success story.

**Clarke**

Actually, if we have time I can give you two. The first is in real estate. I think this is so interesting. Picture this... Someone hears about a rehab project John Doe has going on at an old apartment building. So he says to his buddy, "Boy John Doe was lucky to pick that building up so cheap. Wish we could have found a deal like that."

Although they have driven by this building 100 times they never gave it a second look otherwise that may have seen the sigh that said, "For sale by owner, I am about to just give it away". See the real-estate investor, and I know this because I have been the John Doe in this example, never passes by an empty building without thinking, wonder what I could do with that, as they pull over and do a quick walk around. Its kind of a curse sometimes and my wife used to hate it but she has turned into an animal now. I do most of the driving and it's amazing how many times she says to me, Hon, that looked like a fixer upper. She can't help it and this is a perfect example of enabling the workforce or people around you to get you there.

Now for the second example I promised you. How I ended up talking with you today. It wasn't an accident, it wasn't by luck. I went to a seminar many years ago that had a profound effect on my life. As I put the tools to work in my life I realized what a gift I had been given and decided somehow some day I would pass this gift to another in need. Today, I am fulfilling the promise I made to myself. It all started with a brief conversation I had with a friend and business acquaintance. I casually mentioned my secret plan of passing on my skills and ideas and within a few weeks I was sitting in front of a friend of his who just happened to be the president of the very training company that gave me my start. Had I not been intently focused and consumed by this vision, I would have never brought it up in conversation and my vision would have remained nothing more than a dream. These are both examples of knowing what you want and through intent, focus and undaunted pursuit turning your dream, into reality.

**Wright**

That's an interesting story Paul; I want to go back to something you said a moment ago, because in the book you were also talking about a sense of purpose. You said, "You can travel through life without a sense of purpose, but without a sense of purpose you can have no sense of success." How do you define your sense of purpose?

**Clarke**

Well, it is actually a good question. But, first, let's talk about purpose a little bit. That will help me clarify my thoughts behind making those types of statements. People in general, unanimously need a sense of purpose to have and to hold hope. Let's face it, the mind is a goal-seeking device. People need to identify what they want and what success is. I mean the root causes, not just 'I want to be successful because it looks good in those images of people in fancy cars'. Once they understand what success means to them and why they want it, then they need to have a sense of that purpose. What do I mean by a sense? I think of a sense as an awareness. People need to be able to focus on or concentrate and understand that the steps they are taking are leading them in that direction. When a sense of purpose is missing it is virtually impossible for anyone to achieve predetermined results or what we call success . They must have an awareness of what they are doing and how that action is contributing to their success. Although, people might have what you or I might call success, in their mind they might not realize it is success because it is something that they didn't set out to do. This is why we have so many unhappy people. Let me give you an example that anybody could relate to. Let's say you and I want to go on a road trip. We hop in a motorcoach and take to the street. We drive and drive and drive and after several days we end up someplace. It could be a really nice place. Then what I would do is look over to you and you would look to me and say, "Were we successful". The answer would be, "I don't know". We might not even know where we are and there is a term for that it is called 'being lost'. If you have ever been lost you know it is not a great feeling. On the other hand, if we set out with some type of pre-determined destination, we stand a pretty good chance of getting there, so long as we pay attention to where we are going along the way and pay attention to the turns that we make as we go. Having a sense of purpose is similar in that we need to have awareness in where we are going and why we want to get there. That way we can make the daily decisions that will help us with the navigation of our life's direction. This is really a great tie-in for the two examples I gave you earlier. Knowing where you where your going and enabling the people around you to help get you there. I hope that helps?

**Wright**

Yes, it does help.

**Clarke**

I can give you another thought on sense of purpose. I don't know if you remember this, but when I was a kid we used to play this game. I don't know the name of it but it was the warmer/colder game. We would select and object that the other person had to find or guess. As we would move through the process, the person begins to guess or look and as the person was getting closer we would say they were getting warmer. If the person was moving farther away from the object we would say colder to indicate whether they were getting closer or farther away. If there was no object to this then there would be nothing to accomplish. Inevitably, despite having some fun, people would get tired of this. It is the same in life. When life has no reason, people get sick of their life. At any rate, the subconscious mind is similarly using warmer and colder commands to help you make decisions. When someone has a conflicting destination or no destination or purpose at all, the most powerful tool meaning their brain will have them spinning in circles. This is why we see so many unhappy, frustrated people.

**Wright**

You state that most people never develop the crucial elements of success. Why do you think that is?

**Clarke**

Well, I think there are couple of reasons. I think the biggest reason is most people never look. Most people never seek answers. Most people are so busy living their lives that they never take a look at the direction their live is being taken in. For no other reason than we lead busy lives. We are all busy. We have families. We get out of school and get a job because we have to have a car and all these things. Then, our lives direction starts taking off and moving us, as opposed to us directing our life, our life starts directing us. Unfortunately, they never stop to look at the things they need to do to be successful, let alone what success means to them. They never ask the questions, what are the elements, what are the pieces of the puzzle that they need to put together to design the life that I really want? The second reason is because it is just hard to stay focused. We were never taught how to focus and concentrate. Actually, we were continually interrupted when we tried to concentrate. When it was time to eat, when the school bell rang and so on, What we find is that people spend more time planning their wedding, a one day event than planning the rest of their lives.

**Wright**

You write a lot about the father of a childhood friend of your that you refer to as the "millionaire." Would you say he is credited to your success?

**Clarke**

I would answer that by saying, "Yes, certainly." But, what I would say is that there are many, many people who are credited to any successes that I have had. I include myself in that group. For every success I have had, I have and equal amount of failure. As many people have. I take full responsibility for those failures. As such, I have to take the majority of the responsibility for the successes as well.. I have had the good fortune have many positive influences in my life, I believe all successful people do. I also believe that the people who do not aspire to their full potential have many of those same influences. We find that successful people are nothing more than students who are willing to listen, willing to look at, willing to adopt and seek the knowledge of those individuals like the millionaire. I remember my first career changes. I moved from the farm to a car wash; it was my second job. The owners of the car wash were a couple of businessmen who happened to partner in a car wash. One was a very powerful executive at a big company and the other a wise local businessman. I enjoyed listening to what these gentleman had to say and the different things they tried to teach me. Still, I had the responsibility to take the initiative, seek their knowledge, ask the questions and evaluate his advice. Was I in the right place at the right time? Absolutely. But, knowing you are in the right place, recognizing it, and using it to your advantage is certainly a big piece of it. Although, I have learned from the millionaire and many other people like him, it's important to know that each individual has the responsibility to seek that knowledge and identify those gold nuggets when they find them.

**Wright**

I would like to quote you as saying, "Human beings are born hardwired for success but the software is often poorly programmed." What do you mean by this?

**Clarke**

This is kind of a complicated subject, but it is interesting. As you know from our earlier conversations, my wife and I are expecting our third child and as I think about that, I think about people being hardwired and I think about children. It is amazing to watch children from birth to kindergarten. My oldest son started kindergarten just a few days ago. It's amazing; human beings are born with everything they need in life to succeed. There are very few things left out that we as human beings need to succeed. A newborn is highly evolved by birth however much of it's programming is incomplete. In other words, when a baby is born, many of the electronic connections in their brain are not yet complete. The wiring process goes on pretty intensely until about age seven and then slows dramatically. So, if you think about it, if you have all the things that are necessary to succeed, why is it that some of them get programmed properly and others are not programmed properly? Some of it has to do with environmental conditioning.

Let's take a simple example. As an infant, you don't know that fire is hot. But you learn that fire is hot because mom and dad say the stove it hot don't touch it. If you get your hand near it, what happens? You learn very quickly, your nervous system tells you, Hey! Don't Do That, That Hurts. So, anytime something is hot you move away from it. Anytime something can hurt you then you move away. Your nervous system is what controls how you act and react. It is a basic science that we have known from many, many years. They problem with that is people associate different things with pleasure and pain. Many times people associate hard work with pain. On my fourteenth birthday I got my first job on a dairy farm. Understanding I was a relatively poor, small town kid. My father came to me and said "Hey, a buddy of mine who is a farmer needs some help bringing in hay. Can you do it?" I didn't have any association that hard work was pain because my father was an ironworker. He worked hard everyday. That was something I valued. From a programming standpoint, I was already programmed to say hard work was good, not bad. Not negative. So, I went out and worked on that dairy farm with a smile on my face. Still today, if I could earn the kind of income that I need to earn to live the life I desire for my family and I, I would probably be bailing hay for a living. Many people create mental success barriers, things that won't let them move past the starting line to achieve success. Many people associate money with success and success with pleasure but they also associate pain with the things they need to do to get there. This is where programming comes in. We see people who based on their programming are success adverse.

**Wright**

I also noticed that you teach people to "reprogram mental success barriers". Can you elaborate on this for us?

**Clarke**

Sure, I am happy to. A mental success barrier is something that holds someone hostage. It is something that really prevents them from fulfilling their true potential. Step one with any individual is to identify what mental success barriers they have. Many people go through life with so many of them and never understanding what they are, why they don't succeed, or what is holding them back. Yet, they never spend a lot of time looking at it. Once you can get someone to spend some time understanding what some of their success barriers are you then have some tangible elements to work with. We do this through questioning, counseling, sitting with them and working with them individually. Next, they have to be ready for change. People really only make changes for a couple of reasons. One is because the problem or situation they are in is causing them emotional duress or pain. If you were in pain and I told you there was something you could do to get rid of it would you do it? Certainly you would. The other reason that compels people to do things is something will make them happy, feel good or something that is pleasurable. A lot of research suggests that pain as a motivator and is much more effective than something that is pleasurable. An example of that would be: "If you were to go out today, David— and I don't know if you are a runner— but if you went out and ran a twenty-mile marathon, do you think you could complete it?"

**Wright**

After about three blocks I would be dead.

**Clarke**

Well, we don't want to do that to you. But, now let's say I hung a carrot on it and I said for 10 million dollars I want you to run that twenty-mile marathon. Could you do it?

**Wright**

I would find a way.

**Clarke**

You would want to do it. You would absolutely want to do it. However, as you got running your nervous system would kick in at some point and start sending you signals of tremendous pain. Regardless of the amount of pleasure, the pictures you could place in your head that would say that money would be fabulous, it would allow me to do things I want and have the things I want. Whatever would be driving you, the pain would overcome. The pain would then be greater than any pleasure you could gain by running the marathon and your body would shut down. The problem with people is in everyday life, there are things that need to be done that can cause pain. I don't care who it is, dealing with the boss, dealing with employees, dealing with the spouse handling the kids waking up early. All of these things can have either real or perceived pain. It's what you do with it and how you process things that condition you for success. I was recently watching a special on television about a woman who has conditioned her body to fight off the effects of hypothermia. She is a swimmer now in her mid forties She had just swam 1.2 miles to Antarctica in water 32 degrees f. Water in Antarctica freezes solid at 28 degrees. Scientists from around the world have studied her for years since as a teenager she swam from the Alaska USA to Russia. This phenomenon cannot be explained. In 32-degree water the above average athlete would survive less than two minutes. Yet scientists believe that she has conditioned her body to restrict blood flow to the surfaces of her skin and through her extremities sufficient to not only survive but swim for 30 minutes. So in talking about the possibilities of reprogramming their limiting self-beliefs and success barriers it's important to understand the vastness of our human capabilities. Once we identify these belief and barriers, we use associative conditioning to reveres their effects.

**Wright**

As a motivational speaker, you use the concept of self-developed motivation. Can you explain this in more detail?

**Clarke**

Yeah. I work a lot with sales forces which, is one thing I truly enjoy doing. Many of those types of positions have a type of variable pay program, which is a type of commission basis. So, the harder you work the more money you make. As a result, people have this delusion that people are motivated for and by money. I don't believe that money itself really motivates anybody. What motivates people, and it is different for everybody, are things within themselves they believe to be important. So, in other words, if you think about why it is that any of us want money. Sure, I am like anybody else. Would I like to have money? Absolutely. But why do I want to have money? I remember thinking about this very question as a twelve or thirteen year old kid. The answers to those questions had nothing to do with a stack of money that sat in the basement, in my safe or wherever it might be. The answer was that I wanted to have things that my family didn't have at the time. I wanted to have a bigger home, that when you woke up on a cold morning, in upstate New York, you didn't see your breath. I wanted to have a home where I could look outside my bedroom through a window as opposed to a crack in the wall. I wanted to have the flexibility and freedom to do the things that I wanted to do, to spend the time with my children. I know my father wanted to spend more time with my sister and I. I wanted to have these things desperately and I knew it from a very early age. As I moved through my teenage years, I was always very conscious of this. Many of my friends would stay out late and I would have to get up at five o'clock in the morning to go work at the dairy farm, then the car wash and certainly the business world. So, I missed out on some of those fun activities. I thought to myself each time I had an opportunity to do it, what is more important to me? Going and doing this which is not getting me closer to the things I want, maybe going out with the guys and goofing off and being tired all day on the job and not doing such a good job.

I still remember, when my first son was born. I remember the very moment that I saw him and here within a matter of hours my wife will be giving birth to out third. But, with my first son, I remember looking at him and thinking first, he looks just like me. He did. My second thought was all of my life I have thought of you and now you are here. I just looked at him and said, "Now you are here." You are the one that I thought of all those times when I wanted to give in, when I didn't want to do it anymore, when I wanted to go have fun and didn't want to work hard. When I just wanted to say forget it and it really isn't worth it, you are the reason and now you are here. This was my motivator many years before it happened I was focused on this vision of my life and even I was kind of surprised when I actually got it.

**Wright**

That's a great personal story Paul, you also mention to be successful, people need to work harder on their life rather than in their life. What do you mean by this?

**Clarke**

This is another area I really like to talk about. If you have ever been fortunate enough to be involved in *the EMYTH* by Michael Gerber either reading or by audiotape, he brings up a very good point. He is talking about businesses. He said business owners need to spend more time working on their business than in their business. In other words, working on your business, if you were the president of a company, you would work on the structure and managing things. Many small businesses still start out that way. They start out with a person who knows how to make tools and dies and knows how to do machine work so he buys a couple pieces of equipment. He actually runs these machines on a daily basis thus working in the business as a tool and die maker as opposed to working on his business. The same thing applies to one's personal life. It is the same for you and I. I have heard people say things like, "My personal life is none of your business." I laugh and think to myself whose business is it then? I must be somebody's business. If you were to ask whose business it was, they would probably say, "It's my business." I look back at those people and say, "Well, if it is a business then why don't you run it like a business?"

Some of the things that I talk about in *The Crucial Elements of Success* program is making comparisons between what CEO's does for a corporation and what you as a CEO of yourself Inc. does for your life. One of the things that a corporation does is operates and navigates by a strategic plan, a kind of map or chart. A strategic plan is really just a continuous process of systematically evaluating and communicating the nature of the business to the rest of the employees and the senior. Management team. In you personal life that would be your family, your friends and all the people around you. It is defining overall long term objectives and breaking them down into quantifiable pieces. Developing strategies is very important in life. Once an individual or company has done this it will be possible for them to identifying the appropriate avenues and allocate their resources properly. Those are some important pieces of operating and really running a business. That's working on your business or your life as opposed to in your life.

**Wright**

This has been a great conversation. I have learned a lot here today. I want to thank you. I really appreciate the time you have spent here with me on this subject of success, which alludes a lot of folks.

**Clarke**

It certainly does and I am happy to be here. I am hoping if people can take anything from this, they will spend more time working on their life as opposed to in their life. Focusing on where they want to go, who they want to be and go for it. Make that happen. It is really the most important thing anyone can do. If someone needs additional help with this there is certainly a lot of books and materials that folks can pick up just purely on goal setting. Goal setting is a way for people to get some focus and clarification over what it is they want. As a result they can get there. The mind is a powerful tool and once you send it in the right direction, and put this tool in motion it will help you get where you want to go.

**Wright**

Today we have been talking to Paul William Clarke, a powerful speaker, author and the developer of the Crucial Elements of Success concept and program. Paul, thank you so much for the time you spent with us today.

**Clarke**

Thanks David, it's been my pleasure.

Paul William Clarke is a powerful speaker and a recognized authority on personal and business success. Many attribute his unorthodox high-energy approach and success-driving topics to their personal and professional success. Paul is the developer of the "Crucial Elements Of Success" ® (CEO'S) concept and program, and innovator behind the "Sales Force" ® and the Discovery Sales Process®. Paul is a power learning book series author and was inducted into the National Speakers Association in 2001.

**Paul William Clarke**
Discovery Systems International, Inc
301 Plainfield Road, Suite 195
North Syracuse, NY 13212
Phone: 315.451.5500
Fax: 315.451.5005
Email: pwc@discoverydsi.com
www.discoverydsi.com

# Chapter 5

## BILL BLADES

## THE INTERVIEW

**David E. Wright (Wright)**

Today we're talking to Bill Blades, a professional speaker, trainer, consultant, and author. Bill speaks from experience. While serving as vice-president of sales and marketing for a food manufacturing company, he increased sales 150 percent from $13 million to $33 million in only four years. His firm was named Small Business of the Year. He also served as Finance Chairman for Newt Gingrich, former Speaker of the House of the United States Congress. Bill is the author of the best selling *The Mother Of All Enterprise* as well as a featured author with attorney F. Lee Bailey in the book *Leadership Strategists*. He has served on the faculties of the Graduate School of Banking of the South and College of Estate Planning Attorneys, the National Association of Sales Professionals, and he also lectures at universities including American Graduate School of International Management, the number one rated international graduate school in the United States. Bill Blades welcome to *Conversations on Success*.

## Bill Blades (Blades)

David, thank you very much.

## Wright

You know unless someone is born into wealth they are usually in the same boat as everyone else. At what point did you decide to be as successful as possible?

## Blades

David, when I was 19 years old I was in Hawaii for jungle training preparing to leave for Vietnam in a few weeks. Then Vietnam veterans began joining our ranks and saying things like, "they don't want us over there," etc. I was in shell shock because I wasn't drafted I had joined. So I was double shocked. On the luck of the draw I got sent to Korea instead. I thought I had been given a break. I thought I should make the most of it. I hadn't really thought about college until then, but in essence I thought, "when I get out of this army, I don't ever want to be pushed and shoved again." So the army was good for my maturity, my outlook, and my new goals. My new philosophy became "push myself harder" so I will have newfound self-control.

## Wright

Many people may assume that you achieved your level of success without any struggles. Can you share a few of your most memorable struggles?

## Blades

I've got a couple, David. I was about ready to be discharged from the army and go to an all-black college, but they rejected my entrance application. I thought, "so much for the GI bill I was told about." I also learned the true meaning of discrimination, which was a real eye opener. Without my father jumping on that university, I would be talking to you without any college education whatsoever. Another example would be back in the 1970's. I was seeking custody of my children who were three and five years old. Attorneys wouldn't even take my money, which in itself was amazing. They told me it would be a waste of money and that "no male in this state is going to get custody of children." Well, I did get custody.

The point is that even if you are the President of the United States you're going to experience trials and tribulations. Astronauts, politicians, sports stars, actors, and the like, they've all got their shining moments, their days in the spotlight. But every one of them is going to grieve and suffer. No one is going to escape the difficulties in life. Here's what you do about it: You whine or get back up. It's a personal choice and it's got to be no whining.

**Wright**

Following your discharge from the army, describe one of the prices you paid to move your business life ahead faster.

**Blades**

It took me two days to drive home after leaving the army and I hit the unemployment office at 4:40 p.m. I told them I wanted to get a job that was very close to the university and I remember them asking me "would you mind being a guard?" I said, "Shoot, I wouldn't mind being anything." They said, "Would you like to start at midnight tonight?" "Absolutely." I took every shift that the retired guys wanted to pass on to me. So that meant I often left school at 3:00 p.m., began guard shift at 4:00 p.m., sometimes took another shift at midnight, and then departed for school at 7:30 in the morning. At the age of 21 I actually found those hours not to be that bad. It was just a price I willingly paid. To make a long story short, I went from the guard to plant manager in less than a year. The prices that I paid came back with extra dividends.

**Wright**

So you were taking what others didn't want?

**Blades**

Exactly.

**Wright**

Well that says something.

**Blades**

I had to feed my family too.

**Wright**

The focus with your clients is to help them in the areas of sales and leadership. Aside from your accumulated experience, what did you study to gain your knowledge?

**Blades**

In the army I studied Maturity 101 in a hurry, business in college, and I learned in my early 20's that I couldn't depend on anyone but myself for continual education. That's when I began buying business books and audiotapes as rapidly as I could. I have found, over the years, that many people fight change, but I guess, fortunately for whatever reason, I've always loved it. That love helped me greatly as I was learning new things from books. Most people wanted to stay the same, but I was growing. I still receive over 400 trade magazines monthly, which many people find astonishing. But I remember a quote from Mark Twain. He said, "The man who does not read has no advantage over the man who cannot read." What I got out of that is the books, the magazines, the audiotapes that you don't listen to or don't read may hurt you.

**Wright**

Do you still listen to a lot of audiotapes?

**Blades**

All the time. That makes my car a university on wheels.

**Wright**

I was taught to do that in the late 60's and continue that to this day. It confounds me that every time I get into one of my friends' cars the radio is already turned on to the Top 40.

**Blades**

You got it.

**Wright**

And when you step into my car the first thing that plays is either a tape or a CD of some speaker of international renown talking about whatever subject I need to be learning.

**Blades**

It's more of that self-control, David. You and I both would both like to listen to the radio, and we do listen to it some. But it's called learn to earn, so that's why I take the time in that car to make it a university.

**Wright**

Based on your studies and your results, what message would you share with our readers?

**Blades**

There are two basic components in any business—money and people. Which one is the toughest challenge? People. So our listeners need to read as much as they can about people, how to treat them, help them, and challenge them. If anybody doesn't score a 10 in people skills, they've just got to keep reading and maybe invest in a coach. Without good or great people skills, you're just not going to get to your <u>true</u> potential.

**Wright**

I've heard many times that money never stops you from being great in business. Circumstances never stop you. If you're stopped at all, it's always by the people that you didn't understand.

**Blades**

Exactly.

**Wright**

Do you think the understanding of you is the understanding of me? In other words, do you study yourself so that you might know what other people are about?

**Blades**

He who knows others is smart, but he who knows himself is very, very wise. In other words, in all cases we're not as great as we think we are. So we must deal with the truth, and work on ourselves before we expect better things from other people.

**Wright**

What do you think is the reason many people don't achieve their potential in the corporate world?

**Blades**

I mentioned earlier the words "self control." That's a big part of it. If you want something badly enough, you have to pay the price and go after it. You've got to work harder on yourself than you do for your employer. As an example, if you're in the sales profession and you work harder on yourself than you do for your employer, three groups of people get the benefit—your employer, your clients, and yourself. The second biggest reason that many people don't ever get there is that the American Society for Training and Development reported that 84 percent of all managers in the United States become managers without any previous management training or education.

**Wright**

That's scary.

**Blades**

Exactly. So you can't count on anyone in that 84 percentile to be your mentor or role model. If your employer is too cheap to pay for education, you'd better invest in yourself. It won't be a cost; rather it will be a valuable investment.

**Wright**

You know, I learned that lesson down through the years. I've always paid for my own education and not left it up to my bosses to do it.

**Blades**

A lot of times they won't.

**Wright**

You're viewed by many as a gifted speaker. Do you feel that you have a natural ability for it?

**Blades**

David, I know that I was not a natural. I remember one of my first speeches. I had on a light tan suit, and before speaking I had large sweat rings underneath my suit. I took the suit jacket off and I was in a light blue dress shirt. There were the same sweat rings. I can tell you I never again wore a tan suit and blue shirt while speaking. So other than not being overly gifted, I was nervous and lacked the confidence I needed. As with anything speaking takes a lot of practice, practice, and more practice. One my first formal speeches was in front of a few hundred people at One Times Square at the age of 22. Boy, you talk about nervous! By the age of 29 I was in the corporate life and speaking at least 25 times annually. People started saying, "you should be a motivational speaker." I didn't even really know what a motivational speaker was. Because I had gained so much experience speaking in the corporate world, I didn't have to go through that warm-up period when I began speaking professionally and consulting at the age of 39. I just studied communications, public speaking, consulting, and then got on my feet and started. The key to any new thing in life is to get started.

**Wright**

Right.

**Blades**

It will not go perfectly. Your first French kiss probably didn't go too well either. Parallel parking probably didn't go too well. You just practice, practice, practice at your craft and you get better at it.

**Wright**

I think my first French kiss went really well for me. It might not have gone very well for the other party, though.

**Blades**

Yeah, there you go. Don't forget, you've got to be honest with yourself too.

**Wright**

Prior to starting your speaking and consulting career, you were a Vice-President in Sales and Marketing and a President. What did you learn collectively from those two positions?

**Blades**

David, the list of what I learned would go into the hundreds, but let me give you just a short handful. One: Do every thing you said you would do ahead of time. Two: Your integrity is not negotiable. Three: If you are part of a sales organization, you've got to have a daily philosophy of "no sales equals no eat." Four: Manage your time as if it's your major currency, because it is. Five: When trying to help hard-headed people, just shut up and pray. Six: Don't be afraid of doing new things. Don't even be afraid of how silly it might come off the first time around. Seven: Work at being in the top 1 percent in your profession, in your industry. Somebody is, why not you? Eight: Have more fun than anybody else. At 55 years old, I'm in the business of getting a lot of my consulting clients to laugh and have fun at what they do. It's something that is important to me. It's called bringing joy and value to others. So if you're not having fun, then do everybody a favor and go somewhere else. And nine: Life gets better when you get better.

**Wright**

The second thing that you talked about was integrity and the fact that it's not negotiable. Based on what has happened in corporate America in the last year, year and a half, integrity seems like somebody negotiated it, doesn't it?

**Blades**

Absolutely. That's why there is a big difference in leadership and management. With all the small businesses around the world, strong leadership is called for. People have given up sometimes on our politicians. They have given up on corporations just because corporations like Enron get all the news. But there are tons of great leaders and great organizations around that can be role models to everybody and that's very important.

**Wright**

The fifth thing you talked about was trying to help hardheaded people. I can remember one of the toughest lessons I ever learned. I was raised in a Christian family. We were taught that everybody could make it, but I had to learn that you cannot reach down into the muck of life and pull up people who don't want to come.

**Blades**

Absolutely.

**Wright**

You know it's the hardest thing to do. I wish I had learned that lesson a lot sooner. I remember listening to a famous baseball coach say that the worst thing to do is to work on your weaknesses. He said, "If you are a hitter, hit every day. If you drop the ball every once in a while, that's okay." But he advocated working on your strengths and not your weaknesses. I spent most of my formative years in management of my companies trying to help the weak become stronger instead of helping the strong to become stronger.

**Blades**

It was a lot a wasted time, energy, and money.

**Wright**

Oh yeah. It cost me a few companies along the way.

You said that you try to have more fun than anyone else does. In trying to have fun do you become introspective about whether or not you really want to be in an industry, if it is really what you want to do?

**Blades**

Fun covers a lot of aspects. I have never met an employee yet that wants to work for a boss that doesn't have fun and doesn't believe in fun.

Let's talk sales for a second. Clients hear the same monotonous presentation from sales people over and over. They've heard those things thousands of times. The sales person must focus on joy and value to clients, in other words, I am going to be a lot of fun for you to work with. I am going to be the bright spot in your day. And you won't believe all the personal value of services that I am going to bring to you. That person will stand out from the pack very easily. Now, say you want to start a corporation and let's say there are five VPs. The one that is fun to be around has earned the right to demand excellence from everyone. We're going to get better, but we're going to have fun while we are doing it. What I normally find is that you have an impersonal exchange of money for labor where people arrive in the morning, they do their job, and then they do home. But if it's the most fun place in town, productivity goes up, teamwork goes up, and almost always sales goes up. Clients can tell if that sales person and the sales person's employer are fun to do business with. Fun is very important.

**Wright**

What do you feel from a business viewpoint is the number one attribute someone needs to exhibit for success?

**Blades**

Number one in my mind is that they have to have a passion for what they do. If you have a passion, you'll always want to get better. So the question that everyone needs to ask themselves is, "which is stronger, my desire to grow or my reluctance to change and grow?" In that passion you'll seek positive mentors and role models. Ask for help. A little message to our readers is be sure to pay for the help or do something in return. I get barraged with phone calls such as, "can I buy you lunch?" No, I can pay for my own lunch. What are you going to do to earn the right to ask for an hour or two of my time?

**Wright**

When you and I talked several months ago, I was really interested in something that you said. I haven't forgotten it. You were talking about taking your company from $13 million to $33 million in sales.

**Blades**

Yes sir.

**Wright**

If I remember you correctly, and you'll have to correct me if I'm wrong, you talked about creating within the company a culture of greatness.

**Blades**

Yes sir.

**Wright**

Do you remember saying that?

**Blades**

Absolutely.

**Wright**

Is that what you teach other organizations? If you do, how do you do that?

**Blades**

Well, I initially go in to conduct a needs analysis to find out what needs fixing. I don't have a standard program that I walk in with, but I always start with the CEO. It is important to spend a tremendous amount of time with one-on-one development at the top of an organization. If potential clients don't sign off on their CEO spending time with me and showing everyone that the process of greatness starts with him or her, I don't take the assignment. You can't sit in your ivory tower, hire a consultant and say "go help my people get better."

That doesn't fly. The employees will see the president or other top executives staying the same and there will be no process for greatness. Process for greatness means every single person is going in the same direction with your mission statement for every single client. And that means every person is going to be given the tools to be the best in the world at what they do. If anybody doesn't want to play and participate on a process for greatness, I remind my clients that the only thing worse than employee turnover is no employee turnover when there should be. In other words, if there are 5,000 employees and one bad one out of that 5,000, it can affect another 10 or 25 people around them. The process for greatness means greatness from everyone and greatness in everything that we do everyday.

**Wright**

But it starts with the leader?

**Blades**

Absolutely.

**Wright**

You know it's amazing. I used to go through a lot of management training and I would just be appalled at the CEOs, presidents, and owners that would not attend the sales and marketing training sessions. I just couldn't believe it. When I was in the real estate industry, I had about 175 agents working for me and I never let anybody train unless I was in the room. It was not just so that I could learn, but I was there to let my people know that I endorsed it, if nothing else. Do you find that to be a problem?

**Blades**

It's a big challenge. Sometimes you'll find CEOs that were former corporate attorneys and former bankers. If there's anybody in the organization that's going to need people skills and leadership skills, it's often them. They may know numbers and they may know legalities, but often they don't know people. So they should be sitting on the front row when it comes time for leadership coaching and training.

**Wright**

It's hard to talk about success in companies without talking about success in leadership. I remember once before that you talked about proactive leadership. Could you define that for us as it relates to success?

**Blades**

Oh golly, I guess you could take a look at the airlines right now. The airlines are asking the government for bail-out money again. If I was in Washington, I would want to know "what have you guys done differently over the last five years that will make you go have a profit on your own?" The airlines are having a hard time answering that question. So they are reacting now, not being proactive.

On the people side of proactive, you might see a usually cheerful person in a down mode. It would be very smart at the beginning of the day to call that person in, offer them a beverage and just say, "you seem like you lost the bounce in your step today. Tell me what's going on, is there something I can help you with?" He just might be able, by being proactive, to help that person bounce back quicker.

Sales people with clients, what are you going to do today that will make a difference to help you get to the bottom line faster? A lot of people have a hard time answering questions like that. If they can't answer that question they're drifting. Let's say you've got 20 sales people and you ask a question like this: "Tell me the next 10 clients you're bringing onboard and what's the no-later-than date?" A lot of times people say, "Bill, how can I answer that?" Well, if you can't answer that, who can? So it's being proactive. When I was in sales, I used to send a letter to a client and tell them "here's everything I am going to do to earn your business and here's the date you're coming onboard." When I was 25 years old, the first three letters that I sent out like that resulted in two of three buying from me on my next visit and they were the three biggest potentials that I had in a two-state area. I showed up and two out of the three had the letter on their desk, just waiting for me. I was exercising leadership as a young salesperson.

**Wright**

How about that? As someone that others look to as being successful, where does life take you now to go after more success?

**Blades**

David, I'm 55 years old now and my goals and desires really haven't changed much, other than I guess I should give up on the idea of playing shortstop for the Baltimore Orioles.

**Wright**

Right.

**Blades**

One big change that I made a year ago on my 55th birthday was a shift in my business. I decided to de-emphasize speaking and get and execute more long-term consulting projects. Now by the hour speaking pays better, but through long-term consulting projects I get to see more growth in my client's people. That enables me to be their servant, their confidant, their helper, and their mentor. So I'll be consulting more and speaking less to feed my own personal needs to serve others. Further, after all this time, I've earned the right to be more selective. I've had some great long-term clients over the years that were mixed in with a few not so great ones. If the CEO and VP of Sales don't believe in bringing joy and value internally, I don't want them as clients because receiving joy and value is important to me also. So I'll be working with fewer clients that I care for and respect and they'll compensate me well enough to see parts of the world that I haven't seen yet. David, for me it's a pretty simple formula that keeps me happy.

**Wright**

It will also provide you more stability to do contractual work for longer periods of time?

**Blades**

Yes, because I've got three clients that I'm in the third year with. They all pay a nice six-figure income, and during up times or down times I don't have to worry about where my next dollar is coming from. So I am bringing them joy and value, and I get regular—I'll call it joy and value—checks back. That's a nice win, win.

**Wright**

Yeah, a lot of motivational speakers that I have talked to do it for the accolades and not just the money. They have this tremendous need to stand in front of the people and give them information that the speaker thinks will better their lives some way. Is that the way it happened for you in the very beginning?

75

**Blades**

I've never stood there for the accolade and I've had comments from people who have noticed this over the years. As soon as I'm done, I leave the stage. I don't stand there. I don't say thank you, goodbye, whatever. I give my last punch line and I'm all done. I've seen speakers stand there, and stand there, and stand there, and I watch maybe—let's say there is a group of 500 people, 50 stand on their feet at the end. So the speaker will stand there hoping that peer pressure will get the rest of them to stand on their feet. Get out. You are here to help people, not get accolades.

**Wright**

I always like to play the national anthem at the end of my speeches. It makes everybody stand up.

**Blades**

You got that right. I need to remember that.

**Wright**

Bill, you just don't know how much I enjoy talking to you. You're such a bright spot in the education of American corporations. You've really made me think about the giving of information with pure joy over the last several months. I really appreciate you being with us on *Conversations on Success*.

**Blades**

David, it was fun for me.

**Wright**

Today, we have been talking to Bill Blades. He is a professional speaker, a trainer, a consultant, and an author. The best thing about Bill is he speaks from experience, both good and bad. And he has really taken this success thing to higher levels, taking a sales company from $13 million to $33 million in only four years. Bill, thank you so much for being with us today.

**Blades**

David, it was my pleasure.

## About The Author

While serving as vice president of sales & marketing for a food manu-facturing concern, he increased sales 150 percent from $13 million to $33 million in only four years and re approaching $60 million when he left in year five. Bill has served as Finance Chairman for Newt Gingrich, former Speaker of the House of the United States Congress. Bill is au-thor of the best seller, *Selling: The Mother of all Enterprise*, as well as featured with the attorney, F. Lee Bailey, in the book *Leadership Strategists*.

**WilliamBlades, LLC**
2555 North Windy Walk Drive #55
Scottsdale, AZ 85255
Email: bill@williamblades.com
www.williamblades.com

# Chapter 6

Stephen J. Kraus, Ph.D.

## THE INTERVIEW

**David E. Wright (Wright)**

Today we're talking to Dr. Stephen J. Kraus. He's an author, speaker, and one of the world's foremost success scientists. In his writings and speeches, he teaches the science of success, synthesizes decades of research on personal achievement, and explores the greatest hits of psychology's most fascinating research. At the same time, he debunks self-help snake oil and unmasks self-improvement urban legends. He is the author of *Psychological Foundations of Success: A Harvard-Trained Scientist Separates the Science of Success from Self-Help Snake Oil*. His articles have appeared in *BrandWeek*, *AdWeek*, *The San Francisco Chronicle*, *Contemporary Psychology*, and a variety of scientific psychology journals. He is founder and President of Next Level Sciences, Inc., a peak performance consulting agency that helps individuals and organizations take their performance to the next level with innovative, science-based tools for success. Stephen received his Ph.D. in social psychology from Harvard University at the age of 25. Twice, he won Harvard's award for excellence in teaching. Steve, welcome to *Conversations on Success*.

**Stephen Kraus (Kraus)**

Thanks, David, it's great to be here.

**Wright**

You've been called a combination of Tony Robbins and Mr. Spock because you study the psychology of success, but from a very scientific perspective. Why should we look at the *scientific* research on success?

**Kraus**

The analogy I use for thinking about this issue is prescription drugs. If your doctor prescribes a drug, you probably don't head to the library and review all of the scientific research yourself. But you do assume there has been careful, scientific research documenting the safety and effectiveness of the drug, and you assume that the government has overseen the research and approved the drug. It hasn't always been that way. Prior to the 20th century, no research on drugs was required. Practically anyone could sell any form of medicine and make any kind of claim about effectiveness. Salespeople traveled the country peddling snake oils that they touted as having all kinds of medical benefits. For the most part, those snake oils didn't work. Some actually did make people feel better, as many snake oils contained laudanum—a mixture of alcohol and opium. It pretty much doesn't matter what is wrong with you, if you take alcohol and opium, you'll feel better. But just because something makes you feel better doesn't mean that it works, or that it has helped you, or that it's safe, or that it does what marketers claim. Unfortunately, in the world of self-help and self-improvement, we still live in a world of snake oil where anybody can make virtually any kind of claim and there is very little oversight. Looking at the scientific research on success and happiness is our best protection from being taken in by peddlers of self-help snake oil and self-improvement urban legends. Looking at the scientific research is the best approach for understanding what really works, and for identifying proven techniques for growth and achievement.

**Wright**

When you ask people if they would like to achieve more or if they'd like to be happier, they'll obviously say, "yes." But success and happiness remain elusive for many, many people. Based on the scientific research, what do you believe is the single largest barrier that holds people back in life?

**Kraus**

I think you're absolutely right, David. Most people truly want to achieve more and sincerely desire more happiness in their lives. I don't subscribe to the notion that people have some deep-seated fear of success, or subconsciously undermine their efforts to achieve more. Which brings up the very question you raise: "What holds people back?" My approach to answering this question starts with the scientific research, and there are decades of soundly conducted studies, published in respectable journals, about success, whether it's personal success or professional success or success in making life changes. When I synthesize all of that research, and I ask that question, "What holds people back?" I come to the conclusion it's not that people are weak or lazy or that they don't want to achieve more or that they fear success. I think it ultimately comes down to the fact that true success in life is rare because people too often use flawed strategies for success.

In *Star Wars*, Anakin Skywalker got seduced by "the dark side" and became Darth Vader. When it comes to making life changes, people too often get seduced by "the easy way out." People who want to lose weight too often say, "Gee, it's so hard to diet. It's so hard to find the time to exercise. And I hate to sweat. Boy, it'd just be so much easier if I could take these fat-burning pills or buy this exercise product advertised on infomercials that guarantees rock-hard abs in two minutes a day or listen to these subliminal self-help tapes that will rewire my subconscious mind. Those things are so much *easier*. Sure I want to lose weight, but I want it to be easy." Certainly it would be great if all of those things worked, but the fact is that they don't. They are the easy way out. Marketers are great at exploiting our weaknesses, so we have to remember the old adage, "If it sounds too good to be true, then it probably is."

If you look at the research on making life changes, it is clear that successful people avoid the temptation of taking the easy way out. Those who successfully make life changes are those who devise the best strategies for change. They come up with the largest number of strategies. They thoughtfully apply different strategies to different situations. They work harder and longer at applying those strategies. So the key to success really comes down to a question of *process*—how do you go about making life changes? The good news is that optimal processes for change are easily learned, and improve with practice. The bad news is that implementing these ideal change processes takes effort, and they are often at odds with our desire for the easy way out.

## Wright

Your book, *Psychological Foundations of Success*, outlines a five-step process for making life changes. In it, you review hundreds of scientific studies documenting the effectiveness of these steps, and the fact that these same five factors are characteristic of highly successful people. What are these five steps, and how can our readers perform better in each of these areas?

## Kraus

The five concepts are: Vision, Strategy, Belief, Persistence and Learning. They come up over and over again in the research. Successful people perform well in these five areas; less successful people don't. Similarly, highly successful organizations perform better in these areas than their less successful counterparts. The concepts themselves aren't earth shattering because people have been thinking about success and happiness for millennia. So the big question becomes how to perform better in each of these five areas. And that is really what *Psychological Foundations of Success* is all about— identifying proven tools and techniques for taking your performance in these five areas to the next level.

Take the first step: Vision. It's common knowledge that successful people have the "vision thing" and know what they want. Their lives are characterized by a sense of passion and purpose. Research actually shows that those who are very clear about what they want are psychologically and physically healthier than those who don't. But the big question is: How do you get more vision? How do you really clarify what you want out of life? So in my book I present a number of exercises for doing just that. We also know a lot about how successful people think, and the exercises I present almost force you to think about your future in a manner consistent with what we know about how highly successful people think. We know that very successful people are overly optimistic, flexible thinkers. They take risks. So the exercises really force you to think that way. When I'm doing seminars with limited time, I ask people to think about just one question: What would you try to accomplish if you knew you couldn't fail? That is a very old question that has been used by a lot of people, but it is very thought provoking. It really gets you thinking about your future and helps clarify your Vision. But it does so while almost forcing you to think in an optimistic, flexible way that involves taking risks and has all of those elements that we know are characteristic of how successful people think.

**Wright**

So that's the first step: Vision. Clarify what you really want from your life or your business. What's next?

**Kraus**

The second step is Strategy. Once you've got a Vision and clarified what you want out of life, the second thing to clarify is your Strategy for making that Vision a reality. At some level that's common knowledge, and we all know that successful people make plans for success. But the uncommon knowledge is how you do that. What are the scientifically proven ways to craft better life strategies? This is where I usually bring in the research on goal setting.

Psychologists have studied goal setting for several decades, but there are also a lot of self-improvement urban legends in this area, so it really is important to look at the research. I think that effective goal setting boils down to six ideas that I summarize as S.C.A.M.P.I. goals. In other words, goals should be Specific, Challenging, Approach, Measurable, Proximal, and Inspirational. Each of these dimensions has been shown to boost the performance-enhancing power of goals. Hundreds of studies have shown that Specific, Challenging goals lead to better performance than modest goals, ambiguous goals, or just trying to "do your best." Similarly, people achieve more when they set Approach goals that encourage movement toward desired ends rather than movement away from unpleasant states. Measurable goals boost performance, as do Proximal (i.e., near-term) goals. In fact, people who set near-term goals are more persistent, work harder, and better enjoy the process of making progress. Finally, the I in S.C.A.M.P.I. stands for Inspirational, meaning that you want goals based on your ideals, your values, and your Vision. Again, the research shows that you have a much better chance of making your Vision a reality if you set goals with these six elements. In *Psychologi-*

*cal Foundations of Success,* I've laid out other important aspects of Strategy, like creating an action plan, but setting maximally effective goals is a great start.

**Wright**

So that's the second step: Strategy. Craft a plan for making your Vision a reality. What's next?

**Kraus**

Step three is Belief. Successful people believe they're going to be successful. Psychologists use different labels for this concept; in the research literature, you'll see references to self-esteem, self-confidence, self-efficacy, locus of control, etc. All of the research in these different areas really comes down to the same idea: Belief. The people who believe they are going to be successful are in fact more likely to be successful. As with Vision and Strategy, the basics are common knowledge, but the big question is the uncommon knowledge of: How do you build Belief? In my book I present a dozen proven Belief-building tools. Many of them are based on techniques from cognitive-behavioral therapy, and with practice, they can be quite effective for building Belief and managing cycles of negative thoughts. We all have voices in our head that say, "You can't do that." Personal coaches often call them "gremlins," and psychologists often call them automatic negative thoughts—those thoughts that seem to jump into your head instantly, at the slightest provocation, and say, "You know you are a loser. You'll never amount to anything. You're not worthy." Those kinds of negative thoughts really undermine Belief, and it is difficult, if not impossible, to stamp them out completely. But using various psychological techniques like those in my book, it is certainly possible to keep those isolated negative thoughts from spinning into destructive patterns of negative thoughts and emotions.

**Wright**

I'm starting to see how these five concepts really build on each other. First, clarify what you really want from life. Then craft a Strategy for making that Vision a reality. Then build confidence that you can really make it happen.

**Kraus**

Exactly. You start to build a sense of momentum. And that leads into step four, Persistence. As we all know, successful people work hard, they don't give up, and they persist in the face of setbacks. As with the other steps, the big question is: How? How do you become persistent? I present a dozen proven Persistence-promoters in my book, but I think my favorite is the "deposit-and-refund method." Suppose you want to lose weight. Losing weight is the most commonly set goal, and it's the most common New Year's resolution, but the research tells us that it is the least commonly accomplished goal. Long-term success rates for weight loss are very low. So suppose you want to lose ten pounds. Write a check to a friend for $500. That's the "deposit" part of the deposit-and-refund method. Your friend will refund that money to you at the rate of $50 for every pound you lose. When you lose all ten pounds, then you'll have gotten your $500 back. Commit to spending that money on something that you would be really excited about. That's it! It's very simple, but it's a very powerful tool for Persistence. Research shows it can be very effective, and that the weight will tend to stay off even after the formal reward period ends. This process rewards success, which is very important because people who are trying to lose weight often overlook their successes and beat themselves up over the smallest setbacks. But perhaps the most powerful element of this technique is that it makes instant gratification work for you. There are a lot of great benefits to losing weight—you look better, you feel better—but they are weeks and months down the road. Pizza, in contrast, can be delivered in 30 minutes or less. The essence of many forms of self-destruction—overeating, overdrinking, smoking, sexual indiscretions—is that people get seduced by rewards that are less satisfying but more immediate than the longer-term goals they want to accomplish. The deposit-and-refund method makes instant gratification work for you. You start to think, "All I have to do is lose one pound and I'll get $50 immediately."

**Wright**

What's the final step?

**Kraus**

Step five is Learning. Successful people are committed to learning in a variety of different aspects. They take to heart what Eleanor Roosevelt said about her life, "I have lived my life as an adventurer, and my goal was to taste things as fully and as deeply as I could and to learn from every experience because there is not a single experience that you can't learn something from." Successful people realize you can learn from any experience, even failure, even illness, even personal loss. Some of the research on this is pretty remarkable. For example, over half of breast cancer sufferers report that the disease triggered positive changes in their lives. Even facing a devastating illness, these women find meaning, they draw closer to their families, they develop a heightened sense of what is truly important in their lives. Similarly, eminent figures in history—such as political leaders, scientists, writers, and artists—are more likely than their less famous colleagues to have lost a parent at a young age. In fact, their rates of early parental loss rival that of juvenile delinquents and clinically depressed people. They find ways to draw meaning and inspiration from tragic events. They Learn from them.

But there is another way in which Learning is crucial to success, and to describe that I use story of Sisyphus, the mythological figure cursed to spend eternity trying to push a massive boulder up a steep hill. Each time he neared his goal, the rock rolled back down the hill. Sisyphus had each of the first four steps in abundance: Vision (get the rock up the hill), Strategy (push it), Belief (he was strong and confident), and Persistence (he tried *forever*). He was weak only on the final step: Learning. He never recognized that his Strategy wasn't working. He didn't pay attention to the feedback from his environment about whether his action plan was taking him closer to his Vision. He could have revised his Strategy, perhaps seeking the help of Hercules or trying to pull the rock up the hill with a team of horses. Admittedly, he had limited options, having been cursed by Zeus and imprisoned in the lowest region of the underworld, but, hey, you get the idea.

Successful people Learn when they need to make course corrections in life. As ships, planes, and even space shuttles travel to their destinations, they are "off course" as much as 90 percent of the time. The shortest distance between two points may be a straight line in geometry, but in life it is more often the path of least resistance. Ships take advantage of ocean currents, planes use the jet stream, and spacecraft leverage gravitational fields to propel them toward their objectives faster and more easily than straight-line navigation. They only arrive at their destinations because of frequent course corrections. Life is similar. When clinically depressed people become frozen with inaction, believing they need more information before acting, they are getting hung up on trying to plot straight-line courses of perfect action toward their life destinations. Successful people take action, and rely on course corrections to navigate successive approximations to success. To help people navigate these course corrections better, I recommend the simple process of recording your progress toward your goals each day. It can be very simple, perhaps just using a zero-to-ten scale to record how much progress you've made toward each of your goals each day. Psychologists call it "self-monitoring," and many studies have shown that it contributes to improved performance. It serves as a subtle reward for progress, and a gentle punishment for failure. It forces you to be accountable. It's very motivating. And—getting back to theme of Learning and making course corrections in life—it really starts to give you some insight into what drives success and happiness in your life. You start to see patterns. Maybe you look at your progress data and say, "Gee, I make great progress towards my goal of losing weight during the week, but I kind of fall apart on the weekends." I call those "weekend snowballs." It's letting one little setback snowball into a full-blown relapse, going through that process of lapse to relapse to total collapse. When you record progress toward your goals, you see those patterns, and you start to make course corrections, refining your Strategy based on what drives success and happiness in your life. In this example, maybe you decide to stop going to restaurants on the weekends, or make an effort to take your exercise habit to the next level on weekends.

Goal-setting software not only makes recording your progress easier, but it also allows you to do powerful analyses of the trends in your success over time, all with the click of a mouse. It can really facilitate the process of Learning what drives success and happiness in your life.

**Wright**

Learning ties all of these steps together. You can have the first four steps in place, but, in a sense, travel "off in the wrong direction" unless you are focused on Learning and making course corrections. Just like the old distinction between change and progress—change is automatic, but progress only happens if you are changing in the right direction. That ties in with another interesting point you made in *Psychological Foundation of Success*—the fact that depression and anxiety are 10 times more common today than just a few decades ago. Is that really true?

**Kraus**

That is indeed true. Several studies, each done with different samples and different methodologies, document that depression and anxiety are at least ten times more common today than they were just a few decades ago. In fact, they're up to 20 times more common among women. Equally disturbing is the fact that depression now strikes people even younger—on average almost 8 to 10 years younger today than it did just a few years ago. Certainly some of this change is attributable to the fact that people are more aware of the problem of depression, and there is less of a stigma attached to it. People are a little more willing to admit to these problems. But at the same time, it's also clear from the research that there are real changes going on. Depression and anxiety aren't just reported more often, they are actually occurring more often. And there are some interesting clues as to why. We know, for example, this is primarily a Western phenomenon—this growth in depression and anxiety are evident in the United States and Western Europe, but are much less pronounced elsewhere.

Ultimately, I think it is attributable to two major factors. First, people are more socially isolated today than just a few decades ago. We've very much become a nation of individuals. Many of the social bonds that hold people together—bonds of community and family— are much weaker than they used to be. All kinds of measures tapping an individual's connection to others, and to the community at large, have declined since the 1950's. Many of these are documented in a compelling way by Robert Putnam in his groundbreaking book *Bowling Alone*. The title derives from the fact that bowlers today tend to bowl alone, whereas in past decades bowlers tended to bowl in groups and leagues. That is just one of many examples of the declining "social capital" in the lives of most Americans over the past few decades. People are delaying marriage; in fact, Americans are staying single longer than at any time in the past century. When they do get married, the marriages don't last long—as we all know, divorce rates have skyrocketed. Lasting workplace connections have given way to the "free agent" workplace and frequent job switching. Leisure time spent with neighbors building a sense of community, has been replaced by time alone in front of the television or the computer. All of these contribute to growing isolation, and isolation is a strong predictor of depression. The key seems to be that meaningful social connections help you bounce back from setbacks. We all have setbacks. We all have bad things that happen to us, and we all get sad as a result.

The difference is that successful people bounce back from negative events whereas clinically depressed people don't. They get mired in negative cycles of emotion and thought, and they come to believe that bad times are here to stay. They make "3P attributions" for negative events, believing they derive from causes that are personal, pervasive and permanent. Isolation fuels this negative thinking. Social support, in contrast, helps "buffer" the stressful impact of negative events.

So, clearly, growing isolation is fueling the epidemics of depression and anxiety, and I make that point in the chapter on Persistence in my book. The other big driver of these epidemics brings us back to the first step that we talked about in that five-step program for success: Vision. We know that people with clear, compelling Visions are less prone to depression and anxiety than others. These days, it's just harder for people to identify compelling Visions. It used to be that people felt much stronger connections to ideals or to friends or to families or to God or to country. Connections between the individual and something larger provided a clear sense of Vision. Today, those connections are weaker. If you're going to find a clear, compelling Vision, you've got to work harder to find it than ever before. And if you do find it, it may be something that excites you alone, making it harder to connect with others in terms of a shared Vision. So, I think those two things, lack of vision and isolation, are really driving the epidemics of anxiety and depression.

**Wright**

In your book, you write about "success secrets of superstitious pigeons," based on research by famed Harvard psychologist, B.F. Skinner. Can you explain to our readers what this means?

**Kraus**

I think it's one of the most fascinating studies in psychology. Skinner took hungry pigeons, put them in cages, and then fed them at completely random intervals. The results were amazing. The pigeons responded with bizarre, seemingly pointless patterns of behavior. One twirled in counter-clockwise circles. Two others rocked back and forth like pendulums. Another twitched repeatedly as if using its head to lift an invisible bar. Seemingly "obsessive" patterns of pecking were common as well—one pecked at, but stopped just short of, the floor, while another pecked at the air in an upper corner of the cage. All of this seemingly "neurotic" behavior resulted from purely random feeding times. As it turned out, the birds were being reinforced for whatever behavior they happened to be engaging in when fed. A pigeon that happened to be pecking at the floor when the food appeared, in a sense, came to "believe" that its pecking caused the food to appear. The pigeons developed "theories" that their odd behavior led to the appearance of the food, and those theories led them to engage in what Skinner called "superstitious" behavior—in much the same way that random reinforcement in casinos leads to superstitious behaviors among gamblers. Skinner, of course, would spin in his grave if he heard me talking about pigeons "holding beliefs" and "developing theories" because he believed psychology should concern itself only with observable actions, not internal cognitive processes or emotions. (Leading to an old behaviorist joke that I heard Skinner tell when I was in graduate school: Two behaviorists make love. Afterward, one says to the other, "That was good for you—how was it for me?")

Random reinforcement can lead to superstitious behavior because incorrect theories about why things happen sometimes lead us astray. All of that leads to a very important conclusion for us humans: If superstitious behavior occurs when we don't understand the true causes of our actions and our outcomes, then it is crucial for all of us to understand what drives success and happiness in our lives. Unfortunately, we often do not. For example, research shows that people dramatically overestimate the impact of how much sleep they get on their overall mood, or subscribe to the popular but erroneous theory that overeating provides long-lasting relief from bad moods. Inaccurate theories like these lead to wasted effort and counter-productive actions, whereas more accurate theories, such as recognizing that exercise is a better mood booster than overeating, lead to much more efficient and effective actions. As a simple tool for better understanding their own personal success drivers, I recommend the process of recording progress toward your goals that we discussed earlier. It helps you really understand what drives success and happiness in your life. And it makes sure that you don't become the human equivalent of those superstitious pigeons, turning endlessly in circles while thinking you are engaged in productive action.

**Wright**

That's fascinating. The idea that recording progress toward your goals boosts performance is obviously backed up by sound, scientific studies. But your research also shows that many people are taken in by what you've called "self-help snake oil." Can you think of any examples that you might share with our readers?

**Kraus**

I think the most egregious example these days is these subliminal self-help tapes. The idea is that you listen to these tapes, and although you cannot audibly hear the messages in them, they "unleash the power of your subconscious mind" to produce all kinds of benefits. There are subliminal self-help tapes that claim to help you lose weight, improve your memory, all kinds of things. The one thing that all of these tapes have in common is that they're all pretty much worthless. Every single independent study shows that these tapes don't do anything. Don't get me wrong—I wish these things would work. It'd be great if I could lose weight just by sitting on my couch, ordering a pizza, and listening to these tapes, but unfortunately it doesn't really work that way. So I tell people that whenever somebody promises to "unlock the power of your subconscious mind," hold onto your wallet. That's how marketers of self-help snake oil talk. That's not how psychologists talk.

It's the same kind of thing with "affirmations." Many self-help books would have you believe that if you want better self-esteem, just repeat "I like myself" fifty times a day in the mirror. This also supposedly works by rewiring the subconscious mind. Again, I wish boosting self-esteem and self-confidence was that simple, but it is not. In *Psychological Foundations of Success*, I included a David Letterman style list of the "Top Warning Signs that Marketers Are Trying to Sell You Self-Help Snake Oil." That whole notion of "unleashing your subconscious mind" is right up there, along with guarantees about effortless change and other "too good to be true" promises. You should also be wary of any book that refers to studies or statistics without documenting their sources. Nobody enjoys reading a lot of footnotes in a book, but footnotes play a really important role in science. Footnotes are like those studies proving the safety and effectiveness of prescription drugs. You don't necessarily want to go out and read all of those studies yourself, but you really want to be sure that they exist.

**Wright**

I've been booking professional speakers for about 13 years now, and I used to hear motivational speakers over and over again, saying things like, "You've got to remember that Babe Ruth held the home run record at the same time he held the strikeout record." Then one day I was in a conference and a speaker said, "That's bunk. I've checked it out. It never happened." They'd just been passing that story down, year after year, not knowing or checking the facts about it. It just simply was never true.

**Kraus**

That's a great story. In researching my book, I've gone to a lot of self-improvement seminars, and I've heard a lot of motivational speakers. Some are very good, but some are so focused on telling memorable stories with great punch lines that they lose sight of the fact that it's really important for stories to be true. That's one of the things that separates me from a lot of the speakers out there—I'm a scientist at heart, and by training. I want to see the data and the numbers. You can't just be taken in by a clever story. The fact is that there are a lot of "self-improvement urban legends" out there.

**Wright**

That was one of my favorite aspects of your book—where you debunk self-improvement urban legends, including some fictional studies written up as factual in best selling books. Can you give us some examples?

**Kraus**

There are two in particular that are my favorites. The first is the "Yale Study of Goals." If you've been to a lot of seminars or heard a lot of speakers, you've probably heard about this "study." Here is how the story goes. In 1953, the graduating class at Yale was interviewed, and it was found that three percent of them had written specific goals for what they wanted to accomplish in the future. Twenty years later, researchers followed up and discovered that the 3 percent with written specific goals were now worth more financially than the other 97 percent combined. That's a really compelling study, and it makes a great story if you are giving a seminar on goal setting. Everybody says: "Wow, I really need to start setting goals." There's only one tiny little problem, and that is the fact that this study was never conducted. I have read about it in more than one best selling book. In fact, I just read about it in a book that was on the best seller list within the last couple of years, and it even got the legend wrong, describing it as the "Harvard Study of Goals."

**Wright**

I was just about to say I heard it was Harvard instead of Yale.

**Kraus**

Yes, the legend is "morphing" these days. But as I said, there is only one problem and that is that this study was never conducted. There are literally hundreds, probably thousands of studies on goal setting that have been conducted and written up in reputable journals. I've read virtually all of them. But I've never read any reference to this study in the scientific literature. The most compelling evidence that it is an urban legend comes from Yale University itself where spokespeople are regularly contacted for information about this study and they have done exhaustive searches. Yale has come to the conclusion that this study was never done. It was just a myth. It's like the urban legend that you only use 10 percent of your brain. That's totally false. Trust me, if I removed 90 percent of your brain, you'd notice the difference. Actually, you wouldn't, because you'd be dead, but those around you would. I actually saw an infomercial not long ago where they were promised to give you a photographic memory. All you needed was a credit card, and for only three easy payments of $39.95, you could have a photographic memory. They said the system is perfectly designed based on the way the human brain works because, as we all know, people only use 10 percent of their brains. I thought, boy, whoever wrote the script for this infomercial clearly doesn't know a lot about psychology. They may know marketing, but not psychology.

**Wright**

I've got so many questions to ask you. I find this entire topic so fascinating. I'm sure we'll run out of time, but I do want to ask you one question that I've wondered about for many years. Why do some self-improvement seminars involve walking on red-hot coals? First of all, does it work, and second, what in the world does it mean if it does work?

**Kraus**

That's a great question. I hear it a lot as I'm out speaking and giving my own seminars. The short answer is that, yes, it can work. It can indeed lead to enhanced performance in other areas of your life. First, I should say that it is definitely not a case of "mind over matter"—the ability to walk on red-hot coals without being burned is explained by basic principles of physics, and is sometimes even used as a classroom illustration by physics professors. Still, it can be dangerous, but, as I mentioned before, it can lead to enhanced performance, primarily for two reasons. First, personal growth ultimately requires some powerful emotional experiences. You can't just "think" your way to success. It takes more than learning about techniques for success in an entirely cognitive, rational way. Second, as anybody who's gone through a military boot camp knows, conquering challenges can boost your sense of self-esteem and self-confidence. Those two ideas together—the benefits of emotional experiences and the benefits of conquering challenges—combine to make walking on coals a potentially effective technique, *if* it's done in the right way.

Remember when we talked about the five steps to success? Belief was number three. Firewalking and ropes courses can boost your sense of Belief, but only if you've already got the first two steps down. If you've got a compelling Vision for your future, and you're starting to build a Strategy, then there is some benefit to Belief-boosting activities that give you an emotional boost, or get you really pumped up, or give you that sense of "I can conquer challenges and exceed my old, self-imposed limitations." But if you just go out walking on red-hot coals and you don't have those first two steps of Vision and Strategy in place, then it's not going to do much of anything. If you've got a dysfunctional company with no Vision and no Strategy, and you take them on a corporate retreat to do ropes courses, then you'll end up with a temporarily pumped up dysfunctional company with no Vision and no Strategy. I can't point to any studies comparing people who've walked on fire to control groups of people who haven't walked on fire, but there is a lot of research on "adventure education." These are programs like Outward Bound, which may not specifically include firewalking, but which feature very similar kinds of physical challenges. Literally hundreds of studies on these kinds of programs have shown that, on average, these programs really can help people perform more effectively.

Again, it comes back to that idea of Belief. These programs have been shown to lead to improvements in self-efficacy, self-confidence, assertiveness, independence, locus of control, etc. As a result, these kinds of programs have been shown to lead to more effective management among leaders, reduced recidivism among delinquents, better academic performance among students, and so on. Obviously, not every single course changes lives, and as we discussed, it's necessary to have your Vision and Strategy in place. But there is a lot of compelling research on this. It's also clear that there are lasting effects from these programs—it's not just a "post-group euphoria" resulting from a temporary pump up.

**Wright**

Well, what an interesting time. I certainly appreciate you doing this interview with me. Today we have been talking to Dr. Stephen J. Kraus. He is an author, a speaker, and a success scientist. He is the author of *Psychological Foundations of Success: A Harvard-Trained Scientist Separates the Science of Success from Self-Help Snake Oil.* As we have found today, he is a very interesting speaker. Thank you so much, Dr. Kraus, for being with us today.

**Kraus**

Thank you, David. I had a great time. Live long and prosper...

## About The Author

Stephen J. Kraus is one of the world's foremost success scientists. He teaches the *science* of success, synthesizes decades of research on personal achievement, and explores the "greatest hits" of psychology's most fascinating research. At the same time, he de-bunks self-help snake oil and unmasks self-improvement urban legends. This unique combination—a rigorous scientist who also empowers people with psychological tools for success—has led some to call him a combination of Tony Robbins and Mr. Spock. Steve is author of *Psychological Foundations of Success: A Harvard-Trained Scientist Separates the Science of Success from Self-Help Snake Oil* [citations for all research findings cited in this chapter can be found in Steve's book]. He has published numerous articles, and his insights are regularly quoted in the national media. His research is even cited in major textbooks. Steve is President of Next Level Sciences Inc., a peak performance consultancy that helps individuals and organizations take their performance to the next level with innovative, science-based tools. He has helped many Fortune 500 corporations grow their businesses, build better relationships with customers, and ensure peak performance among their employees. Steve received his Ph.D. in social psychology from Harvard University at age 25, and twice won Harvard's award for excellence in teaching. Steve also taught psychology at the University of Florida.

**Stephen J. Kraus, Ph.D.**

Next Level Sciences, Inc.

3701 Sacramento Street, #349

San Francisco, CA 94118

Phone: 415.346.4974

steve@nextlevelsciences.com

# Chapter 7

## LOUIS MORIZIO, CFP

THE INTERVIEW

**David Wright (Wright)**

Today we are talking with Louis Morizio, CFP, founder and president of The Center for Financial Planning located in Albany, New York. Mr. Morizio is a Certified Financial Planner and has been in practice for nearly 20 years. He is past president of the Financial Planning Association of Northeastern New York, Adjunct professor at two local colleges, Author of *FutureFocus*, an educational program on retirement planning. He is a member of many industry associations. Mr. Morizio, Welcome to *Conversations on Success*.

**Louis Morizio (Morizio)**

Thank you.

**Wright**

Lou, you have achieved notable success in the highly competitive field of financial services. What did you learn early in your career that helped you reach such success?

**Morizio**

Well, a couple of things come to mind. The first of which came from my parents. It's the old "Do unto others" rule. It amazes me today how many people fail to rise to the simplest courtesies we can offer to one another. Clients, peers, community members, and even our competition deserve common courtesies. All are expressions of oneself and directly reflect who we are as individuals. All of us are somebody's client, peer, community member and even perhaps the competition. How do we like to be treated? It's one of the simplest rules to understand and yet seemingly nonexistent for some people. How many times have you patronized a business and never was greeted with a hello or a thank you or even eye contact for that matter. Returning phone calls within a reasonable time period, respecting others and not wasting their time. Don't promise things you can't deliver. Always do what you say your going to do and remember to say thank you. As an old friend used to say… "It's nice to be nice."

The second thing came from a saying I once heard, "Successful people do what their competition can't or won't do". To me this involves taking some risk. Whether the risk is of a personal nature like developing new talents as in public speaking or a financial risk like taking on debt to fund a business venture. In order for us to grow as individuals we need to challenge ourselves and try new things. Each of these risks is essentially a vote of confidence in oneself. The rewards for which come in many forms such as the personal satisfaction of a job well done, increased self-confidence and self-esteem, and of course the financial rewards that follow.

A small example that comes to mind is when I first began in this business, my employer at the time, IDS Financial Services, was planning a seminar for prospective clients. The manager was organizing all the tasks involved and was asking for a volunteer to moderate the seminar, sort of be a Master of Ceremonies. Nobody was volunteering for the position. Being new to the business with little experience I saw this as an opportunity to distinguish myself as having something positive to offer that nobody else wanted to do. As uncomfortable as it was, I volunteered for the position.

**Wright**

So you would say that right from the beginning you had a lot of confidence in your ability to take the lead?

**Morizio**

Absolutely not, I was a rookie—there were advisors in the room that had a lot more knowledge and experience than I did at the time. What I did learn in that moment is none of them liked public speaking. This was something that distinguished me as being different in a positive way. As small a distinction it was at the time, I immediately gained self-confidence for taking on the responsibility. I was taking a personal risk in an effort to effect positive change in myself. It was not an easy decision as I remember my stomach was in knots. The night of the event, I had dry mouth, sweaty palms and the weak knees. But, I did it, and each time I spoke in the future I became more comfortable and had more fun. Never easy though, I still get some jitters before speaking, but I've found that it gives me a lot of satisfaction and I keep looking for opportunities to speak.

**Wright**

Nearly twenty years later, have you found that your willingness to put yourself out front and be a little different from the crowd has continued to contribute to your success?

**Morizio**

Definitely. In a personal service business, the only real value you have is you. Who you are, your character, values and integrity, all the things that makes you a unique individual. It is who you are as much as what you do and what you know that creates value in a relationship, and you have to create value to create success.

What has helped me is that I have always been willing to adapt and change and take risks. Even when things were going well....you know the expression, "If it ain't broke don't fix it." I have a little different take on this. I don't think you wait for things to break. You should be constantly looking for opportunities that will make you better at what you do, create more value for the people you serve. In many cases with running a business things don't necessarily break, they slowly become obsolete.

Whenever I accomplished a goal—you know—if I could only get to there...then I'd be doing really well. Well, as soon as I would achieve one of those milestones, pretty soon I'd become bored. I always need to be challenged so I'd throw it out there again, further ahead. And then I had to work to get to that new point. That can be an uncomfortable place to be in—often it involved serious financial commitments, and especially early on when I was borrowing money to start my business. But that just reinforced my determination to get there. Ultimately I think that this is the real source of self-confidence and self-esteem, to be willing to see a target that's out there far enough that you can't be sure how you are going to get there, but you are just so committed that somehow you will figure it out and get it done.

**Wright**

What makes your firm unique?

**Morizio**

For a long time I've believed the ideal planning firm would be one in which all of the investment, accounting and legal services for a client could all be done in-house—kind of a one-stop-shop. Today's world has become one in which time has become a very important commodity. If you can create more free time for your client I believe you create something very valuable for the client. So we've created a "team" approach if you will with a multi-disciplinary approach to serving our clientele. Too often we run into the situation where the coordinated efforts of an attorney, accountant, banker, and investment advisor are required in order to fulfill the needs of the client. Although we have yet to accomplish all of these in-house we do facilitate the relationship of all disciplines when needed. We advocate for the client and assist with communicating with the client in a way that they can understand. This can be a very complicated business at times so keeping things as simple as possible is the goal. I do not believe one person can be all things to all people and do an effective job. We have service staff and professional staff that focus on particular skill sets in service to our clients. Our clients get everyone, the team, not just one person. The team approach serves our clients very well and for the past several years we have grown through referrals only.

**Wright**

Are there specific characteristics shared by the clients you work with?

**Morizio**

Definitely. A year ago I hired a consultant out of San Diego, Bill Bachrach, to help me better understand my clients and evaluate what we do as a firm. As a result of our relationship Bill asked me to write a forward for his book, *Values-Based Financial Planning.* Since he offers this opportunity on a limited basis to his clients, I thought it would be a good opportunity for me to share with clients an approach I find refreshing. It has been my experience that the clients who work with us have as part of their internal value system a good understanding and perspective on life. They have clearly recognized what is important to them and how to go about living their life. They understand that they cannot delegate away their responsibilities of time with their spouse, family and friends, time devoted to their physical health or spiritual health, hobbies and careers. What they have recognized is that they can delegate away responsibilities such as investment management, financial and estate planning, tax planning, all the things we offer to our clients. In fact, as a result of the work I did with Bill I have created a client profile that I printed as part of my forward. It includes things such as our clients are genuinely nice people—they place a high value on delegating their financial decisions to competent, trustworthy professionals—they place a high value on things they cannot delegate away. We love and respect our clients and take our responsibility for their needs very seriously.

**Wright**

In your *FutureFocus* educational seminar your tag line reads, "It's not just about money, it's about life". Can you explain what you mean?

**Morizio**

Sure. I wanted people to focus more on the "why" and not the "how" of financial planning. I wanted my clients or my audience to keep in mind why they were doing what they were doing. Too often financial institutions pander to our greed in order to entice us to chase investment performance as one example. While I agree it has some importance, it is more important to understand what is truly important to you. I'll give you an example; let's say you want to start a college savings program for your newborn child.

**Wright**

O.K.

**Morizio**

What motivates you more? Envisioning yourself picking the right mutual fund or stock in hopes of accumulating enough money to pay for college or, the prospects of seeing your son or daughter as a young adult, filled with hope and optimism crossing the stage to accept their diploma, prepared to embark on a fulfilling life of happiness?

**Wright**

How about both? Just kidding. Certainly I want the latter. I get your point.

**Morizio**

Again, as I stated earlier we want our clients to focus on the things they can't delegate like time spent raising their children to become happy, productive members of society. Not spending time picking investments, managing portfolios, determining what type of insurance is best for them. All that can be delegated. It's not about the money; it's about life...their life.

**Wright**

Lou, we've talked a bit about how you have gone about achieving success, but let's get really basic. What is success to you, how do you define it?

**Morizio**

You know, that's a great question, and one that we often forget to ask ourselves. I'm sure you can walk into a bookstore and pick up almost any book on personal development, any kind of *"How-To"*, and that's what you'll see—how to do it. But it's even more important to know *"Why-To"*. Why are we doing these things? What is so important to us about having money or influence or respect, or anything that people picture when they think about success? These questions are actually much more interesting because, while I think your readers will find a lot of common ground in these various interviews on success, it is in the *Why* that you will find differences for each person.

I guess in it's broadest sense, success has as much to do with how you lead your life as it does with what you accomplish in it. Its kind of like the saying "Life is in the journey, not in the destination". Success is also about personal growth. Using your brain, thinking about some idea or concept then bringing it into reality. You conceive or picture something that has yet to be done, and then you work very hard to make it come into existence. Something that, but for your existence, would never have come into being. You more than likely had to be willing to go into an area of discomfort, to take the risk of going where you haven't been before.

But as long as you keep a clear picture of your dream, your vision, and are persistent, you can be confident that you will get there. Of course, you have to develop some skill at assessing the risk correctly before you venture into the unknown in order to have a rational basis to believe that you have, or will be able to find, everything that you need to make it happen.

You build a plan one step at a time, and you get a lot of satisfaction from achieving each step along the way because often times the destination keeps changing. But as you move along, step-by-step, you are building the confidence that you can handle the unknowns that are always going to arise.

So, this creative impulse to see something and then make it real is the call to action, but after that it is the whole process that really makes it worthwhile. That's very true of my motivation to succeed—to have that journey, to be on the road to somewhere, and on a road that I chose, instead of sitting back waiting for life to happen. What's enjoyable about working in a personal service business is that a lot of my success has come from the positive influence I have had on other people. To me, there is no level of success that can exceed your service to other human beings.

**Wright**

You mentioned that unknowns are always going to arise. Did you suffer many false starts or stumbling blocks along the way, and how did they help you to move forward?

**Morizio**

Of course. I don't want to reinforce everyone's worst fears about public speaking, but the first thing that comes to mind is a bit of a humorous story about another seminar I was involved with. We were having a large group of clients and prospects to dinner to hear a talk from Harvey Golub, then the CEO of IDS who later became the CEO of American Express Corporation. This was in early 1987, and having survived the stock market crash that came in October of that year, it's interesting to think back about the discussions we were having at the time about the markets. But, I was acting as MC again, and with the large number of people being served dinner, we were running over the time allotted for dinner and short on time for our presentation. The event included my well-rehearsed slide presentation and introduction of Mr. Golub. We are now scrambling to solve our timing problem when Mr. Golub speaks up in his calm and confident manner and says, "Drop the slide presentation, introduce me and I'll take it from here". My prepared introduction is now all out the window with the slide show and I am now to get up and introduce Mr. Golub and his *new* in-prompt do presentation. I take a big gulp of water, stand up, and as I transition from Mr. Golub's biography to his presentation I come to realize that I don't know what his presentation is going to be now that everything has changed. A warm flush comes over my body as I nervously refer to his presentation as a "spiel." Yes. The CEO of one of the largest corporations in the world is going to give a spiel. When I said that, I was looking right at my branch manager sitting in front of me in the audience, and I just remember her eyes going wide as she heard me speak those eloquent words.

Well, I sat down, Mr. Golub stood up, and he handled it extremely well. He said something like, "I've given a lot of speeches over the years, but this is the first time I've had it described as a spiel." The audience burst into laughter, the anxiety left the room and it went on to be a great night. But I learned from that experience, and when I talk now I remember not to become too reliant on prepared notes, but instead be prepared to adapt on the fly. All the mistakes and problems we face in our life are really our "Badges of Courage", if you will. You mentioned David that you're also going to be interviewing Wally Amos for this book is that right?

**Wright**

Yes I am.

**Morizio**

Wally has a great little saying that goes something like "When you trip over a stone in your path, well that's not a stumbling block, it's a building block." That's how you have to look at these things that happen in your life if you're to become successful.

**Wright**

Aside from learning from mistakes, what other things have you done to get better at what you do?

**Morizio**

I have learned the value that a coach can provide. For instance, given that my practice is giving financial advice, people might be surprised to learn that I am not my own financial advisor. I'm as human as the next guy subject to weaknesses such as procrastination and lack of objectivity when viewing my own situation. Therefore, I hired an advisor to advise me and I pay him for his advice.

I have spent tens of thousands of dollars on coaching and professional development. This money has been very well spent, and has been returned with dividends, and not only in business, but personally as well. Learning and growing is rewarding in ways beyond what you can put a dollar value on. Just as my clients come to me for help in my area of expertise, I have always sought the help of other professionals to whom I delegate things I need to get done which are not in the area of my unique ability.

**Wright**

What would you say is the most rewarding aspect of your work?

**Morizio**

I enjoy spending time with the people. It is very rewarding to have spent as many years as I have with my clients. I have learned a lot from them since many of them are older than I. They have watched my family grow and have often offered their caring thoughts and advice to me. Some clients I have unfortunately lost to death, most have passed gracefully into their next life while others have suffered with long-term illness. From this experience I must say I have learned to better appreciate all the blessings I have. Not a day goes by where I don't thank God for my good health and that of my family. I have enjoyed helping people achieve the goals they shared with me years prior. It's very rewarding to participate in the realization of their dreams. You can't put a price on that.

**Wright**

Mr. Morizio, with our *Conversations on Success* book, we are trying to encourage our readers to be better, live better and be more fulfilled by listening to the examples of our guests. Is there anything or anyone in your life that has made a difference for you and helped you to be a better person?

**Morizio**

I think there are many people that have had a positive influence on my life. I think all of us can say that. However, I would have to say my parents have had the most impact on my life. My parents are people who have lead by example. They have been consistent in their behavior and have provided stability for all of us children growing up in their household. We got a lot of love from them and still do. They have come to enjoy the simple pleasures of life and seem to enjoy each day as it comes. They have said on more than one occasion that their happiness comes from watching their children grow up together. My parents also love being grandparents. They would often call us looking to baby-sit the kids and suggest we go find something to do so they could. I took them up on that often! I think anyone who grows up in the environment I did as a child has a great advantage in life. I have very fond memories of growing up with my parents and siblings. I guess I would consider myself very successful if my children grow up to love and respect me as much as I love and respect my parents. I don't think it can get better than that.

**Wright**

What a great conversation and how informative you've been. I really appreciate you taking this time out of the day to talk to me.

**Morizzo**

I appreciate having the conversation.

## About The Author

Louis Morizio is founder and president of "The Center for Financial Planning", a financial planning and investment advisory firm in Colonie, NY. Lou is a Certified Financial Planner and has been practicing for nearly 20 years. Lou is also a member of the Society of Financial Services Professionals, the Financial Planning Association (FPA) and Estate Planning Council of New York. Additionally, Lou served a two-year term as President of the Financial Planning Association of Northeastern New York, the local chapter of the FPA. Lou is a long-standing member of the National Speakers Association and speaks regularly on investing and financial planning. Lou is author of *Future Focus*, a course in financial planning self-assessment, evaluation and financial planning strategies. As an adjunct professor at The College of Saint Rose and Siena College, Lou taught the Certified Financial Planner Board of Standards certification program to students seeking the CFP designation. Lou has lived in the Capitol District his entire life. Lou, his wife, Patricia, and three children Aleksandr, Jacob and Morgan live in Averill Park, NY. Lou enjoys hiking, camping, and working outdoors at home.

**Louis Morizio, CFP**
The Center for Financial Planning
26 Vly Road
Albany, NY 12205
Phone: 518.452.4394
Email: Loum@thecfp.com

# Chapter 8

THE INTERVIEW

**David E. Wright (Wright)**

Today we are talking to Gary Minor. Gary can turn a handful of toothpicks into money, but he is no magician. But it's toothpicks and more sophisticated instruments that Gary Minor uses to illustrate simple principles that transform problems into profits. As the founder of 21st Century Leadership Institute, Gary has been assisting companies both large and small since 1992 to realize their peak performance and maintain a competitive edge in the changing market place. Gary Minor who grew up in Franklin, Tennessee, left for Memphis to attend Rhodes College and stayed to earn a degree in law from the University Of Memphis School Of Law. It was during his 12-year career as a trial attorney that he gained the experience and knowledge that would become the basis for his approach helping people learn how to solve their own problems in the workplace. He is a member of the American Society for Training and Development, ASTD, and a past officer of his local chapter. He also is a member of the National

Speakers Association and an officer in his local chapter of that organization as well. Gary, welcome to *Conversations on Success*.

**Gary Minor (Minor)**
Thank you, David.

**Wright**
By the way, you graduated from a school that my 14-year-old says she is going to attend.

**Minor**
Rhodes?

**Wright**
Yes, her grandmother graduated from Rhodes.

**Minor**
Fantastic! Do you know what year?

**Wright**
I can't remember. It was a long, long time ago though, but she just passed away at 84 so she's a Tri-Delt legacy. That's why my daughter wants to go there.

**Minor**
It is a great school and she'll really enjoy it and really be challenged there.
It's very conducive to a learning environment. It just makes you feel studious when you just walk on campus.

**Wright**
Well, I've been to that church many times right beside it where a lot of the students sing in the choir.

**Minor**
Evergreen Presbyterian.

**Wright**
Evergreen, yes, she was a member there. My wife was as well.

**Minor**

Wow!

**Wright**

My wife grew up in Memphis. Anyway, tell our readers a little bit about how you changed your career from law to training and education.

**Minor**

I am asked that question many times mainly by lawyers that wished that they were able to get out of the profession as well. It's an interesting story, I believe, in that I used to do a lot of commercial litigation. I represented people and businesses in lawsuits that in many cases were being sued by their former customers. The fact that those plaintiffs were former customers is the big key here. What I discovered was that the problems oftentimes came from misunderstandings within my client's company. Sales would sell something that manufacturing wasn't able to manufacture within the time frame that they were given, and then distribution couldn't get it there on time because manufacturing hadn't made it yet. Sales would get calls and blame everybody else for their promises not being fulfilled. So many times sales didn't check with manufacturing to see what could be done first. As a consequence people are too busy protecting their silos to notice that the customer was slipping away and pretty soon that customer became now a former customer that was then referred to as "plaintiffs". Then the finger pointing became even worse because then the lawyer fees were involved and nobody really bothered to notice that their customer base is shrinking. I figured out that if I could help my clients address these internal communication issues on the front end; we'd spend much less time in the courtroom and more time taking care of customers. I would end up representing a more profitable enterprise and they would have a longer list of customers rather than former customers now known as plaintiffs.

**Wright**

I would imagine that the credibility that a law degree has would really be helpful.

**Minor**

The most important thing that I took away from law school was a different way to think. Lawyers think differently. While we spend three years in law school learning what the law is, that information itself has very little value after a year or two because laws actually change. The skill of approaching a problem, thinking in a very analytical way, coming up with a variety of solutions, weighing the alternatives and arriving at a well reasoned conclusion is the lasting skill I use now.

**Wright**

Right.

**Minor**

That's what I have taken from my law degree and my law experience and applied to the business setting because if you have a sales background, you approach everything from a buyer/seller perspective.

**Wright**

Right.

**Minor**

If you have a manufacturing's background you approach things from an input/through put/output perspective. If you have a customer service orientation you see everything through how can we serve a customer orientation. If it's a customer service issue that's exactly the way it ought to be viewed. But what if it's not? The way to approach a problem from a worse case scenario analysis that lawyers are trained to do, allows me to cut through a lot of the fluff and muck inside organizations and help determine what the true problem is. While people often spend a lot of time and energy solving peripheral issues, a lot of times they miss the core problem that actually leads to the real difficulty in the first place.

In the scenario I was giving you earlier from a sales-manufacturing-distribution view-point, people were too busy pointing the fingers at other people's silos and trying to deflect blame from their own to actually look into their silo. And more importantly the larger organization, to ask the hard questions needed to determine whether their processes and systems are actually set up to help their customers or for their own convenience. A lot of companies spend lots of time and money making sure that their policies and procedures are followed for their own convenience. All the while the customer is waving a red flag saying, "What about me? What about me?" Doing what is best for the customer is just not part of the thought process so many times.

**Wright**

Do you like to spend larger periods of time with people that a single presentation allows?

**Minor**

Both delivery styles are quite effective for the correct setting. In a single presentation we have the opportunity to spend an hour or two engaged in one-way communication, keynotes and after dinner speeches and that kind of thing. I am able to share ideas with folks but there is usually not much interaction because it is one way rather than two-way communication. In some cases that is all you want because what you are trying to do is spark a flame or to challenge a small percentage of your folks to view things differently and for them to do the initiating to find a new, more effective solution.

In the other setting, when I spend a considerable amount of time with people often times starting with a keynote and then following up with one on one coaching and workshops, I have the opportunity to do a fairly decent assessment of where individual members of your team are on their development path. Whether you are trying to help somebody become a better salesman, a better frontline supervisor, or a better strategic leader, it takes time to develop the insight and rapport for them to become as effective as they can be. When somebody asks me to work with a 42 year old frontline supervisor or middle manager who's been promoted to a strategic leadership position for the first time in his or her life and you want them to think and execute strategically, that is not the kind of transformation you can expect to see after a single lunch meeting. On the other hand, if you have a group of people together for a two or three day meeting and you need a spark to light some new ideas or jumpstart a new direction, I love to bring that spark to the meeting and deliver that keynote.

**Wright**

Do you prepare differently for those different events?

**Minor**

Certainly. For a keynote, I would have a conversation and perform some research, then have at least a second conversation to clarify in my mind that I am headed in the correct direction, and give my client some comfort that I will deliver what was promised. For a more extended engagement, I would have a series of conversations continually refining direction and methods to be sure we are heading in the same direction and I am delivering what is expected and needed.

**Wright**

Do you give pre-designed leadership courses or do you custom design your presentations to solve specific corporate problems?

**Minor**

I always tailor my delivery and content to what allows me to be as specific as I can with anybody, and that's true whether the engagement is a keynote or a more involved coaching and workshop setting. I've worked with several clients now, two different companies for over four years on a monthly basis, continuing to develop their leaders. Several have since been promoted within the corporation. In order to do that I have to find out where people are because you can't pull something off the shelf and hand him a box and say, "Here absorb this, become one with it, you will be a better leader tomorrow and call me if you have any questions." It just doesn't work.

The principles of how people work effectively with each other and the resources that they are given responsibility for aren't dramatically different from a bank to an architectural firm to a plant using lean manufacturing methods. However, the way that you have to approach them, the situations that you use as speaking examples that they can relate to their own reality dramatically change. How that information is delivered to them changes. How much of it is hand fed, how much of it is self-discovery changes personality to personality. All that has to be tailor-made with regard to several factors such as people's individual learning styles, where they are in their leadership development, what their experience is, what their assessments reveal, among other factors. What I hope to do is to take people from wherever they are and to help them develop into strategic leaders so that they can be as effective as possible for their employer and for their own growth, wherever that may be.

**Wright**

You use an acronym in some of your presentations, "quest", could you explain what that is?

**Minor**

I actually spell it with a "w", qwest.

**Wright**

Okay.

**Minor**

Its' a different way to look at "qwest". I think of it this way:

The "q" stands for question. What I hope that strategic leaders will do is to ask questions of their own people and of their own organization about what the truth really is. I am speaking of questions such as: "Are we kidding ourselves about our market share? Are we kidding ourselves about how our customers feel about the physical environment inside our stores, or how our employees about our environment? How do our customers feel about our services and goods that we deliver to them? Do we really know who our customers are?"

Tom Peters tells us you need to question all you assumptions every three weeks. That might be a bit rash but I think he is heading in the right direction because the reality that you use to form your assumptions about how business ought to be even as recently as just a couple or three years ago, those assumptions are based on a world that no longer exists. If you don't continually question these assumptions, I think that you will be targeting a market that doesn't exist, you'll be trying to sell to the customer that isn't there; you'll be relying upon old, antiquated systems hoping they can deliver goods and services that people are no longer interested in having.

The "w" stands for wonder. Think of a senior leader, somebody that's in an executive position, in the policy business rather than the daily firefighting business; he's sitting back in a desk chair staring at the ceiling or they're out on the plant floor or they're up in the office in the project room looking out the window; they ask themselves a question; "I wonder what it would be like if we—If we did something differently, if we pitched our clients in a different way, went after a different market statement; I wonder what it would be like if we did something, anything, everything, differently?" Michael Dell set up a new way or marketing and selling PC's completely sidestepping the middle retailer and look what that company has accomplished.

Asking these "wonder" questions about what it would be like if any particular variable in your business model were different, I think, would likely lead you to a conclusion that would address the first problem that I mentioned about operating when many of the old reliable assumptions are no longer accurate. People become so attached to their in-baskets, processing daily information and dealing with day to day things where they have a high comfort level; they forget to look out the window and figure out where the company ought to be two to five years from now. So they need to spend more time just wondering about what it would be like if it were different. The real key to the "wondering", however, is in the execution of your decision after you decide to do something different.

I use the "e" in qwest for emotions. You need to mine deeply into your organization to determine its emotional reality. Some people would call this morale. I think it's deeper than that. While morale is a component of it, it really involves more than just that piece. Are people emotionally engaged in the work that they are asked to do? This question applies to the receptionist at the front desk all the way to your Chief Operating, Chief Financial Officers and even your CEO. Are they really engaged in what's going on? Do they (or you) know your own emotional strengths and weaknesses? And are you able to utilize those strengths positively or are you able to render your weaknesses irrelevant by either strengthening those weaknesses or putting those particular aspects of the business in somebody else's control so that the fact that you are not particularly good at it becomes irrelevant? I know engineers, architects, retailers and accountants that are so married to the numbers that they really have a hard time in senior leadership positions because they want to spend the majority of their day executing skills in their core competency. They fail to realize that if senior leadership wanted them to continue that role they would not have promoted them. Well, if they have time to actually continue drawing and formulating plans for clients, that's great. But if their role is principally as a rainmaker to go out and find new business or to manage customer contacts and keep people happy, look for new ways to serve, if they are in a strategic position where they are designing the future of the organization, all that has to be done to the exclusion of the technical skill. The question is, "Are you able to turn those things over, let go, and actually spend your time where you need to spend your time?"

The "s" stands for strategy. As I said earlier I want everybody that I touch whether or not it's in a keynote or after dinner speech or after years with working with them through their organization, I want everybody to be a strategic leader. I use strategy to mean not only do you know where you are going, but do you personally, or at least your business unit, have a share of the strategy of the organization? Do you have a stake in making sure that your vision and mission are accomplished? If you don't, what can you do to put yourself into a position where you have an opportunity to influence execution? Frankly, management is easy compared to leadership. Warren Bennis has been quoted as saying "Most organizations are over managed and under led." I agree. I think he means that most organizations have a good handle on their policies and procedures and they follow the rules accurately, but they are not sure where those policies are taking them, or how those procedures add to their bottom line.

**Wright**

Right.

**Minor**

The "t" in qwest stands for tell. Tell everybody everything. The more people know about the organization, what it stands for and what uniquely positions it in the marketplace, what distinguishes it from its competitors, the better they can serve their customers and their communities. The more employees know about that, the more they know about the tools they have at their disposal, the deeper the commitment is going to be to your strategy, to your vision, to your goals or project.

You also need to tell people where they stand. You need to share their triumphs and successes with them and their peers and acknowledge the great work that they do when they do great work. You also need to tell them when they are not meeting expectations or when they are just plain messing up. To be effective and help your team be effective, you must tell them the score whether it's good or bad news. You have to give them specific examples so they know what behavior to repeat and what to avoid. By giving people specific examples of what they do well and what they don't do well, they have a clear understanding of what behavior you want more of and what behavior you want less of, and it gives them a clearer indication of what they ought to be doing with their time and how to set their priorities. It should be fundamentally easy to tell people what it is you want, but over the last 11 years I've worked with thousands of people in a couple hundred organizations and people just don't do this. They assume that people know what their jobs are, what their priorities should be, and what actions bring the most value to the organization. Since execution is really the only measure of an organization's worth you would think that clarity would rule. However, so many people rely on assumption rather than clarity when clarity would be so easy to ensure, merely by being sure all know what needs to be done.

**Wright**

Right.

**Minor**

It's just really bizarre to me that people think that somebody can step into a brand new role they have never had before, and they would know what their expectations are and what they ought to be doing. It's just not reasonable.

**Wright**

You have used the words "management" and "leadership" several times. Do you think there's a difference between management and leadership? And if so, could you point out some of the differences for us?

**Minor**

Certainly. I think there is a big difference. It seems to me that a managers' job is to get "it" done, and they have to get it done by ensuring the policies, procedures, budgets, boundaries and deadlines that have been set for them are being fulfilled. Leaders decide what "it" will be. That's a pretty high level view. It doesn't give you much detail, but if you thought with that premise in mind, I think you'd understand the fundamental approach that I take. When you are talking about managers, they must see the rules I mentioned a minute ago are being used accurately and effectively. When you are talking about leaders, they must actually be leading and not still managing. If you are in the senior leadership position and you are still managing, nobody's really looking out the window figuring out where you are going for the next couple of years, where you need to be in three to five years. That's one of the big differences.

**Wright**

I was talking to a famous management guru the other day and he stated that in his opinion the difference between management and leadership was vision. Would you think that was one of the things?

**Minor**

That is the "it" that I am talking about. You have to be able to see it. You have to be able to create it in your mind first before you can convey that message to anybody else. And if you are in a leadership position, you have to be able to determine what 'it' will be.

**Wright**

I think that makes sense.

**Minor**

You've seen General Motors go from a car manufacturer to a finance company that has some cars to sell. They are doing a good job of weathering the uncertain economic times by focusing on the financing end of the business rather than the car manufacturing. They are already good at that.

**Wright**

By the way, I noticed that in your company 21st Century Leadership Institute, you refer to you associates as "coaches" rather than trainers. Is there a difference?

**Minor**

I believe there are some differences between the two. From my experience, trainers teach you what they know, but that may not be what you need to know. A coach, on the other hand, is likely someone who will spend more time working with you to try to assess what your current situation is, figure out where you are, figure where you need to be, and help you reach the outcome that is best for you rather than just teaching you what they know. I think of the difference as much a matter of the type and length of relationship as anything else.

There is always usually some value to that or some relevance to what a trainer can teach you, but it might not be exactly what you need to be doing. I use coaching in both the one on one reference as well as in the large group. When I am in a group setting and working with a group of people in an organization for a half day, full day, or periodically over longer periods of time, I like to set the conditions in a place where they can do a lot of discovery rather than me spoon feeding them what I know. I think of that more as coaching rather than training. It's a little bit narrower definition than some people have, but I think if we think of ourselves as coaches we're more responsive and we do a better job of meeting people's needs rather than telling them what we know.

**Wright**

I've kind of found down through the years that the very term "coach" is one of not only reverence, but also endearment. I can remember my old coaches when I see them now I know their names: Johnson, Smith, Black, but I still call them coach. Some of them are in their 80's and to me that is who they will always be. I noted that I saw a television interview of Joe Namath one time call Bear Bryant coach, still. There is something almost reverent about a coach.

**Minor**

I agree with you and if you are going to use the term you have to treat that relationship with reverence as well because people really put their future in the hands of their coach. Whether it's Joe Namath learning how to be a professional football quarterback after a successful college career, or in a business situation when you're trying to make a change from a tactical manager who's in charge of day to day operations to a strategic leader who will have the responsibility to chart the future of the organization.

**Wright**

I read that your staff is skilled at team tuning. Do most companies use teams in today's competitive businesses and what is team tuning?

**Minor**

Well, a lot of companies say they use teams. What I have discovered is that many use the term to refer to a work group where there is very little interaction, where there is very little communication within the work group itself. They either work on a common machine or use similar processes or systems to achieve similar outcomes, but they don't really work together as a unit. I think of them as groups. Some organizations are more like mobs, but I think of them more as groups rather than teams because there is no true plan or discussion about how the team is supposed to do what and how certain outcomes are going to be achieved. Someone who is not on the team hands all of that to them.

We call it team tuning because most people think of team building as an initial process. We're going to formulate a new team so we need to do some teambuilding. Then you go into a manufacturing plant or you go into an architecture or engineering firm and observe what is called a project team and there is no interaction whatsoever. People aren't working together at all. They are just working on different parts of the same piece. They say, "Well, why would I want to do any team building when this team's been functioning for two years?" The short answer is because it was called a team two years ago but it has not been functioning as an effective team does.

To give a more positive example, an organization may have a team that has worked together well for a number of years. Then, the mission changes a little, the personnel changes a little, and the team is not as effective as it once was. This team only needs tuning up, not a re-build. We think of tuning as getting everybody on the same page playing the same music, so that all the different pieces of the orchestra, if you will, all come together and all play their respective roles because they have effectively communicated and understand what every role is. Everybody knows whose job is whose, who is good at what tasks, and the team has clear communication both inside and out. When you put all the pieces together, you get beautiful music because the mission is clear, the roles are clear, the practice was good and when this happens, the outcome sounds great.

**Wright**

I was interested in one of the topics your firm offers to your clients, namely, emotional intelligence. What is emotional intelligence and how does it affect business?

**Minor**

Emotional intelligence or "EQ" for emotional quotient is a theory that was popularized by Daniel Goleman. I think 1995 was the year when his first major work came out about the topic entitled simply *Emotional Intelligence*. The initial proposition was that your emotional intelligence or your ability to understand and be aware of your own emotional state, understand and respond to the emotions of others and the like had a larger stake in your success than your traditional IQ or intellectual quotient. I am sure you have known people that were mediocre or poor students in school, had trouble reading even as an adult, yet were wildly successful in sales, owning and running a restaurant or in an organizer's or motivator's role in a community or volunteer setting. I had a friend in Memphis that was quick to tell you that he was not the smartest guy on his company's sales team, yet he consistently broke sales records and was professionally quite successful. This was due to the fact that he exercised his skills in connecting with and taking the time to understand his customer, clearly articulating his value proposition and delivering on his promises. These skills were more than enough to overcome his lack of raw intelligence.

Part of that is because your ability to use your intellect to absorb and analyze data doesn't necessarily produce the outcomes that will make you successful in any particular venture and it is very difficult to achieve anything in this world without working with and through other people. People are really emotional beings. They like to think of themselves as rational, logical, thinking folks, but if you think about the last time you bought a car, did you buy the most sensible, logical car or did you buy one that made your blood flow? If we all bought only the logical ones, I think the road would be full of Toyota Tercels and panel trucks. When you buy new clothes, do you buy the ones that are most practical for your use or do you buy the ones that you think make you look the best, even if they are not the most comfortable ones? That would be an emotional reaction to some extent. We really are emotional beings and the whole idea of emotional intelligence is to find out where people are through the assessment process, which I can provide and score for you. You can use either 360° assessments or just stand alone ones that measure only your input to find out where your emotional intelligence skills lay, where they are lacking, what impact that might have on your outcome and the results that you are striving to achieve. You have to reach a certain tipping point within the 19 or 20 competencies that make up the array of emotional intelligence skills, to truly be as effective as possible. The value of doing an assessment process and analyzing the results is in finding the areas where you are strong and capitalizing on those, and then finding where you are weak and working to either strengthen them or render them irrelevant within your organization.

You know, when two or more organizations merge, oftentimes the senior leadership team spends 95% of its time focusing on the operational structure, such as the new corporate pyramid, which vice presidents will survive, which locations to leave operational and which ones to close, how they are going to mix computer systems and whose software will be used. Things like that are important, but many seem to just forget the fact that all those processes, systems and decisions will only be effective when people use them. They totally ignore the fact that they are merging two different cultures out of which a new third culture will spring. Some people think that the large organization's culture will be able to absorb the new group, smaller group, and it just plain doesn't work that way. It will take a large group of people with high levels of EQ or emotional intelligence to read the culture, tune into people's feelings and respond in a way that keeps the newly merged entity on course and the people engaged in the new mission.

**Wright**

In some of your writings, you quote Aristotle who said "What we learn to do we learn by doing". I've found that for me at least, experiential learning is the best and the longest lasting. Have you found that to be true and if so, could you give us some examples of learning by doing?

**Minor**

I will. Kids are just sponges. They soak up anything you throw at them and they don't have to test it at all. If they have confidence and trust in you, if you say it they believe it. Adults aren't like that. Adults aren't sponges; they are more like the Teflon frying pan that new things bounce off of without sticking. Every time that an adult is given a new proposition or a new approach or a new way to do something, the first thing they are going to do is to test it against their own reality. They will ask themselves questions such as "Does this make sense with what I already know?" When you have 25 people in the room, you are going to have 25 different sets of experiences. The same proposition will be tested 25 different ways instantaneously. Some will embrace the idea, others will reject it, and others will be in denial that there is the need for any change. I am in front of a group in a keynote, training or coaching setting about 120 days per year. I spend about 50-60 of those days dealing with change in some way every year. If you give adults an opportunity to practice things and to experience the new way of doing things even if it's as simple as a new process to have some forms filled out when somebody opens a checking account or places an order and let them come to their own conclusion that they can do it and it actually works, you will have a much better chance of success that you would if your announced the new method, announced that you expected them to do it, and punished those that didn't.

I can give you an example from the toothpick story that you mentioned earlier. In creativity workshops or when I am doing keynotes dealing with people expanding their thinking into the new reality because they are about to undergo a change, I'll give people six tooth-picks. I'll ask them to form four equilateral triangles. If you remem-ber geometry, "equilateral" means all three corners are the same an-gle and all three sides are the same length. There are three or four ways to do this by laying your toothpicks down on the table or a flat surface. In every group, some find one of these ways and some don't. I always ask the question, "Why, when I give you three dimensional tools like toothpicks do you come up with a two dimensional outcome of laying your toothpicks flat on the table?" They usually give me a puzzled look. What I'll do is lay three toothpicks on the table flat and then I'll take three other toothpicks and stick one in each corner of the triangle on the table while holding the other end in my hand in the air. I will have one triangle lying flat and three in the form of a pyramid standing up in the air. You were given three-dimensional tools, why don't you have a three dimensional outcome? The reasons I am given are usually a stack of assumptions that were not part of the exercise, such as "I didn't know you could keep your hands on it" or "that isn't fair; you didn't tell us we could put them in the air".

**Wright**

It's fascinating.

**Minor**

It's a simple tool and it's something that I can do with a cast of thousands literally or in a workshop with just two or three folks. The idea is to challenge people's thinking to incorporate the capability of the tools that they are given even when they are as simple as tooth-picks. The way you approach the problem always dictates what your outcome will be. If you approach it from exclusively two-dimensional possibilities with a stack of assumptions not are not part of the exer-cise, you will miss a wide variety of other outcomes that are possible. People often approach their strategic planning this way, with thought of what is possible in the future except a repeat of what was possible in the past.

**Wright**

This has been an exciting interview for me. As a matter of fact, I have learned a lot. I certainly appreciate the time you've given us to-day.

**Minor**

It is certainly my pleasure to spend the time with you.

**Wright**

We have been talking today to Gary Minor. He is the founder of the 21st Century Leadership Institute and, as we have found out, knows a lot about leadership. Gary, thank you so much for being with us today.

**Minor**

Thank you, David.

Gary says his job is to "wake people up"! He spent thirteen years practicing law, and then in 1992, he began helping people reach their full
leadership potential through speaking, coaching and highly interactive
adult learning experiences. He is an Eagle Scout, designated an International Training Fellow by the Junior Chamber International Training
Institute, member of his Local ASTD chapter and National Speaker's
Association. His clients include Motorola, Department of Defense, Veri-
zon of New England, Kraft Foods, Books A Million, & Aventis Pharma-
ceutical of Canada.

**Gary Minor, JD, Exec. Dir.**
21st Century Leadership Institute
2236 Oakleaf Drive
Franklin, TN 37064-7413
Phone: 615.790.3296
Fax: 615.595.9169
Email: gary@garyminor.com

# Chapter 9

## JEFFERY COMBS

## THE INTERVIEW

**David Wright (Wright)**

Today, we are talking with Jeffery Combs, an internationally recognized trainer, speaker and author in the network marketing and direct sales industry. Jeff specializes in prospecting, leadership, teleconference presentations, personal breakthroughs, prosperity consciousness, scripts, mindset training and all levels of effective marketing. Jeff has personally consulted with more than 1,200 clients in the past five years and is highly sought after by start-up companies as well as established businesses seeking to expand their profitability through distributor training programs. He is the author of the highly inspiring book and audio series *More Heart Than Talent* as well as fourteen other motivational and personal development products. His many audio training programs benefit entrepreneurs and direct sales people at all levels of consciousness development. Jeffery, welcome to *Conversations on Success.*

**Jeffery Combs (Combs)**

How are you this afternoon, David?

**Wright**

Great! I read an interesting article you wrote a few months ago about listening. In it you stated, "Listening is one of the most under-developed skills in sales and entrepreneurship." You went on to say that "Most Americans are average listeners." Would you tell our readers what you mean?

**Combs**

Actually, most of us are average listeners at best. Very few have been taught how to listen well. Most of us are typically taught how to react. Many of us operate from the position that we have to say the right thing and that we have to be perfect to get our point across. So instead of really listening or being in the moment or operating from the present, most Americans are already operating on thinking. They're already thinking about what to say halfway through someone else's sentence; henceforth, they miss the second half of almost every sentence spoken.

**Wright**

So we're just waiting to talk and not listening.

**Combs**

That's correct, because most of us want to be heard. We want to get our point across.

**Wright**

I've always heard that listening employs more than just hearing. Would you agree with that?

**Combs**

I teach people how to listen from the heart, not from the head, and I teach people how to hear what is really meant and not just what's said.

**Wright**

So you're looking for wants and needs and meaning?

**Combs**

"Need" is a word I never use. I teach all the people I personally coach and do business with to look for words of decision and words of indecision. For instance, if you ask someone a direct question, the average person is going to use two words to set up his or her statement—"um" and "well." This is a statement of indecision. So if you really learn how to listen, and if you're doing any kind of effective communicating from a business perspective, then you learn how to understand what is meant, not just what is said. The two most common excuses you'll hear when it comes to a business transaction are, "I don't have the money" and "I don't have the time." But what is really meant when someone says he doesn't have the money or he doesn't have the time? That's the real question. You have to really hear what someone means, not just what he or she says.

**Wright**

In the same article, you write that "listening begins by learning how to read people by the energy they are emitting." Tell our readers what you mean by that.

**Combs**

It takes a tremendous amount of patience, and it takes a tremendous amount of being in the moment, of being in the present, to be able to read body language and what signals are sent—how people are projecting, how they are radiating, how they're transmitting, what they're vibrating.

For instance, I do motivational and inspirational speaking, and afterward, people usually approach my sales table. I've taught the people who work at my sales table, who collaborate with me, a whole different level of free enterprise. I show them how to ask direct questions and then read what happens before the other person answers. If, for example, someone steps up to my table and I ask him what he is going to buy, a lot of times, a right-handed person will take a direct step back with his right foot and then look directly up to the right with his eyes. A left-handed person will do the exact opposite; he'll move a step back with his left foot, and his eyes will move to the left, or they'll move up and left. What did this message really say? It says that this person just disengaged from the process. However, people who make emotional purchases or buy emotionally, like a lot of us do, will just walk up and purchase. You don't have to ask what they're going to buy.

Here's another example. You give someone a compliment, and if this person is uncomfortable with herself, she may deflect the compliment. You say, "That is a very nice dress," and she'll look down, bring her arms in and say, "Oh, this old thing?" What did her body language just show you? She pulled her hands in, she went into a fight-or-flight situation, and she just showed you how uncomfortable she is with herself.

Then there are other people whom you can feel come into a room. You can feel them without even seeing them. It's their energy, it's their presence, it's what they are radiating. I've been asked before, "How do you close?" and I always say, "The minute I open my mouth" or "The minute I walk in the room." You don't necessarily close with what you say; it's how you are, what you're becoming and the way you transmit, transcend.

**Wright**

In your book *Money is My Friend For The New Millennium*, you write of money and spirituality. I had a great laugh over the mental image of God riding around with me in a Mercedes. I know that you were being serious in a humorous way, but would you expound on your ideas about spirituality and money?

**Combs**

Absolutely! First of all, I don't believe God wanted anyone to be poor, and it's easier to assist the poor when you're wealthy than when you are one of them. We have a lot of misconceptions when it comes to money. For instance, here's a fill-in-the-blank exercise I do with audiences all across the world: "Rich people are ____." Rich people are crooks. Rich people are cheats. Rich people are liars. This is the standard misconception that is conditionally handed down, typically during what I call the "20,000 meals with the wrong financial planners." By the time you're eighteen years old, you've spent 20,000 meals with your parents, and you've heard the word "no" 144,000 times. In society, there is a great misconception about money: If you have it, you are different than the rest of us "folks." However, money is neither good nor bad. Money is not evil. Money is nothing more than strips of paper and pieces of metal, but it's the perceived value and the perceived energy that we place upon it that keeps us either close to it or distant from it. A huge percentage of our population puts a great deal of distance between themselves and not only money but love. So I teach people, number one, that money is not going to make you happy, but it's not going to make you miserable either. It's all based on your own perception. Most people believe that it is hard to make money. First of all, you don't make money; governments do. In free enterprise or as entrepreneurs, we get paid for value and service. If you create a value and a service in free enterprise, then you get to dictate what the free market will bear. Like in the Bible—and many people misconstrue this statement—"Money is the root of all evil." But it doesn't even say that in the Bible; it says, "The *love* of money is the root of all evil." Even that, to me, seems somewhat contradictory. You can love money, and that doesn't mean that you're good or that you're bad. You can hate money, and that doesn't mean that you're good or evil. It's really all based on your own perception.

**Wright**

In your book *Money is My Friend For The New Millennium*, you also write, "I have found that a large number of people fear failure but that just as many people fear success." Do people really fear success?

**Combs**

Absolutely! If they don't fear it, why are so few people successful in the great land of opportunity? Why is it that only seven percent of our population achieves a six-figure income? Why is it that only one tenth of one percent of our households in America have a net worth of a million dollars? When it comes to women and money, it's really staggering. For every five people who achieve six figures, four are men. When it comes to women, only *one tenth of one tenth* of a percent are women who have a net worth of a million dollars.

There's a tremendous amount of emotional resistance to success. Here are several reasons, David. First of all, many people fear the responsibility that success brings—that you're going to have to be smart with money, that you're going to have to pay a lot of taxes, that things can go bad in the stock market if you put money in, et cetera. Another great fear that most people have is that if they become successful, then they will upset their loved ones. Many people unintentionally hold themselves back so as not to upset their loved ones. That goes back to the notion that if you're rich, then you're different than they are.

**Wright**

One real barrier to financial success has to be the way we think about money. Your chapter called "Past Money Thinking: A Family Legacy About Money" really brought the problem home to me, especially your "connect the dots" exercise. Will you tell our readers what you mean?

**Combs**

Yes. I'll use myself as an example first, David. I grew up in a household in the Midwest where my parents were not wealthy and they were not poor, yet they were very prosperous. I never heard the phrase, "We can't afford it." We always had very nice cars, and my father always had money. It wasn't like he was wealthy, but he taught us the value of money. We were taught the ethic of earning. I had two jobs during high school, still playing four sports for four consecutive years. I saved a lot of money before I went to college and put myself through college on my own. So my money conditioning was very good. I got a college degree, continued to work two jobs and was very entrepreneurial throughout my entire life, always looking for ways to create wealth on my own. I knew I was never going to get rich or be able to teach anything about money consciousness unless I understood it myself.

Now most people in America are not in that situation, because they grew up in situations where they heard, "We're from the wrong side of the tracks." They've heard that money doesn't grow on trees, that you have to work real hard, that you have to go to college and that success is hard—all through those "20,000 meals with the wrong financial planners." I say that in jest, because I'm not suggesting that our parents were bad people. But many people grew up in extremely dysfunctional homes, with alcoholism, abuse, neglect, emotional abuse and situations like that, and there are all sorts of direct correlations between the distance one has from money and the distance one has from love. So most of our money conditioning as we grew up was very negative. Most of us were not taught prosperity.

Have you noticed that in colleges there aren't any books by any of the money masters who can really teach you anything, like the Suze Ormans of the world? She's not found in most college courses, and Napoleon Hill's *Think and Grow Rich* is not taught. The only conditioning and schooling we really get on money is economics and business classes. College predominately teaches you how to be employable and how to get a job; it doesn't teach you how to operate in free enterprise, it doesn't teach that you have to have a good, healthy money consciousness, and it doesn't teach you how to be entrepreneurial. It teaches you how to set your life up for a series of job skills, and it teaches you how to trade time for dollars. It doesn't teach you how to create any value in yourself so you can step out into the free market.

**Wright**

Through your company, Golden Mastermind Seminars, Inc., you speak a lot about coaching and how important it is. Would you define coaching for us and perhaps tell us a little bit about how it differs from managing?

**Combs**

Managing is a job. Managers manage, leaders lead. In my coaching practice, I have personally coached well over 1,200 people in the last five years. Most of them were very entrepreneurial by nature, and that is what I specialize in—showing people how to liberate themselves from many of their own fears, many of their own issues. Most coaches will coach "how" situations, but to me, "how" is completely irrelevant. For instance, why do you sabotage yourself? Why do you do what you do? Why do you have challenges in your relationships? Why do you have challenges with money? Until one understands these issues, what difference does "how" make?

For instance, if someone has issues with phone fear when it comes to prospecting, and I sit there and tell him how to pick up a telephone, how to read a script and how to converse with people, that's not going to get to the bottom line. That's not getting to the emotional issues that this person has—what he perceives to be rejection. So in my coaching, I always coach from "why you do what you do." The word "management" doesn't even register, because I don't teach any kind of management skills. I teach how to volunteer for success and how to become the leader that people are looking for. To me, everything is voluntary, and what I'm seeing is a group of like-minded volunteers that I can develop into a team. That's the area I come from, David.

**Wright**

It's obvious from your writings that you believe in action. You talk about being a goal getter instead of a goal setter. I've heard that most failure comes from not trying or from giving up too soon. What do you think?

**Combs**

That's a great question. The word "failure" does not register. It is not in my emotional dictionary, because I personally believe there is no such situation as failure. I was an addict and an alcoholic for fourteen years, and I can look back at all the situations that I created. I was arrested for drunk driving twice. I was arrested for public intoxication. I was arrested for drug possession. I can look back and give you a laundry list of all the situations that I've put myself in, and I can list hundreds of failures. Then I can look at my own entrepreneurial career. I actually ended up $65,000 in credit card debt at one point. Now I could look at that as a failure or I could look at that as a reason to succeed, because for every yin there is a yang, and for every cause there is an effect.

First of all, I teach people how to have a different perception of the word "failure." The great writer John Maxwell even refers to it as "failing forward." I just teach people to look at it as a privilege to go through what you go through, because the journey is based on a process, not just on a payoff. The average person consistently focuses on the payoff rather than the process. The process is where you learn all the great secrets. The process is where you incur action.

It's kind of like basketball: You shoot free throws from a line that is exactly fifteen feet from a cylinder—the basket. Now if you look at the cylinder and you look at the size of a basketball, you'll see that the basketball barely fits in the cylinder; however, with a little bit of practice, you can get the proper form and the proper technique and get a handle on being able to drop this round object through a cylinder that is just a little bit wider. And with a lot of practice, you can actually get quite good. I can go anywhere from five to ten years between picking up a basketball, but I can walk up to that stripe and still drop it in and get nothing but net. I can drop in eight out of ten, just because I recalled the proper technique and had practiced millions of times between the ages of eight and twenty-one, including six years of high school basketball and two years of junior college ball. That is called diligence. That is self-motivation.

It's okay to be motivated and positive, but that is not enough to get you to your promised land. If you just stay positive over and over, typically all you do is spray paint rust. You have to have an action plan coupled with a positive mental attitude. I see a lot of people who go to workshops and seminars who become spiritual, get pumped up and excited and gain a lot of the insight and wisdom that are required. But the great majority of people fail to ever create compounding, David. Compounding comes from performing a consistent action over time to develop what I refer to as "a compound effect." Compounding in success is just like compounding interest with invested money. David, if you invest $100,000 in a market at ten percent interest, it's going to take around seven years for that compounding to double your money. And most all of that compounding takes places in the last one, two and three years. That is exactly what action will do. You have to learn from your actions. Most people only give themselves room to fail, but I teach people how to give themselves room to succeed.

**Wright**

You know, success is defined differently by different people.

**Combs**

Like beauty is, David. It's in the eye of the beholder.

**Wright**

Right. I seem to get the feeling from your writing that cleaning up old thoughts and habits is vital to becoming successful. To be successful, does one have to establish a different set of beliefs?

**Combs**

Not always, but even that question is going to be like beauty. It's not like you have to develop a different set of beliefs, because many of the beliefs that we have may be strong, valid and good. But the beliefs you have that do not empower you are the ones you learn to address. You see, David, even the way you phrased that question is very interesting. Really, the reason people don't succeed is because they resist change. To them, change represents death. I'm not talking about death on the physical plane but death in a spiritual environment. I'm talking about death meaning the end of an era. For the average person to succeed or to change, he or she would have to give up struggling. So what I'm saying is that the average person will continue to struggle, because if he gives up struggle, then that will mean the end of an era, and he won't know how to operate, especially if he has struggled his entire life. You want to look at the beliefs you have that empower you, but you want to look at all the beliefs that disempower you even more, like hard work. Is it important to work hard? Or is it important to start to produce results over time? Hard work alone will never make you successful; diligence is required. Your per-

135

ceptions of what you do will allow you to make some of the simple changes. It's so much easier than the average person perceives it.

**Wright**

Jeffery, with our *Conversations on Success* book, we're trying to encourage our readers to live better and be more fulfilled by listening to the examples of our guests. Is there anything or anyone that has made a difference to you, that has helped you to become a better person?

**Combs**

Are you asking me if I've ever had any mentors?

**Wright**

Yes.

**Combs**

I strongly suggest that our readers do find mentors. I've never really had any mentors myself, although there have been people whom I've modeled. My parents exhibited certain examples that I modeled and certain examples that I didn't model. For instance, my parents were very diligent, highly educated and prosperous. They were both very athletic, but they didn't know anything about mentoring me. I grew up in the '70's, with a father who was a very successful basketball coach, and there was a lot of pressure on me to perform. There are very good traits that I got from both my parents, but athletically, I never had a mentor; I never had a good coach.

I never had a good coach or mentor in business either; however, two models that I really followed throughout my journey were Tony Robbins and Jim Rohn. Even though I never got to meet them, I always new that one day I would, and that absolutely happened. I actually ended up speaking on the same stage as Jim Rohn, whom I consider to be one of the most brilliant speakers in all the world. I got the opportunity to be on a tape series with him at one point. He was someone I really admired. Napoleon Hill, the author of *Think and Grow Rich*, was someone I studied from afar, even though he is no longer on this earth plane. I read his book over and over. Florence Schovel-Shinn, a brilliant writer who wrote a little book called *The Game of Life and How to Play It*, was someone else I modeled myself after when it came to spirituality and universal law and universal truth and understanding the give-and-get method.

A mentor, a coach or a leader is someone who can assist you with trimming time off the learning curve. But even the greatest mentors and the greatest models and the greatest leaders still can't produce the action for you. When it comes down to it, you have to volunteer for your own success. When it comes down to it, you have to stay in the game, and you have to stay in the process long enough to learn the life skills that will allow you to succeed in any endeavor, whether it be life, spirituality, business, a job or any situation. First of all, you have to have the talent, you have to develop the skills and then last, but not least, you have to have the heart. That is what will separate the average from the exceptional—having the heart. I just produced an eight-CD audio program that is my signature product, called *More Heart Than Talent*. It came out in December 2002 and the book form came out in June 2003. In that book, I really talk about the heart of a champion. I talk about what it means to have more heart than talent. I personally believe that heart beats talent every time.

**Wright**

Of course, I don't like to rehash bad things and failures in my own life or others' lives, but did I hear you say that if you had to do it over again, one change you would make would be to seek out mentors?

**Combs**

Actually, I would never do it over. I wouldn't even want to, because every blade of grass I've walked upon brought me to this moment, in this present moment of consciousness. I believe everything happens for a reason. I believe we choose our parents. I believe we go through what we go through. What I am suggesting to the readers is to take a look back at their past and let go of it. What I am suggesting is that there's a tremendous value right now in finding someone you can either model yourself after or someone you can mentor with. Hire yourself a coach if that is a possibility. Always go to someone who is actually doing what you seek to do. What I find so many people doing is getting advice from people in the exact same situations that they are already in. I always point people in a direction that goes up. Go up for advice; never go down. It's much better to fly with eagles than to hang around on the ground with turkeys.

**Wright**

What an interesting conversation. I really appreciate your taking this time to talk to me, Jeffery. Today, we've been talking to Jeffery

Combs, who is an internationally recognized trainer, speaker and author in the network marketing and direct sales industry. We will need to be on the lookout for his book *More Heart Than Talent*. Thank you so much, Jeffery, for being with us on *Conversations on Success*.

**Combs**
   Thanks, David.

## About The Author

Jeffery Combs is an internationally recognized speaker, trainer, and author who specializes in prospecting, leadership, personal break-throughs, prosperity consciousness, spiritual enlightenment, mindset training, and all levels of effective marketing. He is the author of the highly-inspiring book and audio series, "More Heart Than Talent," along with many other motivational and personal development products. His books and audio training programs benefit entrepreneurs & direct sales people at all levels of conscious development. He has personally consulted with thousands of clients in the past 5 years, and is highly sought after by start-up companies as well as flourishing businesses seeking to expand their profitability through distributor training pro-grams. He has developed a special package of training materials and professional guidance that will assist you and your company to create maximum results now! Jeff's unique style, sincerity, and genuineness have elevated him to become one of the most highly demanded speak-ers today. He is the President of Golden Mastermind Seminars Inc., and is committed to assisting people change the way they feel in order to achieve their goals and dreams.

**Jeffery Combs, President**
Golden Mastermind Seminars, Inc.
6507 Pacific Ave. Suite 329
Stockton, CA 95207
Toll Free: 800.595.6632
Email: GMS@GoldenMastermind.com
www.GoldenMastermind.com

# *Chapter 10*

## WALLY "FAMOUS" AMOS

## THE INTERVIEW

### David E. Wright (Wright)

Wally Amos was born in Tallahassee, Florida. He lived there with his father and mother until he was twelve then, he went to live with his Aunt Della, who first baked chocolate chip cookies for him in her Manhattan apartment. As a senior at Food Trades Vocational High School, Wally dropped out to join the air force. In the air force he earned his GED high school equivalence diploma. That certificate helped change his life, the GED diploma made him eligible to train at a New York secretarial school after he received honorable discharged from the air force. Wally Amos is an icon and his name is a household word. As founder of Famous Amos Cookies in 1975, and the father of gourmet chocolate chip cookie industry, he has used his fame to support educational causes. Since 1979, Wally has been national spokesman for Literacy Volunteers of America he is also a board member of the National Center for family literacy and communities and schools. His latest enterprise, Uncle Wally's, has been critically acclaimed by the media and consumers alike for their tasty high quality muffins. Wally "Famous" Amos I appreciate the conversation today, thank you for being with us.

## Wally "Famous" Amos (Amos)
Well David it's my pleasure, thank you for wanting to talk to me.

## Wright
Wally, you seem to have always been around success and achievement. I understand you worked as a theatrical agent at the William Morris Agency, where you worked with Simon and Garfunkel and the Supremes. What did you learn working with super stars?

## Amos
Well, you know at the time I was working with them they weren't necessarily superstars. I was the first agent to work with Simon and Garfunkel and I was with the Supremes on the very first day before they even had a hit record. I later worked with Marvin Gay. I worked with a lot of acts early on and watched them develop. I had been around show business now since 1961, when I started working with the William Morris Agency. So, I have seen some big ones, I've seen some not so big ones, I've seen all kinds. One of the things that I have learned is people are people and it doesn't matter what your title is or how famous you are, we all have the same issues that we are dealing with. I have learned to treat people with respect; the way I want to be treated because in reality everyone is a superstar.

## Wright
Was there anything about the ones that have been really successful that you could see in the very beginning?

## Amos
When I first heard Simon and Garfunkel, I knew that those guys were going to be a major, major act. First of all, their look. They had a very unique look. Arty Garfunkel was this tall guy with hair going every which way. Paul Simon this little guy that looked like Napoleon and the blend of their music was just absolutely out of this world. That combination said to me, "Wow these guys are really hot and they are really going to go somewhere." Now, the Supremes. I had been working with Motown and actually I wanted an act that had a hit record on Motown, called Brenda Holloway. Brenda Holloway had a record called *Every Little Bit Hurts*. So, we wanted her for a tour. I

called Ester Edwards ,who is Barry Gordys sister. Ester was handling the management of Motown acts and I offered her five hundred dollars for Brenda Holloway. We supplied bus transportation and they had to pay their own hotel. So, Ester, who had been trying to sell me these three little girls she had called the Supremes, said, "You know we will give you Brenda if you'll buy the Supremes." I said, "But Ester, the Supremes do not have a hit record and I can't have them if they don't have a hit record. They are not going to be any value to me." We talked on and on and she said, "We just recorded them, let me send you a test pressing." I said, "fine." There was no Fed-Ex overnight then. She sent it special delivery and we got it a couple of days later. We listened to it. During those years everything Motown produced was a hit record. We heard it, it was in the grooves as they say, and we said, "yes, let's do this, let's go for it." I offered her eleven hundred dollars for the two acts. Six hundred for the Supremes to be split three ways and five hundred dollars for Brenda Holloway. So, their record broke on that tour. I can remember seeing theme in Atlantic City at the Steel Peers towards the end of the tour. The Supremes were one of the last acts for Motown to have a hit record and they were just crying. They were saying, "We are never going to have a record. We are never going to have a hit. Everyone has got a hit, but we are never going to have a hit." Well, their first record, *Where Did Our Love Go,* broke on that tour. They had six number one records and never looked back. But you can see Diana Ross, she was clearly the leader of the group, she had a certain charisma, a certain entertainment attitude about her that said she was a superstar. It was wonderful. It was a great experience.

**Wright**

Knowledge, someone had said, is power and you are a teacher and host of fifty episodes of state of the art programs for adult basic learners on PBS stations nationally. Do you think this is a major step towards their ability to achieve and follow a success path?

**Amos**

I think so. I would also question whether knowledge is power. An automobile is not transportation, it is only transportation when you drive it.

**Wright**

That's true.

**Amos**

Knowledge is only power when you use it and when you use it properly also. But, to have access to knowledge, to understand the importance of knowledge and to be willing to do whatever it takes to avail yourself of that knowledge I think is absolutely critical. The work that I have done through the years with literacy and helping adults learn how to read and creating awareness for literacy; I have never said I was fighting illiteracy, I'm always promoting literacy. I always look for a way to give it the positive spin because I think what you resist persists and if you constantly focus on the negative then that's what you are going to have in your life. I think that education is the foundation of a well lived life. No question about it. I'm really proud of the work that I have done with literacy since 1979. I'm the national spokesperson for literacy, I've been a literacy advocate since 1979.

**Wright**

I had read that since 1979, you had been the spokesman for literacy volunteers.

**Amos**

Well, now here's the thing. There were two major organizations that worked with adult non-readers. One was Literacy Volunteers of America the other one was Labock Literacy Council. Those two merged last year. They are now pro-literacy worldwide. Both organizations were headquartered in Syracuse, so, their headquarters is still in Syracuse but now it is just one organization.

**Wright**

Can you tell us a little bit about their work? Especially the volunteer part of it.

**Amos**

What they do is one on one tutoring. So, I'm not saying it is an adult, it could be a teenager. I have known of high-school teenagers and college students who have actually tutored adults also. So, if a person knows how to read, has the desire to teach someone who cannot read to read, then, pro-literacy worldwide has the skills, the tools, the resolve to train that person in the techniques of teaching an adult how to read. An adult already has a vocabulary. It's not like you not dealing with a blank page. They've got experiences, they've have vocabulary, they have context, they have ideas so, the progress that an adult makes is a lot quicker because they are motivated also. There are techniques but you know it requires a lot of patience. Is also requires a lot of love and respect for that adult who has spent all of their life never really acquiring literacy skills, so they have low self-esteem. I have spoke to so many tutors, who are volunteers, that have said a student come in and they have hunched shoulders and head is down; it's low self-esteem. A lot of negativity that is attached to that. Watching them learn how to read is like watching a flower bloom. The more they learn, the more they grasp the alphabet and the English language and the more they are able to master those words on pages, it's like their posture becomes more erect and the attitude changes. They see a transformation right before their eyes. That's a wonderful experience for the volunteers. Both people get something from it and lasting friendships are formed also. It changes their relationship with everyone in their life. A volunteer did that, there's a wonderful quote that says, "Volunteering is reaching your hand out into the darkness to pull another's hand back into the light. Only to discover that it's your own."

**Wright**

Well, I'm glad to hear that because I just signed up to be a volunteer in Sevierville, Tennessee.

**Amos**

Oh you did, you pulled me right into that.

**Wright**

Now I can't wait.

**Amos**

You are going to love it. They are just the most wonderful people. There is another quote that says, "If you give a man a fish he eats for a day. Teach a man how to fish he eats for a life time." I have often thought when you teach an adult how to read you are literally giving them the tools the skills to enhance their life for the rest of their life. It's wonderful.

**Wright**

Wally when you speak to corporations, associations and universities you talk about such things as inspiration, motivation and overcoming adversity. What caught my attention was one of your topics titled *Spirituality in Business.* Do corporations really care about spirituality?

**Amos**

Well, some of them do and some of them don't. It's taboo in some areas, but it's more and more accepted now. I remember one day a number of years ago, I was taking a morning walk in Phoenix, Arizona. It was a Sunday morning. I am passing churches and the parking lots were just overflowing. It occurred to me that many of those people worked in corporations. Some of them were even CEO's, vice presidents, treasurers, human resource people in a corporation and every Sunday they go to church and then they don't want to acknowledge the God in them and the God in others five days a week. They want to only acknowledge it on Sundays. And so, those same people have a spirituality and often times they try to deny it. I'm finding that more and more people now are really dealing with their spirituality. They are understanding that it's more than just material, it's more than what we can see, touch, feel, smell or hear. There's something behind all of that, that breaths your lungs everyday that formulates the words and pushes them out of your mouth. There is absolutely something to all of this that beats your heart twenty-four hours a day. So, more and more corporations, more and more CEO's are acknowledging their spirituality and that's a great signal for everyone else in the organization to acknowledge theirs also. There was a time when I heard people saying, "don't say God." I go, "Why not? God is all there is." Now I never get that anymore and my talks are always laced with spirituality. I get more and more people after my talks that come up and thank me for acknowledging the power greater than all of us. The power of the one that created us. I think we are becoming more and more open to spirituality in the workplace. There are companies now that do seminars on that. There is a good friend of mine who has written books and he gives seminars. He has done tremendous work in that area.

**Wright**

Great. You have an audio cassette tape out titled, *You Have the Power.* In the program you talk about unlocking your dreams and experiencing success, embracing love and letting go of fear. What really caught my attention was your comments on not getting bogged down with expectations. What do you mean by that?

**Amos**

Well, you know you've to have some expectations. So often we expect things to be a certain way. When they are not the way we expect them to be, it absolutely throws us for a loop. We cannot function after that. We are just totally out of whack. I always believe that you got to let it go. You have got to turn it over to God. We've got a plan, but God's got another plan and I'm just so happy that God's plan overrides my plan. It has happened so many times when I have wanted it to go a certain way but it didn't, but it was so much better. As a matter of fact, I created a quote for myself years ago that says, "Life is never really what it seems. It's always more." It's always more. God knows what you need before you do and he has promised that he will provide it and provide it in abundance. So, we don't always know what's best for us. You have expectations but I think you cannot necessarily be married to your expectations. There's something far greater than what you expect and you have to be open and receptive to that you have to allow a little serendipity to come into your life, those unexpected gifts.

**Wright**

My minister used to tell me people would say, "God doesn't answer my prayers." He used to say, "He did he just said no."

**Amos**

Absolutely, absolutely and you know sometimes he answers them in different ways and he doesn't always answer them when you want him to answer them. As a matter of fact this morning, every morning, I read a book called, *A Streams in the Desert,* it's a wonderful book on faith and this morning it was about patience.

**Wright**

What's the title?

**Amos**

*A Streams in the Desert.*

**Wright**

*A Stream in the Desert.*

**Amos**

No, just one stream. *A Streams in the Desert*. It's by L. B. Cowman. The message this morning was about People having this idea that we are suppose too be doing something all of the time. We are suppose to be making things happen. You can't make anything happen. You can prevent it from happening, but you can't make it, it's happening anyway. Often times what we do is interfere with it happening. Just wait and see what God has in store for you.

**Wright**

Well, you certainly have the reputation of someone who walks the walk.

**Amos**

Sometimes I trip up. Sometimes I get impatient. That one that I am challenged by is patience, because I want it and I want it now. I need it now because I've got all of these other pressures and so I forget sometimes.

**Wright**

One of the greatest statesmen in our time, I think, is secretary of state Colin Powell. May I read a quote from him?

**Amos**

Please.

**Wright**

"Drawing on his own life experience over a quarter of a century of passion for enriching his fellow man, Wally gently hammers home the point that the stones we occasionally find in our paths are really building blocks not stumbling blocks." Those words must have made you awfully proud.

**Amos**

It did. I mean, what a neat guy he is. You know, when he gave me that quote he said, "Wally you know everybody calls me for quotes. I just don't do it, but I'm going to do one for you." That was for my book, *The Cookie Never Crumbles,* so I was very honored and very pleased.

**Wright**

I was going to ask you about *The Cookie Never Crumbles*. Could you tell us a little bit about it? I know it's a best seller.

**Amos**

Well, it's not a best seller but it has helped some people along the way. The book was published in 2001, and it's a series of personal antidotes really structured in the form of recipes. I'll talk about an experience I've had then that represents the dish and then after that I'll give the recipe on how I overcame the challenge involved in that particular episode of my life. The answers on how I came through that are really structured: A half a tsp. of commitment, a cup of desire, positive attitude, all those kinds of things. It's a neat little book and it's easy to read. Just little short antidotes so you can really turn anywhere too the book and get a meaningful message.

**Wright**

That's great. You know almost every person that I talk to about success and achievement points to some form of goal setting as the first step to success. Do you agree with that?

**Amos**

Well, I think we are always setting goals because, it's just like if you want to go to Cleveland, how are you going to get to Cleveland unless that's your destination. I think people establish goals in different ways. We don't necessarily always have a very clear way of how were going to get someplace. Everyone is just different in the point relation of their goals and how they achieve them. But, I think either subconsciously or consciously you are always establishing goals. Now I don't necessarily sit down and say you know at three o'clock March 1st, I'm going to accomplish this and I'm going to do that. I had a goal a long time ago to get back in the cookie business. That was really a goal that I had and I got back in it too. I started this company under a new name that wound up not being cookies, but muffins. It turned into Uncle Wally's. But, I still wanted to be in the cookie business. I held to the thought that I really wanted to sell cookies again because I'm really passionate about cookies, about chocolate chip cookies in particular. So, I'm back in the cookie business. But, it took a long time to have that come about. I was a lot of set backs and a lot of ups and downs but I just held to the desire. Along the way, I met people that bought in to that dream of mine and people that were very instrumental in helping me and that had the skills to help me accomplish my goals. It's like a discussion whether you make a decision or don't make a decision, it's a decision. I think goals are the same way. You could have a goal—you could just be sitting down saying, "Wow, I want a new house." That is a seed of a goal that germinates and it grows and you water it and then you start figuring out how to do it. Then, other people come into your life because the only thing you can do by yourself is too fail.

**Wright**

Well, your Aunt Della is probably glad. She's probably smiling down from above and saying, "he's back in the cookie business."

**Amos**

Oh yes, yes. She has always smiled down. I've always thought Aunt Della was my guardian angel who just saw me through the rough spots. I'm just convinced that this time around she's going to be more than a guardian angel because this is named after her. She has to have a very active part in having this come to be.

**Wright**

The only reason I asked the question is, of course, I believe in goal setting. You know, I'm sixty-three now and some of the things that have happened in my life that I was very successful at happened because I was open too it and didn't resist it when the opportunity came. I didn't plan for it but sometimes opportunities just jump up in your face and I think we all have a decision to make whether we are going to follow our instincts or just resist it.

**Amos**

That's serendipity in life. You just never know where it's going to come or how it's going to come. I'm telling you if you have faith, if you trust, if your intentions are good and if you are doing everything you can too succeed at your goals and realizing your dreams it will happen eventually. You've got to be patient and you've got too know it's not your time, it's God's time.

**Wright**

Wally with all your success and achievement did you ever think that someday you would actually become famous?

**Amos**

Never crossed my mind, that was never a goal.

**Wright**

Isn't that something?

**Amos**

It was never even an idea to become famous and yet, I became very famous.

**Wright**

I see your picture on things and now I recognize your picture.

**Amos**

I always tell people if I can succeed on the level that I have, then surely everything is possible. Without a doubt, everything is possible.

**Wright**

I have known Les Brown for many, many years.

**Amos**

He's a good guy.

**Wright**

He really is. I think he was either thirty-four or thirty-seven when he discovered he was dyslexic and boy that changed his life forever. Because, everybody up until that time had told him he was dumb and stupid. He found it was just a reading disorder. The things that you are doing, I can just imagine why all these people talk about you the way they do. Do you have any plans for the future that you can share with our readers and listeners.

**Amos**

Well, my plans are to continue to be a part of the Uncle Wally's team and develop Uncle Wally's muffin company into a successful company. My plans are to really establish Aunt Della's to be a major, major cookie company. My plans are to be a good father, to be a good husband. I don't have any long-range plans, things just kind of come and I grab some and watch some go by. I guess if I have a long range plan it is to get all of these business' really in a good solid state so that they're supporting me and my family financially and I don't have to travel quite so much. I'm on the road seventy, eighty sometimes ninety percent of the time. I would just like to stay home a little bit more and just enjoy Hawaii and enjoy my wife.

**Wright**

The last time I talked to you it was cold in Tennessee and you were sitting on your back porch watching the ocean.

**Amos**

Well I'm in Houston today and it's a little chilly here. I'm watching the freeway today.

**Wright**

I remember that conversation very well. I was freezing to death and you were looking at the ocean. I really appreciate you being with us today. It's always a pleasure talking to you.

**Amos**

Anyone interested in more information about Wally Amos can go to wallyamos.com. There is a lot of detailed information there on Aunt Della's cookies and Uncle Wally's muffins. Also my lecture schedule, my books and that kind of stuff.

**Wright**

Well, by the way that's www.wallyamos.com. What really caught my eye was— sometimes I try to keep up the best I can with readings I'm suppose to be doing daily and you have got some great tapes. One is called *Faith*. The message is about beauty and the wonder that faith could bring into your daily life. I think they are taken from the *Daily Word Magazine* aren't they?

**Amos**

Yes, the *Faith* messages are *Daily Word* messages and the *Let Go, Let God* tapes are *Daily Word* messages.

**Wright**

I also was reading about those. I intend to get those.

**Amos**

The *Let Go ,Let God* tape is one of the most powerful things I have ever done. I mean truly, truly, truly my friend.

**Wright**

That's the one on *The Man With No Name*, did Deepok Chopra write that?

**Amos**

*The Man with No Name*, no that's my book.

**Wright**

Oh is it.

**Amos**

Yes, I wrote that when I was going through a law suite that Famous Amos was suing me. I think Deepok might have given me a quote for it.

**Wright**

A quote for it, yes I see now. So that was all of your trials and tribulations, going through the lawsuit?

**Amos**

Going through the lawsuit when Famous Amos sued me.

**Wright**

Well, I'll get those too then. Now, I may look funny in the Wally melon top hat.

**Amos**

But who cares. My daughter thinks I look funny in mine but I don't care. What you think of me is none of my business. It's what I think of me that matters.

**Wright**

I really do appreciate it. It's always a pleasure.

**Amos**

It's my pleasure. Thank you.

Originally, Wally Amos, a true cookie lover, baked his cookies to share with his friends. Once he perfected the ultimate chocolate chip cookie, he started using them as his business calling card and as thank-you gifts. As Wally made his rounds in the entertainment business, more and more of his friends and clients asked for another bag of cookies. Finally, Wally launched the Famous Amos® Cookie Company in 1975.

**Wally "Famous" Amos**

www.famous-amos.com

# Chapter 11

## STEPHEN BLAKESLEY

THE INTERVIEW

**David E. Wright (Wright)**

Today we're talking to Stephen Blakesley who is founder and CEO of Management Systems, Inc. He has personally assisted in over 100 start-ups. He is a speaker, writer, trainer, and facilitator. One of his most cherished efforts is chairing two CEO groups for TEC International, an invitation-only organization of top executives working together to solve common business issues. Stephen spent 25 years as founder and CEO of The Flagship Group, Inc., a financial services firm in Houston, Texas. He has designed numerous training and educational programs for some of the larger financial service organizations in the United States. He holds two Masters Degrees from American College. He is a sought after speaker and writer. Stephen has a great body of work in the marketing, sales, customer service, and recruiting fields. His direct approach and passion for clarity bring big chunks of value to any corporate setting. Stephen, welcome to *Conversations on Success*.

**Stephen Blakesley (Blakesley)**
Thanks, David.

**Wright**
Stephen, recently I read an article that you wrote for *The Insurance Record*, a publication established in 1934 as the voice of Texas insurance. In it, you stated that today's new economy business is focused on staying one or two steps ahead of ever-changing customer desires. You also state that the insurance industry is different and slow to change. To what do you attribute the difference in such an important industry?

**Blakesley**
There are really many aspects to the term "new economy," far too many for us to cover them all today. There is one aspect, however, that I think is very important to your question and that is the need and necessity for organizations to be extremely flexible. In today's business world, companies need to be able to move quickly to take advantage of changing market conditions. The insurance industry is a very structured, hierarchical, command, and control managed industry. As a result, it is lagging behind other industries. So maybe we can talk about that in detail in a few minutes.

**Wright**
So, you'd say flexibility?

**Blakesley**
I would say the insurance industry is one of the most "unbendable" industries in the marketplace. As a result, other industries stay two or three steps ahead of them. I'm not certain why that industry is so reluctant to change. If I were to pick the most likely reasons, I would say that it is because of heavy government regulation and lack of real competition. Many industry icons are struggling today because of their lack of flexibility. If they don't make changes, they're going to be gobbled up or they're going to be out of business before this decade is over.

On the other hand, companies like Progressive have set the pace for change, built a flexible infrastructure designed to meet ever-changing customer needs, and, as a result, have taken a substantially large share of the automobile market in a relatively short period of time. They have done so largely because of their willingness to get out on the cutting edge and take new approaches that set them apart from many of their stodgy competitors.

## Wright

In that same article you said that you hear a lot about paradigm shifts, but you see most people spending their time trying to drag the past into the future. How do we reverse this kind of behavior?

## Blakesley

It's just human nature for us to resist change. The truth of the matter is that in the last ten years change has come upon us so rapidly it has left us almost breathless. The best way I can describe it is that many people have their arms around the past with their hands clasped together in a "death grip." Quite honestly I think it's a lot like surfing. I think it's a lot like getting up on the crest of a wave, in that, if you keep hanging onto an anchor rope you're never going to be able to ride the crest. You've got to have enough confidence in your organization to be able to release the past and "go with the flow," as they say. You know, there's an interesting story that I always tell about my first experience with water skiing that describes what I mean. A number of years ago, quite a large number of years ago to be exact, I was water skiing for the first time. Back then the boats and the motors were considerably smaller. This day the boat was a 14-foot aluminum boat with a 35 horsepower Johnson engine. I was about 14 years old, and the instructions were, "Grab hold of this towrope, keep the tips of your skis out of the water, and whenever you see the rope getting tight wave at us and we're going to take off and you will pop right out of the water." I have to admit that I was a little skeptical, but I was willing to give it a shot. If you can remember the first time you ever water skied, just coordinating all of those activities was a major task. So, I was working real hard to keep the tips of my skis out of the water, trying to keep my head above water, trying to hold on to the towrope, while watching it as it got tighter and tighter. While juggling all these activities, I was really worried about how I was going to wave and hold on to the rope. In any event, while I was watching the rope my ski tips got turned downward instead of up, but since the rope was tight I gave the "take it away wave" and off they went. So there I was holding on to the towrope expecting to "pop" on top of the water as they said I would, but instead, I kept going deeper and deeper and deeper. I kept thinking, "Is this the way it's supposed to work? Am I going to pop up any moment?" After a period of time of only going deeper, I decided, "You know, I better let loose of this dude. I'm not sure I'll come up if I keep hanging on." I think change is a lot like that experience. It was a mistake to hang on to the towrope when I was headed in the wrong direction just as it is a mistake to keep doing things that are taking an organization in the wrong direction. It's human nature. People want to hang on to what they believe will work. In our lives and in our business adventures we hang on to the past because we think we know what the outcome will be. But, if we would just let loose of the rope or the past we will pop up and be carried to new heights on the crest of that wave of change. I don't know if we'll ever be able to overcome the tendency to hang on to the past, but I think it's important to know that change is coming at us more rapidly than ever before. We've got to learn to make it work for us rather than against us.

**Wright**

In an article that you wrote for sales and marketing executives, you posed the question "are you customers apostles or terrorists?" Can you help us understand what you mean?

**Blakesley**

I believe there are only three kinds of customers, David. The first is the satisfied customer, the second is the very satisfied customer, and the third is the very dissatisfied customer. Let me set this explanation up by first defining the middle ground, the satisfied customer. The satisfied customer is the one who is happy with the product and/or the service but may or may not come back to buy again. In today's marketplace, customer satisfaction is only the price of admission. People expect to be satisfied and there are many businesses that deliver satisfactory products or services. A satisfied customer is in the middle of the customer spectrum but is no more likely to return to buy again than not. Those customers that are on opposite ends of the spectrum represent what I call the "terrorist and the apostles."

Let me explain what I mean. Let's talk about the very satisfied customer who not only makes frequent purchases from you but also purchases more than one product or service. They also buy your premium product or service and, most importantly, tell others about you and your product or service. They are those I call the "apostles." They are your most magnificent sales force. They have used your product or service, like it, and are actively telling others about their experience. The beauty of the "apostle" is that they are selling for you but are not on your payroll. Their message is more likely to be heard than that of any salesperson. A strategy to create more of these customers is where you and your company can make quantum leaps in growth and profits.

There are actually two types of very dissatisfied customers; the customer who is dissatisfied and lets you know it and the customer who is dissatisfied and doesn't tell you. The customer who is open about their dissatisfaction can often be appeased and sometimes even become an "apostle." They are not really too dangerous to your company, provided you act to correct the problem. Most customers accept mistakes but where they really get lit up is when they express their dissatisfaction and do not get the proper response. The proper response being; one, listen to the complaint; two, offer a sincere apology; three, correct the problem; and four, do something extra.

It is the other type that is really the one you want to be aware of and avoid at all costs. That is the very dissatisfied customer that never lets you know it. This guy is extremely dangerous and can do more damage than fifty of the openly dissatisfied type. This dissatisfied customer is the one I call the "terrorist." Unfortunately there are many more of these guys than the vocally dissatisfied kind. In fact, some researchers say that only 4 out of 100 dissatisfied customers ever complain. That leaves ninety-six out of one-hundred that never complain to you but go out the door of your establishment and within 24 hours tell five people about the lousy experience they had at your establishment or with your product. Now that is what I call terror!

Just think about the last time you went to a restaurant recommended by a friend and found the experience less than exciting. The manager comes over in a nice way and gets down at table level as they are taught and asks, "How was everything?" You say, "fine," even though it was nothing special. He asks, "how was the service?" and you say, "fine," even though it was just okay. You leave and tell everyone what a disappointing experience you had, every opportunity you have. Now that is terrorism. I work with companies that recognize the impact of the terrorist and the apostle to create a memorable experience for the customer that will enable them to tip the balance in their favor.

**Wright**

I can remember going into a restaurant the other night and it was late and I think they were kind of disgruntled that I had gotten there so late. Anyway, I ordered a substantial meal and when I got my check I went to the front to pay it. I had laid 20 percent down on the table and when I got outside I noted that they had charged me a 15 percent gratuity on the check. So, I tipped 35 percent! I was really angry. Not only have I never gone back there, but I don't even know how many people I've told that story to. You're probably the hundredth.

**Blakesley**

That's exactly my point. I think many businessmen and women today really don't think that process through. Yet small changes in customer retention can have a very dramatic impact on profits.

**Wright**

In the same article you further write that while many factors impact customer loyalty, indifference is responsible for nearly 70 percent of all customer defections. What do you mean there?

**Blakesley**

What does the word indifference bring to mind when you hear it, David?

**Wright**

Somebody that just doesn't care about anything.

**Blakesley**

Absolutely. You know what I think about is calling an organization to complain about a product or a service and before I can get the complaint out of my mouth they say, "Just a moment, I'll have to transfer you to Mr. Jones." Or they'll say, "I'm sorry, that's not my department. Let me connect you with the complaints department." And then you get in voice mail jail for the next fifteen minutes.

**Wright**

Voice mail jail.

**Blakesley**

Has that ever happened to you?

**Wright**

I've never called it that. I feel like I'm in jail.

**Blakesley**

That is why I call it voice mail jail. You get in, but you can't get out. I think it happens to all of us, David. How many times have you walked into a retail operation, walked up to a counter or to a cash register ready to buy or to give some of your money and the person behind the cash register is either talking on the phone or talking to a colleague or doing something other than the most important thing that they have to do which is take money from customers and put it in the cash register. It really grinds on me when I am in an establishment to spend money and I have to do the work. I have to almost ask for the opportunity to spend money. Have you ever been there? I call that "counter-indifference." This matter is so critical. I am surprised it is not on the "top ten do not do" list. Indifference is really a matter of education, monitoring, encouragement, caring, explaining, and educating your people about how important it is to engage with the customer and how important it is to take ownership of every problem when it comes to you. Teaching employees focus is almost a lost art today. We spend a lot of time teaching employees the value of customer focus when we work with companies.

**Wright**

You know I have read more books, I've attended more seminars, and I've listened to more cassette tapes on the subject of customer service in the last 20 or 30 years than any other single subject. Yet, customer service seems to be at an all-time low. How do you account for that?

**Blakesley**

I think it is affluence. I think people have drifted into a mode that says, "It doesn't matter what I do, people will buy anyway. Nobody is going to notice. What I do, my interface with the customer, is not meaningful." The issue really is, again, an issue of education, encouragement, monitoring, feedback, and directing people to the right solutions. There are many good companies today. Oftentimes, I think employees take the performance of their product or service for granted and believe that the product or service will sell itself. As a result of that, they lose focus on the single most important thing—the customer.

**Wright**

You take the position through your writings that it is not enough to satisfy customers, you've got to dazzle them to keep them loyal. Can you give us some examples?

**Blakesley**

Well, that is what we have been talking about, isn't it. There are a lot of good phone companies. There are a lot of people that offer good service, good prices, good response, but people aren't impressed, are they? What I mean is, they expect good service. The minimum expectation today is "good." In fact there's a classic survey conducted by Xerox Corporation in the middle 90's. Xerox Corporation was focused on selling imaging equipment at that particular time and they wanted people that bought their imaging equipment to come back and buy again. So, they embarked on quite a large campaign to determine what it was that made people come back and buy again. They thought that they needed to measure customer satisfaction and did so by creating five stages. They had very satisfied, satisfied, neutral, dissatisfied, and very dissatisfied. What they believed was that if they could get every single customer that had an experience with their imaging equipment to have a satisfying or very satisfying experience they would experience an increased level of repeat sales and that would be good. So, they went out to do that. In fact, they did do that. Over 80 percent of the customers who bought imaging equipment said that they were either satisfied or very satisfied. You would think that if that were the case that people would come back and want to buy that same Xerox again and again. But what they found was, people that said they were only satisfied were no more likely to buy another Xerox copier than the people who were either neutral or dissatisfied. That meant that it was only the people who were in the very satisfied category that came back to repurchase the Xerox copier. So, expectations in the marketplace have been raised today and people expect to be satisfied. You've got to be good just to stay in business, and if you want to grow you must do something more—you have to "dazzle" the customer. You're going to have to do something special. One of the most popular things we do in our Customer Service Workshops is teach employees how to dazzle customers.

To dazzle, you must do something beyond the norm and building a loyal customer base should be the focus of most businesses today. Customers have got a lot of choices and they're going to go to the place of least resistance, the place that's most convenient unless there is a reason and the reason is to be dazzled. If you want a loyal customer, you're going to have to find something that will dazzle them.

**Wright**

Your taped study is titled *Six Secrets to Success in the New Millenium*. It talks about teams and teamwork. How important is teamwork in the American company?

**Blakesley**

Warren Bennis, in his book *Creative Genius* said, "One is too small a number to produce greatness." I agree. Most of the great, truly great, accomplishments in the world have been a result of teamwork, not individual efforts. Teamwork is certainly not a new concept in business organizations. Teamwork has been an important aspect of growing companies for many years. But, in this current day, in this new economy where flexibility is so extremely important, the value of the team concept is really magnified.

I believe that to do or to accomplish extraordinary results, the team is the only entity that's going to be able to do that consistently. The reason is that in today's multi-faceted business setting, you know, there are just too many demands. No one person can have all of the skill sets that are necessary to move the company to its corporate objective.

What I have found, David, in working with companies on many different teambuilding efforts, is that companies with high performance standards understand the value of teamwork and teams and seem to spawn more "real teams" than companies that just talk about teamwork.

Truly, high-performance teams are very rare. Many companies talk the team talk but don't walk the walk. To build a high performance team there must be a certain passion, a real commitment by management to build high-performing teams.

I have found that teamwork is the primary unit responsible for increasing corporate performance. I would like to take this all the way back to your first question regarding the insurance industry. I believe a commitment to teams and teamwork is the driving factor creating the ever-widening gap between the haves and have-nots in the industry.

The team provides multi-faceted assets that can be applied to business problems that change with ever-increasing regularity. They can just do the job much better than the individual. The faster our world moves, the more important teamwork will be. Those companies that are still hanging on to the old command-control management style will be overtaken by those more flexible, team oriented companies of the future.

**Wright**

Another of your success secrets has to do with thinking as an entrepreneur. How does an entrepreneur think differently from others?

**Blakesley**

That's a good question. When you hear that word, what does it mean to you?

**Wright**

Two things really, someone who has excitement about forming new businesses and also someone who doesn't work very well for someone else.

**Blakesley**

An entrepreneur is a very unique individual. There are a lot of people who walk and talk like an entrepreneur, but they are not really. The truth of the matter is that the entrepreneur is very unique and they're very unique in one particular aspect. It's the aspect of risk. An entrepreneur is a person who is willing to take a business concept and pursue it even at the risk of great personal loss. Let me tell you that risking great personal loss is far more stressful than risking corporate loss. I hear "would be" entrepreneurs working for a multi-million dollar company talking about "intrapreneurship" and how it is the same, but it is not. There is nothing like "betting the farm" that your concept will work.

If you go to a lot of seminars, like I do, you hear "wannabe" entrepreneurs all the time talking about how to do it, but they have done it only in their dreams or so long ago it doesn't matter. Entrepreneurship requires courage greater than walking on coals. And to do that, they must think differently. They're classically self motivated. They're almost always people that are seekers and learners. They're self-promoters. They don't need a management team to get them directed. They seem to have a unique ability for self-management. So, if you put these four together, self-motivation, learning, self-management, and self-promotion and then you add to it the willingness to accept what others see as unbearable risk, you've got quite a unique individual.

**Wright**

Your Six Secrets theory is the only one that I have ever seen that discusses how to market and sell to the wealthy. So, will you give our readers a few tips on how you sell the wealthy?

**Blakesley**

David I am going to play the cynic here for just a moment and say that there is no better place to sell than to those who have the money to buy. In my view, Dr. Thomas Stanley has done the most comprehensive work in the field of selling to the wealthy and affluent. One of the things he points out is that, as a class, the wealthy are often under-prospected and undersold. From his work, and that of others, we have crafted some of the finest and most productive sales workshop focused on selling to the affluent.

One of the many things we zero in on is how to find the wealthy and affluent. Many salespeople miss the mark by focusing on the wrong clues. Remember the scene in Raiders of the Lost Ark where Indiana Jones is pacing up and down in the desert concerned that the Nazis are going to beat him to the ark? Meanwhile Indie's Egyptian Fakir friend was translating from some ancient writings and he stops and says, "They're digging in the wrong place." Well, that is the case with most salespeople when it comes to finding and selling the wealthy. They are "digging in the wrong place." They are looking for the wealthy in the wrong place. The best place to find people who have enough money to buy is to look to the self-employed or the small- to medium-sized business owner. Nearly 80 percent of the millionaires in this country are still working and 80 percent of them work for themselves.

Let's look at a snapshot of the average millionaire, (is that an oxymoron?). The average millionaire is 57 years old, has been married for 32 years to the same woman or man, owns a small- to medium-sized business, and takes an income of $100,000 a year or more.

So, one of the keys that I use in selling to the wealthy and teaching others to sell to the wealthy is, first of all, find out who the wealthy are. How do you do that? I mean, how do you know who's wealthy? Do you just look at who's driving the Lexus and the Mercedes? You can't do that today because you've got people who are leasing those cars for $299 dollars a month and 36 months from now they're going to have a $45,000 bill due. You can't really tell by the cars they drive or the houses they live in. One good way to tell, David, based on what we have said earlier, is to look to those people who own businesses. Seventy percent of the millionaires today are either business owners or have owned businesses in the past and sold them, becoming millionaires as a result. So, let's just say if we were selling things, we would want to try and sell things to people who have money and if we were looking for the most likely place to find people who had money, I would go directly to people who are in business for themselves.

Now there are some unique aspects about people who do business for themselves. People in business for themselves like to get personal recognition for their accomplishments through the things they buy, like nice cars, homes, and clothes. But also in other areas, like where they go on vacation. Instead of just going to Disneyland, they take the family on a photo-safari in Africa. So if you are selling something that can transmit success, you are likely to have something that will appeal to the wealthy.

So, business owners are seekers of self-recognition items. For instance, a business owner, a wealthy person, is much more likely to have a personal coach. Why? Well, not so much maybe because they want to benefit from the personal coach, but because that's a symbol of what they've become. That's a symbol of what they've achieved. Maybe they want to drive a nice car and live in a nice house. Why? Well, because that's the symbol of their achievement and they're their own recognition system. So, you know, when you ask, "How do you sell to the wealthy?" the first thing you do is zero in on where you are most likely to find wealthy people—people who have the money to buy what I'm selling. Second, you want to appeal to their self-recognition system. You want to position your product or your service such that it's a unique item. Third, wealthy people typically want to do business with experts. They want to do business with people that are the top in their field. One of the best ways to establish that kind of credibility is to write in publications that wealthy people read, to speak at events that wealthy people attend, and to become an expert in your field. Now that doesn't necessarily mean that you know more than anybody else in your field, but you can position yourself as an expert in your field and it's not difficult to do. We do a two-day Selling to the Wealthy Coaching Clinic that is jam-packed with great tips and methods for selling to those who have the money to buy. So, did that answer your question?

**Wright**

Absolutely. I have one last question for you. You've obviously been successful in your career. To what do you attribute your personal success?

**Blakesley**

There are three things that I attribute to my meager success. First, I want to say that it is my faith in God that keeps me grounded and focused. I am reminded everyday that I am God's instrument and that I need always to yield to that calling.

Second, it is my wife who keeps on encouraging me, even in the midst of failure. My wife, Lillian, has never let me stay discouraged for long. She is always right there to encourage me and dust me off and tell be that she believes in me and I thank her for that. Many go through life without any encouragement.

Finally, I believe that it is my ability to see the "glass half-full" as opposed to "half-empty." I am an optimist and I believe in one's ability to accomplish and continue to get better. That is my goal in life, to perpetually get better. I strive to get closer to God, become a better husband, father and grandfather, and be a better businessman. So, I think that pretty well sums it up.

**Wright**

Well, I sure have enjoyed this, Stephen, and I've learned a lot as well. I really appreciate you being with us today on Conversations for Success.

**Blakesley**

Well, David, I want to thank you for inviting me. I've enjoyed talking with you. Obviously we could talk a whole lot more, and maybe we'll have another opportunity sometime in the near future.

**Wright**

I'll make sure we do.

**Blakesley**

Okay.

**Wright**

Today we have been talking to Stephen Blakesley who is founder and CEO of Management Systems and The Flagship Financial Group.

He is a personal coach for CEOs. He is a speaker, writer, trainer, facilitator, and, as we have found out today, a very intelligent man. Thank you so much, Stephen, for being with us.

**Blakesley**
Thank you, David.

## About The Author

Stephen graduated from the University of Oklahoma with a B.S. degree in Chemistry. He holds two postgraduate degrees from American College, a Masters of Science in Management and a Masters of Science in Financial Services. He was CEO and Founder of The Flagship Group from 1974 to 1997. He is currently CEO and Founder of Global Management Systems in Houston, Texas. Additionally, he serves as Chairman of several CEO groups for TEC International (The Executive Committee, an international organiza-tion of CEOs).Stephen has served as Board Chairman for Something's Hap-pening, a youth organization in Houston. He currently serves on the State Board of Directors of Prevent Blindness Texas. Additionally, he has served on many Trade Organization Boards. He is a speaker, writer, teacher, coach, and master communicator. His passion is seeing others excel. He teaches a Bible Study class and is the husband of Lillian. They have six children and twenty grandchildren. His Life Mission is guided by the following quote; "We all must die, but few of us ever really live."

**Stephen Blakesley**
Management Systems
14550 Torrey Chase, Suite 255
Houston, TX 77014
Phone: 281.444.5050
Cellular: 281.687.9255
Home: 281.370.3856
Email: sjb@globalmanagementsystems.com
www.TheSpeakerMan.com

# Chapter 12

## KINGSLEY BISHOP

## THE INTERVIEW

**David E. Wright (Wright)**

Today we are talking to Kingsley Bishop who has been an international speaker for over two decades. She has presented over 800 seminars, workshops, and keynotes for businesses, organizations, and educational institutions across the United States, Mexico, and Europe. She's a former university instructor who taught her students that life doesn't get better by chance, it gets better by choice. Her degrees in English, French, and International Literature, plus her graduate work in counseling and educational psychology, and her multilingual abilities enable her to conduct dynamic presentations in several languages. Mrs. Bishop was the producer and host of *Common Cents*, a financial program on PBS, the producer and host of *The Money School*, a three part program teaching money matters, and the producer and host of *The Pride of Las Vegas* featuring the best in art, literature, music, architecture, dance, and fashion in the Las Vegas, Nevada area. She is the author of five books, the winner of numerous business awards, and the mother of six children. Her goal is to enrich women's lives through books, tapes, and seminars which excite and inspire health, financial wellness, lifelong learning, and organization at home and at work thus affording more time and energy for self, family, home, and career. She is often called the Goddess of Less Hassle. She includes future women of the world and therefore a portion of all her books and tapes of sales is donated to the Girl Scouts of America or to scholarships. Kingsley, welcome to *Conversations on Success*.

**Kingsley Bishop (Bishop)**
Thank you, I am delighted to be with you.

**Wright**
The title of your book, *Household Winners for Working Women*, is an attention getter. Often we don't associate working women with household work.

**Bishop**
That's somewhat true, but this is not a book about housework. It's a book about household organization because there are 65 million working women in this country and 3.7 million of them are multiple job holders needing to make every minute count. Their huge numbers really floored me. Although some of them are involved with paid housework like maids and cooks and laundry workers, we usually think of working women, David, as bankers, secretaries, teachers, managers, realtors, and interior designers. Whatever our professions, we all start out in the morning from a home base and retire to it at the end of the day. We all need clean clothes, clean dishes, and clean beds. Over the years I have found that when the home base is in order, the career is free to sing. Organization affords these women more time, energy, and money.

**Wright**
So you actually advocate or teach organization at home and career?

**Bishop**
Yes, and I don't teach, I guide. I lead. I'm like a forest ranger pointing out the tiny ponderosas and the big forest at the same time. I show that forest fires are possible and how to prevent many of them. I don't believe I want to say I teach, because you can't teach anyone anything. People learn when they want to, when they are ready.

**Wright**

Why is it that 85 percent of Americans say that they want to be organized or more organized and why aren't they?

**Bishop**

There are several reasons for that. One is that according to the American Demographic Society, Americans waste over nine million hours per day. That's a lot of hours looking for lost items—keys, warranties, glasses, and bills. When you add the piles of junk mail and the mad dash to retrieve a child at daycare plus the mountain of laundry stacking up, you have pure chaos. So organization is a very powerful wish and one of the top three New Year's resolutions. Why aren't people organized? Over the years we have conducted surveys at all our seminars, and we asked women, "Well, why aren't you more organized?" They narrowed it down to six things: 1) They don't know how to do it. 2) They don't trust themselves to try. 3) They worry about other people's opinions; maybe someone else won't like it. 4) They don't really know what they want in the first place. 5) They feel overwhelmed. They don't know how to eat that elephant a sandwich at a time. 6) They give up. So that's why they aren't more organized.

**Wright**

I guess that goes along with the statistic I read a long time ago that 98 percent of all failure comes from quitting.

**Bishop**

Yes.

**Wright**

What is the cost of being disorganized, not just to working women but to the rest of us as well?

**Bishop**

Chaos or disorganization has three main detriments. We took surveys of questions and answers in seminars and found many ways disorganization costs us. These costs fall under three main headings—Time, Energy, and Money. Take Time for example. How often are we late to meetings or appointments? What did it cost us? Or have you ever missed a plane? Or more tragically, have no time for those we care about? We say we care but do we give our loved ones the time they need? Corporations calculate that they lose thousands of dollars or hundreds of thousands of dollars due to inefficient time management.

Now when it comes to Money, how often have we had to buy another pair of scissors because we couldn't find the ones we own? Have you ever bought duplicates of something because you didn't remember you had one...somewhere? Have you ever lost a contract because you weren't with the project? Or have you ever lost your purse or your credit cards? These are things that organization helps to stem and you, consequently, don't waste your life.

Then when it comes to Energy, energy depends on its own generation and maintenance. You need something to get it started and you need something to keep it going. And that something is usually mental and physical health, which are both impaired by chaos. How many dollars do we spend on stress related illnesses? How much work or pleasure do we lose because we feel too tired to participate in the "pleasure of excellence"? These apply to all humans, David, not just working women.

**Wright**

One of the things that I've decided to do is write down the titles of all the movies that I rent. I don't watch that many, but I've found that I can't remember from time to time so I go ahead and pay the $3.50 and get the movie and play the first five minutes of it and come to the conclusion that I've seen it before.

**Bishop**

Yes, that happens to us, but you have a very good idea there. You carry that around in your little day planner or your Palm?

**Wright**

Palm, yes.

**Bishop**

And then it's all at your fingertips.

**Wright**

How can I determine what kinds of organization I should be doing?

**Bishop**

Well, David, first of all, know that organization is a very individual thing. You're the one who determines what's driving you crazy. That's the way you do it. You don't go by what other people say. You determine what is driving you crazy or what you want to streamline. You may not know why things are not working, but you know what isn't working. So zero in on the worst offender. How can you vaporize it? You do this a few times and you're on your way to more sane living. After a while it gets to be a habit. You start vaporizing all the bad things and you're organized.

**Wright**

You know I'm a head of a company. It's a pretty large company and I'm a pretty big deal, to myself at least. But to be honest with you I'd be embarrassed to call a professional organizer to help me. I guess that's a bad thing, right?

**Bishop**

Yes. Don't be embarrassed. Never be embarrassed because that's like cleaning your house before the maid comes. The professional organizer has a purpose—to help you. Professional organizers are not judgmental. They have seen houses and offices that are much worse than yours. They will think you are pretty special because you not only have the brains to realize you have a problem, but you have the guts to call them. You know the organizing profession is growing by leaps and bounds and there are organizers in every state. The members of the National Association for Professional Organizers have a strict code of ethics and are also very caring individuals. So never be embarrassed.

**Wright**

Why include carjacking in a book about organization?

**Bishop**

It's hard to be successful when we don't feel safe. How can we concentrate on our goals or our loved ones if we're in the middle of a physical or mental trauma? Today there are many more dangers than existed 50 or even 20 years ago, David. That's why I wrote that *Emergency Preparedness* booklet. Some things we can control and some things we can't. Besides being basically prepared, which does give us a sense of control, we must look at what's also likely to happen (like carjacking) and then become informed.

According to the Bureau of Justice, this nation averages 49,000 completed or attempted carjackings every year. This is one nightmare that no one should experience, but it can be more traumatic or even tragic if we are not aware of what to do. How does it relate to organization? Well, carjacking takes your time and peace of mind, even when no one is physically hurt. We talk about organization saving time, money, and energy; carjacking takes time, money, and energy from us. So being prepared is a way to de-clutter the junk in our lives. This is one of the reasons I put in a whole chapter on what to do or not do. For example, never, ever ask a carjacker if you can get your child out of the car, because the answer is always "No!" But if you know what to do then you're ready.

**Wright**

Are there any organization skills that I could use today to get an instant result?

**Bishop**

Yes, we live in the world of instant gratification and there are dozens of things that you can do. You would need to start with something small like a drawer or a shelf. I coined the phrase "time packets" to describe minutes available to do something. For example, do you have 15 free minutes? Then you have a 15-minute "time packet." What can you do in 15 minutes? Well, if you're at home, you can sort and straighten your sock and underwear drawers or throw away all the junk mail or magazines that are over two months old and any newspaper that is over a day old. Those are instant results. When you start with the little things like that, you can think of dozens of ways you can get instant results. But if you are thinking about big things, it does take time.

**Wright**

How did your formula for organization, the **Azure System**, come about?

**Bishop**

Everybody likes that system because it works! Years ago when my children were small, we used to take them out in the back yard and we'd read or paint or sing or whatever the project for the day was.

Then somehow we always wound up looking at the clouds and saying, "Oh, there's a pie or there's an elephant!" or whatever our imaginations could invent. Then one day we were looking up and there wasn't a single cloud up there. It was just the azure of a clear and unclouded sky, and I thought, "Oh, that's my symbol, my life direction, a clear blue and unclouded sky." Then all of a sudden words jumped out to define the acronym AZURE.

A stands for **Assess**. We assess most things when we plan...even wars, a trip to the grocery store, or any project. This helps zero in on what we want. Then **Z** stands for **Zone** or mini zones. We're used to zones—the parking places at the mall or the lines at the bank. When we assign mini zones in our homes or our offices, we create a place for everything. That's the big secret. You know where things belong. Then **U** stands for **Unclutter** or unload. It's another way of saying junk the junk. The **R** stands for **Regroup** or rearrange because now that you've assessed you know what you need and what you don't need. You've found a place for everything and you've gotten rid of the junk. Now all you have left are the good things. So you arrange them in ways that they make you happy. And **E** is for **Enjoy**. The word enjoy comes from the French "live in joy" and how many of us really do that? How many of us feel huge surges of joy and how often? We don't experience that often enough.

I use this Azure System in almost every chapter of the book and in every room in my house. You know it does create a lot of joy when you walk into a room and it's beautiful and it's clean and you know where everything is. I know that I can go out and do a seminar or write a book or just sit and watch a sunset and there's not that much clutter in my life.

**Wright**

What is the greatest benefit, in your opinion, of being organized?

**Bishop**

Well, David, I think one of the greatest benefits is like a big beautiful web in incredible colors. The web itself is your reinvented life because you weave around you benefits which include peace of mind, less stress and exhaustion, more time for yourself and for those that matter, harmony and simplicity around you even though the world is in a very bad state, and better money management. All of us could use more of these. And when we experience these joys, we can also help make a better world.

**Wright**

You know I was talking to a man recently about the amount of information that we receive daily from periodicals and e-mails that we really need to be reading. He told me he felt like he was sitting in front of a fire hydrant that was going full blast and he was drinking through a straw.

**Bishop**

Yes.

**Wright**

We started talking and I had to admit that I have less and less and less time and less and less and less energy all the time. What definite steps can we take right now to get organized since we have so little time and so little energy?

**Bishop**

We don't have so little time. Each and every one of us has always had 24 hours a day. It's what we do with that time. So, how do you start? There are three basic steps to start—**DPA**. Keep in mind that you want to start simply so that you can get the hang of it. The first step would be to **Decide**. Decide that you want to be organized. Don't be overwhelmed all the time. Make up your mind to have harmony instead of chaos around you. Step two is **Plan**. I know you are very good at this because of all the things you do. You're going to start small and keep it simple, but you still need a blueprint. So you zero in on your most important priority challenge for the day and then everything else is just detail. The third step is **Action**. The best intentions in the world are useless if you don't apply them. So you make a list of all the things that you can do to make your chosen challenge better. Then you sort the list into big things and little things. The little things will take 5, 10, 15, or 30 minutes. The big things take from 31 minutes to a week. If you have little energy, then you can go with what you can spare until you feel better. If you only have 10 minutes then you just do something that takes 10 minutes. For example, the women at the seminars always ask me this. "What can I do in 10 little minutes?" You can rinse a few dishes, wipe down a few counters, throw out junk mail, get the trash out of your car, write a note, or make a phone call to someone important to you. Even in the seminars I will not let them leave until they have organized something. Sometimes we organize purses. They take everything out of their purses, throw away the old Kleenex, trash those lifesavers that were there for six months, and get rid of old notes. They simply junk the junk. And when they leave, they have one thing organized and they can start with all the others. Remember, you're not killing time, it's killing you! So make it work hard before it gets you.

**Wright**
What is the real purpose of or the point of being organized?

**Bishop**
In one simple sentence, the purpose of organization is to make you happier.

**Wright**
Because you'll have more time?

**Bishop**
You'll have more time, more money, and more energy. That makes everybody happy.

**Wright**
There are people who consider themselves hopelessly disorganized. Is it possible for someone with lifelong bad habits to learn organization?

**Bishop**
Yes, people ask me that all the time. I just say if you can rinse a plate, you can learn organization. *Household Winners for Working Women* does help you organize most or all of your house. You must never think of yourself as hopelessly disorganized because you are not. Think of yourself as temporarily disorganized. You have reasons for being that way. You may have too much on your work plate or your home plate. Maybe no one ever showed you what to do or you never took the time to explore better habits. Or you may have your own inner reasons—like your mother was terribly disorganized so you are too. Or your mother was terribly disorganized and you're a rebel so you're the opposite. But being disorganized never has to be permanent unless you enjoy it.

**Bishop**

That depends on four factors: 1) Your level of organization. How much do you want? Some people just want a little bit, like being able to find their socks, and some people want it all. Could you guess that CPAs are wonderful about wanting tons of organization? 2) How much time are you willing to devote to getting organized? You may want to be totally organized, but you only want to put in five minutes a day. That doesn't work. 3) How fast you work. Some people get organized faster because they pace themselves. If they are type "A"s, like me, they go until they drop. If you are in no hurry, like my sister-in-law, take your time, enjoy it, and you'll still get there, just not as fast. 4) Your maintenance plan, which is simpler than most people think. So with those four factors you can determine how long it takes to be organized.

**Wright**

Where's the best place to start for someone who feels overwhelmed all the time?

**Bishop**

Start with your purse or billfold. Then at least something on your person is organized. You have a measure of success. Then when you get home or at the office get one drawer, just one drawer, in perfect order. Then, in your kitchen, start with a silverware drawer. Then the bathroom counters. When you have done a little bit in each area of your house or in each area of your office, then you keep those areas in order every day. It's important that you can see something that's not in chaos. You can do this. Then little by little you'll branch out. Choose what you want to organize or simplify each day and continue this process. The secret is always put things back. If you have to define organization, I can give it to you in two steps. One, have a place for everything. And two, and this is the killer, put it back.

**Wright**

That's good advice. I'm going to ask you a personal question. You may not want to answer it.

**Bishop**

Okay.

**Wright**

How could you possibly be organized with six children and a career?

**Bishop**

Everyone asks me that. But you're a parent. You know one child takes all your time. Two children take all your time. Six children take all your time. So it's not the number of children that produces chaos; it's the number of family members that produce harmony that counts. Everyone helps. It helps to be able to keep work at work and home at home. Sometimes I'd become a little basket with an idea to start a child in a different direction. Sometimes I'd be a wheelbarrow with lots of ideas and methods for family or coworkers, and sometimes I'd be a very large bridge from chaos to order without a lot of hassle. In short, that's where the title "The Goddess of Less Hassle" came from.

**Wright**

What an interesting time we have had together. I've really learned a lot and I really think I'll implement some of your suggestions.

**Bishop**

I'd welcome yours too because I'm sure that you have plenty that we can learn from.

**Wright**

Today we have been talking to Kingsley Bishop. She is an international speaker and has been for over two decades. Her degrees in English, French, and International Literature plus her graduate work in counseling and educational psychology and her multilingual abilities enable her to conduct dynamic presentations in several languages and, as we have found out today, she absolutely knows what she talks about. Thank you so much today, Mrs. Bishop.

**Bishop**

Thank you, David.

## About The Author

Dr. A. Kingsley Bishop, working mother of six, has been a college instructor, financial planner, TV host/producer and advisor and counselor for working women. She is currently a professional speaker, a professional organizing consultant, and author of five books.

**A. Kingsley Bishop**

Greystone International, Inc.

PO Box 70

Las Vegas, NM 87701

Phone: 866.566.BOOK (2665)

Fax: 505.427.1192

Email: kingsley@greystone-international-inc.com

www.greystone-international-inc.com

# Chapter 13

## RANDALL BELL

THE INTERVIEW

**David E. Wright (Wright)**

Today we're talking to Randall Bell. Randy is an economist with Bell Anderson and Sanders LLC of Laguna Beach, California, which specializes in damage economics, strategic planning and crisis management. Prior to this, he founded and directed the real estate damages practice at PricewaterhouseCoopers.

His assignments and research include, Chernobyl, September 11th, the Laguna Niguel landslides, the Jon Benet Ramsey crime scene, the Durham Woods pipeline explosion, the Malibu floods and firestorms, the O.J. Simpson crime scene, the Northridge earthquake, the Heaven's Gate mass-suicide mansion, the Hollywood Boulevard sinkhole and many others. He was retained by the Nuclear Claims Tribunal to determine the damages caused by nuclear weapons testing on the Bikini Atoll and the Marshall Islands. For years, Randy's career has been profiled in dozens of newspapers, magazines and by every major television network.

Randy is an award-winning author and has published numerous articles in various professional journals. He authored the textbook, *Real Estate Damages,* as well as *Out of Bounds: My experiences with high-profile disasters and what they tell us about failure and success.* Two other books, *Master of Disaster* and *Right Line-Left Line-Bottom Line* will be published next year.

He has developed The Bell Matrix®, a strategic planning tool that has been used in many high-profile consulting assignments. Essentially, his studies show that disasters are caused by either negligent or excessive management styles, while operating within the in-between results in achievement. Mr. Bell, welcome to *Conversations on Success.*

### Randall Bell (Bell)
Thank you, David.

### Wright
What is your specialty, Randy?

### Bell
Well, essentially I work with disasters. I go into situations and measure the economic damages that were caused by a disaster. On top of that, I consult on ways to mitigate the damage and develop strategies to manage the crisis.

### Wright
Boy, those were some high profile cases. The Jon Benet Ramsey crime scene, O.J. Simpson, September 11th, the Bikini Atoll nuclear test sites, my goodness. The Hollywood Boulevard sinkhole, those are some pretty heavyweight cases.

### Bell
Well, many of them are. Most of the cases that we deal with involve millions or even billions of dollars. They are disastrous not only from a lives lost and economic standpoint, but also in terms of disruptions to business and people's lives. I've learned that every disaster has both emotional and practical issues.

**Wright**

Randy, I'm curious; will you describe your typical day at the office?

**Bell**

Okay. This morning, I received two Fed-Ex packages. One involved a flood and the other dealt with a major landslide. I still need to finish looking at documents that I got yesterday dealing with widespread contamination in Colorado. One client called this morning from Hawaii regarding a major pesticide spill. My partner just left my office to go to the airport. Before he left, we talked about one of our cases where a deranged woman went into an office building and started shooting people.

Two weeks ago I was in Pennsylvania with the owner of the land where September 11th's United Flight 93 crashed. My secretary just handed me an itinerary to go to St. Louis next Tuesday to inspect a nuclear waste landfill. On the way out she made some comment about the nuclear fuel pellet on my bookshelf and said that it was making her nervous, and then she made some wisecrack about Homer Simpson.

**Wright**

So, you actually go on-site to these high-profile cases?

**Bell**

Sure. Yesterday I was at a site where contamination spread throughout an entire neighborhood in Northern California. Last week I was at a site where explosive materials were found at a residential subdivision. I'm at these types of sites all the time.

**Wright**

Goodness. How did you get involved in this field?

**Bell**

I started off in real estate—both with investments and consulting. I live in Southern California and, if you'll recall, back in the early '90's we had a rash of problems. We had the Malibu floods and firestorms, the Northridge Earthquake, O.J., the Laguna Beach firestorms, and the L.A. riots. We just had a whole rash of problems.

My clients would call me and say, "Would you please go and evaluate a shopping center in Los Angeles." I would go and see that it

My clients would call me and say, "Would you please go and evaluate a shopping center in Los Angeles." I would go and see that it had burnt down in the riots. I got so much experience with so many disasters in the early '90's that I decided I would specialize in damage economics from that point on. That led to a contract to write a text-book, which was the first book of its kind. From there I have never looked back.

**Wright**

Now, I know that your career has been profiled everywhere from *People Magazine* and the *Wall Street Journal* to dozens of newspapers and every major television network out there. How did the media learn about you?

**Bell**

Lou Brown, the father of Nicole Brown Simpson, asked me to do some work for him. To do my research, I called a colleague of mine who worked on the Menendez Brothers case. His wife happens to be a reporter for the *L.A. Times* and she called to ask me a couple of questions about the O.J. Simpson case.

She put *one* sentence in the *L.A. Times* that mentioned my name, and from there every single media outlet you can imagine called including: *Entertainment Tonight, The O'Reilley Factor, Time Magazine,* and the *New York Times.* It just keeps coming. Just last Sunday there was an article about my career in the *Seattle Times.*

So, I've been doing this work for many years before the media came along, but from that one sentence in the *L.A. Times* a few years ago, they've been calling ever since.

**Wright**

I hear that the mass media calls you the "Master of Disaster." Where on earth did that come from?

**Bell**

A producer at CNN got the idea to call me "Dr. Disaster," and then ABC News came up with "Master of Disaster." At first, I'm not sure that I liked the nicknames, but I decided to have fun and just go along with it. Now I even have a website called MasterOfDisaster.com.

**Wright**

You've turned into a major media sound byte.

**Bell**

Well maybe, but I enjoy my career just as much today as I did before the media ever called.

**Wright**

So you are the "Master of Disaster." What is your business philosophy?

**Bell**

Well, I believe that disasters provide excellent case studies for both failure and success. In fact, I don't believe that you can have a real discussion about success without also discussing failure.

For years I've been measuring these economic damages, but I think that it involves a lot more than just walking around with a clipboard and a calculator. We have to understand the behaviors, management styles and mindsets that lead to the disaster, and then evaluate how effectively or ineffectively that disaster was handled.

When I was in graduate school at UCLA in the late '80's, I developed a tool, which I call *The Bell Matrix*®. It basically lays out the ten categories of a business or personal strategic plan. So for the last several years I've been working on finding links between this business management strategy and the disasters that I study.

Ultimately, my research has shown that all damages are caused by one of two factors: either negligent or excessive behavior. I call negligent behavior "Left Line™" and I call excessive behavior "Right Line™." In between those two areas is an area that I call the "Bottom Line™". I call it this because when we are talking about genuine success, this is the "bottom line" of what we are really talking about.

## THE BELL MATRIX®

| MOTIVATIONAL BEHAVIOR™ | | |
|---|---|---|
| Left Line™ | Bottom Line™ | Right Line™ |
| **Philosophical** Unprincipled | Flexible Principled Passionate | Fanatical |
| **Intellectual** Ignorant | Teachable Knowledgeable Brilliant | Arrogant |
| **Sociological** Illicit | Lenient Lawful Considerate | Annoying |
| **Influential** Insensitive | Independent Reliable Supportive | Controlling |
| **Physical** Apathetic | Relaxed Fit Competitive | Excessive |
| **Environmental** Careless | Comfortable Orderly Extraordinary | Harsh |
| **Financial** Insolvent | Generous Budgeted Wealthy | Greedy |
| **Developmental** Regressive | Creative Proactive Determined | Irrational |
| **Operational** Negligent | Easy-Going Organized Aggressive | Compulsive |
| **Consequential** Denial | Forgiving Accountable Grateful | Obsessive |

David, we can see what management styles work and don't work from looking at how a crisis is handled. I'm probably the only person in the world who has consulted on so many disasters. I've consulted on the September 11th tragedies, the Heaven's Gate Mass Suicide situation, the O.J. Simpson case, the Jon Benet Ramsey case and nuclear test sites. I don't say that to impress you, but I say that to impress *upon* you that I've seen the most extremes of human behavior.

What is fascinating is that for every disaster and achievement I have studied, I have found a direct link between this business model and the actual mindset involved behind the scenes, as well as the economic impacts that they have.

So you might say I've established that the "Left Line™" or "Right Line™" is going to impact your "Bottom Line™".

**Wright**

So, let me see if I get you on the "Left Line™" and "Right Line™" thinking. As I look at a management model—which, you know, we've all studied a lot of management models—but as I look at yours, the "Left Line™" would be someone managing almost through apathy and neglect and the other, the "Right Line™", would be someone that was autocratic and domineering. Is that what we're talking about?

**Bell**

That is exactly right. "Left Line™" is an unprincipled mindset where people are ignorant and illicit. They're insensitive, apathetic and so forth. The "Right Line™" is a mindset that goes overboard. People with this mindset are fanatical, arrogant, controlling, harsh, and greedy.

**Wright**

Huh. And there is actually a correlation between that and disasters?

**Bell**

Absolutely. With every disaster that I study, I have identified a direct link between the management style associated with it and the disaster that results. Not only that, but as an economist, I can put a dollar amount on it.

In fact, with every disaster and every achievement I am able to identify the "Left Line™", "Right Line™" or the "Bottom Line™" concept behind it.

Some people say, "Well wait a minute. In some cases Mother Nature causes the disaster." My response is, "You're absolutely right. But I still see people building subdivisions at the base of active volcanoes. I see people who develop shopping centers in flood zones and expensive homes in avalanche zones. I see people who ignore warnings and evacuation notices. We can't blame Mother Nature, or anything else, for our situation. We have to be accountable for our results."

Once we understand the behavior that inevitably results in a disaster or a crisis, we inherently understand how to better avoid it and build success.

In fact, while I work with crisis after crisis, many of the lessons that I learn are really about success. I see people who are highly effective in dealing with a crisis and taking a bad situation and solving it.

When you think about it, we are all in the "business" of solving problems, so these lessons have an important lesson for all of us.

**Wright**

I was in Anaheim a few years ago when there was a 7-point-something earthquake that scared this Tennessee boy half out of his wits. I mean, it lasted so long and I was so stunned and so surprised and so fearful that, you know, it would be hard to understand. Of course, here in Tennessee there is a fault at Memphis. So, what you're saying is building on a fault, you take your chances. So, for example, in California the building codes are supposed to be some of the finest because of the lessons learned from hazards like earthquakes.

**Bell**

Exactly.

**Wright**

And if builders don't follow those earthquake safety codes in building, that would be "Left Line™" management or "Left Line™" thinking?

**Bell**

Yes it would. But every disaster isn't always bad news. Sometimes calamity comes along and you see some very effective management styles in dealing with it. We all see a crisis everyday, whether we're talking about Three Mile Island or a copier breaking down.

A crisis is a crisis, and the management style is the same whether you're talking about a big incident or a little incident. You can make the problem worse or successfully solve it, depending on your mindset.

**Wright**

So, what lessons have you learned, personally, from studying disasters?

**Bell**

Well, when I went to Chernobyl, I learned that the first thing to really consider is the philosophical mindset that the people have. The whole Chernobyl accident was caused by some guys who went to work one day and thought that the rules did not apply to them. That's classic "Left Line™" thinking.

I've learned philosophically that, "We are what we value." If we have an unprincipled mindset or a fanatical mindset, that can lead to disaster. Whereas if you have a principled mindset with some flexibility on one side and passion on the other, that's a good, effective mindset.

"Intellectually," the whole Love Canal environmental problem was caused by some Ph.D.s who ignored direct warnings and built an elementary school smack on top of a hazardous waste dump. That is "Right Line™" arrogance. We see that intelligence is not measure by I.Q.; intelligence is a way of thinking. Also, I learned that real "Intelligence is never above learning."

From my research in Hiroshima, I learned that the Japanese started rebuilding their City just two days after an atom bomb had been dropped on it. From a "Bottom Line™" developmental standpoint, this teaches us that "Problem solvers progress."

I've learned other great lessons throughout the whole spectrum of The Bell Matrix®, which also includes "sociologically", "influentially", "physically", "environmentally", "financially", "operationally", and all the way down the road to "consequentially".

From the O.J. case, we saw examples of "Left Line™" negligence from the L.A.P.D. and Marcia Clark's prosecution. Clearly, O.J. himself was over the "Right Line™" with his obsessions over Nicole.

As far as the "Bottom Line" goes, we see how the Brown family focused their anger and grief into forming the Nicole Brown Simpson Foundation, which helps battered women all over the country. This has been a great "Bottom Line™" achievement.

I always tell both my kids and my clients, "Problems create lessons, lessons create value, and value creates achievement." So, even though we have setbacks, and inevitably we all will, those can be great lessons for going forward.

From all of this I've learned that, "There are great lessons in both triumphs and tragedies."

**Wright**

Those are some great lessons. As I understand it, you tell people to forget "win-win" and think, "win-lose." Why would a nice guy like you be telling someone to do that?

**Bell**

I am a nice guy, but I do tell people that there is a much more effective way than "win-win."

The reality of both life and business is that we all have competition and we've got to beat the competition, whatever it is.

I developed this concept further when I met Maureen Kanka, the mother of the little girl that "Megan's Law" is named after. She told me that the whole point of "Megan's Law" was to give parents a fighting chance when competing against society's predators.

I'm a parent myself. I have four little kids. If I went around with this sugarcoated concept of win-win, I would be trying to help child molesters and drug dealers and other people like that. Frankly, I have no interest in seeing that group of people "win." In fact, I want them to go to prison.

Now I know that's an extreme example, but you know that with any football team in any high school, the coach doesn't go tell them to think, "win-win." That's just nuts. They're trying to out-strategize and beat the competition.

Business is no different. If we're going to gain market share, that means that our competitor is going to lose market share. So, it's important to define just whom we want to win and whom we want to beat.

In other words, what I'm saying is I want "you to win." I want "me to win." I want "society to win." I want "my clients and my customers to win." But, I want to protect my family against predators. I want to win out on the basketball and tennis courts.

One of the great lessons I learned in business school at UCLA was to "create barriers to the competition." I want to gain market share. In all kinds of ways, I want to out-smart my competition.

"Win-win thinking" is what I call "Happy-Valley Sunshine." When you promote the notion of "everybody winning," people risk losing their competitive mindset. Competition is a reality in both life and business. When people forget that, somebody else is going to beat them. I want my kids and my clients to be smarter than that.

**Wright**

Could you give me an example or two of what you mean by creating barriers to the competition? I'm not sure that I get that.

**Bell**

Sure. I have competitors in my own business, but I was the first one to write a book on the subject of damage economics. While they were playing at the beach, I was working hard and writing a big hardbound textbook. Today, that's a real barrier to my competition.

Now, I'm the one who gets to play a lot more. In fact, I bought an office building by the beach and I take a walk there every day that I'm at the office.

I'm not saying that we have to go around and be mean and tear people down or be unpleasant, in fact, I'm against that.

But on the other hand, if we want to be outstanding we have to standout. In order to stand-out we have to be willing to do things that other people aren't whether that be improving our product, bettering our customer service, being more attentive, doing more for our clients and customers or just going the extra mile.

This type of thinking will gain market share in our businesses. If we are willing to do more and outsmart the other guy, we are creating barriers to the competition.

**Wright**

Wow, now there is some new stuff. Tell us more about how "Left Line™" and "Right Line™" impacts the "Bottom Line™"?

**Bell**

Sure. Speaking as an economist let me put it in economic terms. I have determined that there are really only seven types of economic outcomes. Types I and II are good. Type III is okay and the rest are bad. With each type, you can see a direct link to the "Right Line™," "Left Line™" and "Bottom Line™" mindsets.

THE BELL MATRIX®

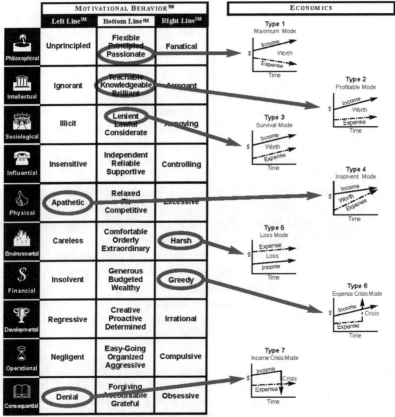

**Wright**

That's fascinating. What has been the reaction from those who have studied it?

**Bell**

I frequently get the comment that for the first time this model actually makes a direct link between the business model and actual economic performance.

What is unique about this position is that after I give a presentation or a speech, the CEO and CFO often invite me into their offices to discuss it even further. They recognize that it is an effective way to create a better, more enjoyable, more accountable and more profitable organization.

When you're talking about the "Bottom Line™", they take that very, very seriously. It's more than just some high-profile cases and some fascinating stories; we're talking about the actual mindset that drives bottom-line profits.

## Wright

Most of the management models that I have seen are models of how to manage people and how to treat people. They're geared towards making employees happy with incentive motivation or whatever. Is that also included in your model?

## Bell

Absolutely. In fact, that's the key objective. When we understand and avoid the "Left Line™" and the "Right Line™," then we are automatically getting to the "Bottom Line™" of success. Believe me, that's a great place for any person or organization to be.

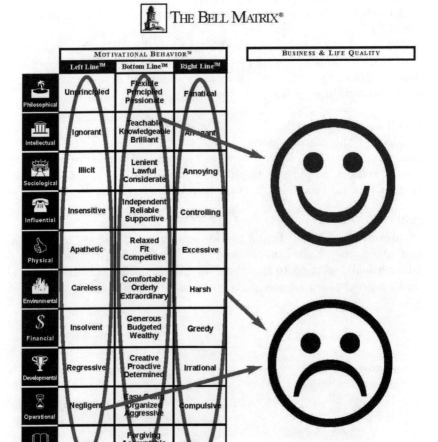

THE BELL MATRIX®

| MOTIVATIONAL BEHAVIOR™ | | | | BUSINESS & LIFE QUALITY |
|---|---|---|---|---|
| Left Line™ | Bottom Line™ | Right Line™ | | |
| **Philosophical** Unprincipled | Flexible Principled Passionate | Fanatical | | |
| **Intellectual** Ignorant | Teachable Knowledgeable Brilliant | Arrogant | | |
| **Sociological** Illicit | Lenient Lawful Considerate | Annoying | | |
| **Influential** Insensitive | Independent Reliable Supportive | Controlling | | |
| **Physical** Apathetic | Relaxed Fit Competitive | Excessive | | |
| **Environmental** Careless | Comfortable Orderly Extraordinary | Harsh | | |
| **Financial** Insolvent | Generous Budgeted Wealthy | Greedy | | |
| **Developmental** Regressive | Creative Proactive Determined | Irrational | | |
| **Operational** Negligent | Easy Going Organized Aggressive | Compulsive | | |
| **Consequential** Denial | Forgiving Accountable Grateful | Obsessive | | |

This mindset leads to being principled, creative, passionate, fit, competitive, accountable, determined...and wealthy. The mistake that a lot of management models make is that they ignore or leapfrog over the "Left Line™" or "Right Line™" elements and just dive directly for success. This is not really a grounded approach, and the results are short-lived. When we talk about success, we must also have a sober talk about failure. Then we get the full picture.

Remember, the Menendez Brothers had goals. Their goal was to eliminate bad relationships and to build personal wealth. On the surface that sounds good, but they obviously crossed the "Right Line™" to get it.

When we have the complete picture, we know both what to do, as well as what to avoid. That is real success.

**Wright**

Well, this model and all of its components sound kind of leading edge to me. I've been studying management principles now for 20-30 years and it sounds really good. How much time is spent in communicating the model to employees, or is any of that done in your consulting work?

**Bell**

I am asked to speak to businesses and organizations all over the world.

It's really amazing because within 10 minutes, people get the concepts. After showing them the disaster case studies virtually everyone buys into the concepts because I can prove a link between the concepts and failure or success. It's also an easy concept to explain to others.

Almost immediately, people throughout the organization start talking the same "Right Line™," "Left Line™" language. We're taking common sense and good and bad mindsets and simply putting better labels on it.

Once everyone starts identifying these behaviors, and they see the effects that they have on a quality workplace and the bottom line, you really see incredible improvement in the organization. It's very exciting to see the change to an organization and to watch their "Bottom Line™" grow.

**Wright**

So, this is not a tool just for management and leadership. This is something that incorporates personal growth within the entire organization, no matter how large?

**Bell**

Absolutely. We have taught it to all kinds of organizations, such as small start-ups, schools and church groups and some of the world's largest businesses. No matter where we are, we start with the philosophical mindset, and work right down through the consequential, bottom-line results.

**Wright**

Do you maintain that through the years, or do you turn the maintenance part of it over to in-house training directors and that sort of thing?

**Bell**

It really depends. One thing that I am proud of is that this business model is so effective that it can be taught quickly and implemented immediately. That's all that some organizations need.

Other organizations don't want to be just profitable. They are more aggressive and demand maximum performance. In those cases, we can add some horsepower through ongoing training and maintenance seminars.

**Wright**

That sounds really good. I've certainly learned a lot this afternoon and I really appreciate you being with us on *Conversations on Success.*

**Bell**

David, I've enjoyed our discussion.

**Wright**

I appreciate you taking all of this time. Today we have been talking to Randall Bell. Randy is the principle of Bell Anderson and Sanders LLC in California, which is a consulting firm that specializes in environmental damages, strategic planning, and crisis management. As we have found out this afternoon, Mr. Bell knows a lot about management styles and can influence your organization as well. Randy, thank you so much for being with us.

**Bell**

David, it has been a pleasure, thank you.

## About The Author

Randall Bell is the CEO of Bell Anderson & Sanders LLC. Prior to this, he founded and directed the property damages practice at PricewaterhouseCoopers. His firm specializes in strategic planning, crisis management and damage economic studies. An award-winning author, Randy wrote the textbook *Real Estate Damages* and sits of the Advisory Board of the Bureau of National Affairs in Washington DC. His assignments often involve complex matters, such as oil spills, floods, earthquakes, riots, fires and pipeline explosions. They include the September 11th United Flight 93 Crash Site, the OJ Simpson and Jon Benet Ramsey crime scenes, the Heaven's Gate Mansion and the nuclear weapons test sites on the Bikini Atoll. Randy's career has been profiled by all major television networks and the print media ranging from the *Wall Street Journal* to *People Magazine*. Randy has a MBA Degree from UCLA.

**Randall Bell**

Bell Anderson & Sanders LLC

496 Broadway

Laguna Beach, CA 92651

Phone: 949.497.7600

Fax: 949.497.7601

Email: Bell@RealEstateDamages.com

# Chapter 14

## DELORESE AMBROSE

### THE INTERVIEW

**David E. Wright**

Today we are talking to Delorese Ambrose. Since 1982 she has shared her inspiring messages on emerging workplace issues in conferences and seminars internationally. A student of Pathways to personal and organizational mastery, Delorese has traveled and studied with practitioners from various world cultures. She holds a Doctor of Education Degree from Columbia University, and has authored two books, *Leadership, the Journey Inward* and *Healing the Downsized Organization*. She's also co-author of the training video series *Diversity Dilemmas*. Delorese was named one of the city's 25 most powerful women by *Pittsburg Magazine* in 1995 and has been profiled in other industry and media publications including *Black Enterprise Magazine*, *The Pittsburgh Business Times*, and *CNN Financial News*. Among her many honors are the 1994 Athena Award for women who attain and personify the highest level of professional excellence and the 1993 A.S.T.D. Human Resources Development Excellence Award. Delorese welcome to *Conversations on Success*.

**Delorese Ambrose (Ambrose)**
Thank you.

**Wright**
How do you define success?

**Ambrose**
Well, you know, in reflecting on the question of success, I realized that I have a personal definition of success that might be quite different from traditional definitions, which I will get into later. I want to start by saying that one of the most powerful exercises in my leadership development seminars involves posing two questions, "How do you define success?" and "Whose definition of success do you live by?" The answers fall into three categories invariably. The first category is people who define success as *doing* something, achieving riches, accomplishing goals, triumphing over adversity, raising successful children, or owning one's own business. The most frequently cited examples of success fall into that first category, the *doing* category.

Then there's a second category of answers that have to do with being *seen* or remembered in a certain way. People in this category define success in terms of how others regard them: "I will feel I'm successful if I'm seen as a good person, as trustworthy, or if I earn the respect of others, or if I'm regarded as an expert in my field."

The third category, which is least often cited, is what I call "being" a certain way. These respondents say, "Success is being at peace, or being self-accepting, or living one's faith, or freedom from fear, or living in the moment." I tend to gravitate, as I get older, towards the latter. But success is also about discovering a path that's right for you and being on that path in a conscious way. It really involves following what I refer to as "your call". I believe you are successful if you discover the unique thing that makes your heart sing and if you are able to follow that. For some it might be a call to be a craftsman, or a parent who is a guardian of the home and does not enter the workplace until the children are grown. Or it might be that you are called to climb the corporate ladder and to lead in that arena, or to be a technician, or to be a free wheeling artist. It's that unique thing that energizes and sustains you. In fact some people are successful just living a life of inquiry and reflection. There have been great spiritual masters who simply walk the path of inquiry and self-reflection.

How do you know what's right for you? I tell my clients to listen to their bodies as well as to their psyches at the end of the day, and to ask themselves, "What energizes me, When do I feel really at peace, When do I feel connected with who I am and with the life I'm living?" This means that success requires a certain degree of consciousness, a certain degree of devoted attention. I meet people every day, for example, who fall right out of school or college into their first job and 20 years later when I work with them, they are still fantasizing, still planning their exit from this job because they weren't conscious about "Well, what is that I am trying to create in my life?" So, I think that being truly successful is not just about making it in the traditional sense. It's not just about doing this or achieving that. I think that some so-called successful people are so busy climbing the metaphorical ladder or winning the next big accolade that they go past where they're potentially happiest. So they make a good living, but they are not successful at living a good life.

**Wright**

Right.

**Ambrose**

I mean that's biblical teaching, what does it profit you if you gain the whole world but you lose your soul. When I think about success, I think about how to move to a more conscious, more elevated experience of success, to move away from the external definitions of success, the looking good, to a more internal definition of being a certain way. To discover that, I often ask clients, " What is the question or the inner stirring that keeps coming up for you that won't go away year after year?" You know that question that just doesn't go away. And your logical mind might be saying, "This makes no sense." But your intuitive mind knows that your life won't make any sense until you choose the path of that inner stirring. That's what I mean when I say be very conscious about what would satisfy your soul? If you can find that, I think that you are close to true success.

**Wright**

How compatible is your definition of success with the traditional corporate definition of success?

**Ambrose**

Well, I think the corporate definition of success is about winning. It's about achieving. It's about attaining goals, making profits, and in the western world, it often has an underlying assumption that bigger is better, more is better, faster is better. We really knock ourselves out trying to do more and more, bigger and better, and get better results faster and faster, and now we have to do it with fewer and fewer resources. The question I think under girds all of our lives in the corporate sector and in government, and not for profits very often, is "How can I succeed in that expert, competitive, more ambitious way?" Very often what happens, and what is happening increasingly today as we downsize and restructure and people are putting in longer and longer hours, is that the soul of the worker doesn't get nourished. So we have a lot of people who are burned out, who set the alarm clock at night, go to bed then they are awakened by the alarm clock in the morning. They scurry about getting the kids ready for school and getting themselves ready for work. They dash off into what we call "rush hour" traffic. They get to work in their cubicles, they rush around and they try to do as many things on their "to do" list as possible. They try to win. They try to attain goals. Then they turn around and they come back from work in the "rush hour" traffic, and now they're tired, harried, and honking horns. They get back home and they rush around preparing dinner, overseeing the kids' homework then they set the alarm clock and start over again. They do this 40-hours a week, 60-hours a week, over and over again with perhaps two weeks of vacation. I'm not so sure that if you do that well, make a lot of money, buy bigger and bigger homes, more and more cars, and do it better and better, that is really success at the level of human psyche and a level of the soul.

**Wright**

Do you think our culture is overly preoccupied with success?

**Ambrose**

Yes. In those terms, yes. I think that it has gotten us to a place where there are many people making six figure salaries who have zero net worth because success means buying a larger home with each promotion and having several cars in the driveway. We are a consumerist society, big on acquiring. We have walk-in closets full of clothes even though we wear the same five pieces of clothing each week.

**Wright**

You've been in my closet then.

**Ambrose**

Oh yes, we have more shoes than Imelda as the saying goes, but we only wear a couple of comfortable pairs. But it's really about getting more, doing more, and less about being contented and being in the moment, and transcending the rat race. I think that we're being called to rethink that. I think many of the events that we have experienced in recent years on the global scene are forcing us to rethink how we structure our lives, and what "success" really means. Our downsizing economy is also forcing us to take stock and redefine our relationship with work and our notions about success.

**Wright**

Do you consider yourself to be successful?

**Ambrose**

I consider myself to have achieved much success in the traditional corporate sense in my work. I'm well known in my field. I make a good living financially. I know my work and do it well, so people see me as an expert. I have found that on turning 50 those victories became kind of hollow. At midlife you are called to take time to reflect more deeply on the next stages of your life. In my own case, I came to a place where I virtually had to stop. I actually shut my business down and relocated to Atlanta. It was the only way I could find to slow things down long enough to get in touch with who am I really and what is it that I'm needing to do with the second half of my life. That was a very powerful experience because now I have returned to my work with new vigor. I'm working solo and still doing the same things. I'm still a management consultant, a writer, and a speaker, but I'm now also coaching others in how to stop and reflect and how to re-energize their work lives in a new way. So what is happening for me is that I am beginning to embrace an inner definition of success. I am considering myself more and more successful, but it is very difficult to walk the talk. I find that I have to constantly work on my own life to have enough integrity to model effective leadership or to coach others. I'm getting closer and closer to that. I am now surrounded by family. For the first time in years. My mother, who is much older now, lives nearby and I am able to support her. I enjoy living near my grandchildren and watching them grow. I'm making time for other interests like art and travel for leisure. These choices are causing me to feel much more successful than I did when I was just going after professional goals.

**Wright**

Did you miss those things when you were in Pittsburgh? In other words, was it a conscious decision that you wanted change just to get out of the rat race, or did you really miss the kind of life that you are living now with your family?

**Ambrose**

I missed it. I felt like here I was achieving—going to meeting after meeting, board meeting after board meeting, making lots of money. But I didn't even have time to enjoy it. My weekends were spent preparing for the weekdays ahead. I had good friends, and I would take vacations, but even my vacations were hectic. I took my laptop on vacation, which I no longer do.

**Wright**

You've been talking to my wife again, haven't you? You were preaching, now you're meddling.

**Ambrose**

It's really pretty amazing because you know weddings and funerals and other family events don't happen on your date book timetable. When you get to a point where such events feel like interruptions of your work, you've lost perspective. One day I woke up and I said, "This makes no sense. These events should not be events that are difficult to fit into my schedule with my clients. I've got to get some balance here." Now I wouldn't think twice about making sure that when I'm setting my calendar for the year, I'm also making sure that there are blocks of personal time set aside. I don't work usually in the month of December. I take off for several weeks in the summer. I actually "X" out those days at the start of the year so there is no chance that I'll schedule them with clients. It's just a matter of shifting the balance.

**Wright**

Is it possible, do you think, to be successful and not know that you are?

**Ambrose**

I think that to be successful requires that you be conscious. So if you are successful, you feel at peace, you feel like you are living your life on target. You feel like you're living with integrity. There's a certain release that come with that, a certain freedom from fear, a certain ability to live in the moment. I think that if you don't feel successful, then you are not. If you feel like you are struggling and there's something missing and there's something more, then you are not really successful. So I don't think it is possible to be successful and not know it.

**Wright**

To what extent is upbringing related to success?

**Ambrose**

I think it's quite related because we get our early developmental markers from our birth family, our ethnicity, our place of geographic location and the people around us who teach us how to live. So, for example, I grew up in the Caribbean, in Jamaica. This is an island that struggles. It's a third world economy brimming with potential, yet troubled with poverty and making it. So, one of the early markers for me was the sense that education is important. Acquiring land is important. The most important thing is to own a home and acquire land. We also learned somehow that risk taking is okay. I'm not sure where that comes from in our culture, but we happen to be a small island with a big vision. So there are a lot of high achievers that come out of Jamaica. There is a funny, true story of the young people watching the Winter Olympics and seeing the bobsled competitors and thinking, "No problem!" which is one of our culture aphorisms. "No problem! We can do that!" then going out and actually trying it, competing in the Winter Olympics. You know we have a music form that's heard around the world, known as Reggae that's made popular by Bob Marley. So no matter which culture I visit, whether I'm in Brazil or in Italy or in Africa, I hear Reggae all the time. It's just amazing to me that a small island can achieve so much even in spite of its size and economic challenges.

So I think of cultural heritage and upbringing with its focus on risk-taking and education as keys to my success. Even the way that we as immigrants come together, we pool our money with each paycheck in order to help each other succeed. Then my mother is a woman who grew up in a relatively poor family, but had a big dream about making it professionally. She became a schoolteacher and was quite successful at it. I got possibility thinking inculcated into me. So, of course, I pursued the path of education and so forth. I think your family values do help. Then there are the spiritual underpinnings. I think one of the reasons that my early successes felt hollow was that I wasn't attending to my spiritual life, and that was an important family value. Once I began to focus on that I could feel even more successful.

**Wright**

Down through the years as you consider the decisions that you have made in your life, has faith played an important role?

**Ambrose**

Absolutely, yes. I believe very strongly that the work I'm doing is work that I am called to do in some deeper, more spiritual sense. I also tune in each day to how I'm feeling and I ask myself at the end of the day when I've worked, "How do I feel? Do I feel filled up and energized or do I feel depleted?" That very often tells me when I am on the path and when I'm not. So there are certain assignments that I take on that just don't spiritually fill me up and I very quickly move on from those.

**Wright**

What factors in your own background contributed to your personal success?

**Ambrose**

As I mentioned before, I think that education is important. I'm very hungry for knowledge and learning. I'm very open to learning from anyone, from children, from people who are not formally educated, or through travel—I travel a lot. I love to study in different world cultures. I've also had incredibly wonderful mentors—parents, teachers, supervisors and friends have all been generous in offering guidance and positive feedback, which buoys me up and gives me a sense of direction.

Another contributing factor is the willingness to keep learning and growing. The older I get the more conscious I am of how little I know and how much more there is to learn. So, I'm learning to be more humble and more open to learning. When I was in my 30's, I thought I knew everything.

**Wright**

Right.

**Ambrose**

Now in my 50's, I am just so amazed at how little I know, and yet much clearer about the things that I do know and the things that I do believe in. So there's a contradictory way in which I'm simultaneously growing in humility and yet becoming clearer about my values and gifts as I get older. I'm also a risk taker and I embrace change. In fact my friends and family tease me because I'm always moving things around. But it's also a metaphor for change. So I'm constantly changing colors, changing things, and have even changed homes frequently. I experiment with living in different places and doing different things. I often ask others, "What would you do differently if you had no fear of failing?" I often ask myself that too and then I go do it.

**Wright**

I interviewed, within the last couple of days, a famous interior designer. I had never thought about redecorating as being a manifestation of change, but it really is, isn't it?

**Ambrose**

Oh yes, in fact when I'm coaching clients one-on-one, I often work with their space, their office space and their home space. I study Feng Shui principles and other principles related to Proxemics and Kinesics, the use of space to get meaning. I ask people, for example, to move things around physically in their offices, clear out their closets, introduce color. Just really do things to shake up their physical space as a metaphor for them shaking up themselves mentally and spiritually. I have got such great results with that. Even with experimenting with dressing differently. I am coaching a woman now who is coming out of a very difficult marriage. She has actually cut her hair into a completely different style, and bought new clothes, and experimented with colors that she had always admired on others but never had the courage to wear. That shift has caused her to shift a whole series of other areas in her life.

**Wright**

Isn't it strange how an exterior, a dramatic exterior change really does lots to change the inside, how that happens? I think women find it easier to do than men because a different hairstyle on women makes a different look completely.

**Ambrose**

Yes, yes. Women are encouraged more to experiment with difference and with change. The converse is also true: When you change the interior, it manifests externally as well.

**Wright**

You speak of different stages of success. What do you mean?

**Ambrose**

Well, you know, success is experienced differently at different stages in your life. So far I have talked about external manifestations of success such as making a lot of money and living well physically. Internal manifestations of success include being a peace with who you are, being at peace in the world, and so forth. I think that in the earlier stages of our development we almost have to move toward the external manifestations of success. When you are 20 years old, trying to make enough money to pay for your apartment or to buy your first car you are naturally preoccupied with being successful in the physical, or financial sense in order to be able to just survive. It's like Mazlow's Hierarchy of Needs. The lower rungs of the ladder have to do with getting your basic physiological needs and your safety needs met, before you can attend to higher level needs. So it's virtually impossible in the early stages of your life not to be preoccupied with success in those more external senses, which is why I need to say I don't want to dismiss that definition of success as worthless because if you're not physically successful, it's hard for you to self-actualize. Often hard times make it difficult to turn your attention to how to transcend the ordinary and how to walk in a more spiritual path,́ and so forth? You need both. I think that I would say up until the middle of your life you are living through the stages of success that have to do with questions of survival, growth, and achievement. Then in the latter stages of your life, after that great big mid-life crisis that we talk about, that crisis of integrity where you come to a place where you say, "Okay, I've figured out how to live in the world in a physical sense, but I need more. What else is there? Who am I really?" Then you move into the inner journey that I write about in my book, *Leadership, the Journey Inward*, and that Janet *Hagberg* writes about in her book, *Real Power*. Now you are asking the questions: How can I find meaning? How can I go deeper? How can I connect with my passion? How can I instill wisdom, because at this stage you are emerging as an elder? Success as an elder is about being the conscience of your organization, being the conscience of your community, aligning you inner world with your outer world so that you show up in a way that says, "I am living what I believe."

I like to cite Rosa Parks, the black woman who refused to give her seat up on the bus. She had been giving her seat up all along in order to succeed, in order to survive in the world as it was at the time, but she came to a point one day, tired and worn out, where she said, "I can no longer go on giving my seat up. I cannot live with myself if I give my seat up." That was her call to embark on a different definition of success where her inner life that was saying, "I am worthy of more than this" was now in alignment with her outer life—what she's doing in the outer world. So when they said, "If you don't give your seat up, we'll have you arrested," she said, "You may do that, because I've got to live in a way that is consistent with what I am feeling on the inside."

**Wright**

How does one make the shift from a focus on external success to inner success?

**Ambrose**

Well, I think it's something that you can't force, but that you can speed up if you are aware of what is the question you are living with. If it's a basic question like: How can I survive until the next paycheck? You then know that your concerns are about basic, external success considerations. If the defining questions in your life are questions like: What can I do to get support to build my skills, to build my self-esteem? Do I need to change jobs? Do I need to go back to school? What do I need to do differently to move to the next level? Who are the people with information that can help me grow to the next level? Then, you can't help but have success be defined in these more external ways. You can't help but worry about having enough or doing things right.

To move beyond this elementary, externally defined notion of success towards inner success requires a leap of faith. It also requires risk taking, because often when you are trying to make a shift from one way of being to another, you feel like you're stepping off a cliff and you don't know what's on the other side. You have to step off and grow wings on the way down, as they say. You have to resolve to redefine success for yourself, trusting that you will find the resources and the people and the wherewithal to grow yourself to the next level

211

where success is intrinsic. It also requires a whole lot of work on the self or on forgiveness. For example, if you are preoccupied with blaming others for the situation you find yourself in, you can't experience success in this way. I was coaching a manager the other day who at age 53 was still blaming his father for the mistakes he made in raising him. He was saying, "Well, I treat my staff badly because my father never hugged me; never said I love you." His father has long since died, but as long as he has his father to blame for his not being able to be more caring with his staff he doesn't have to change his behavior. So I have to work with him to learn to forgive and to let go of that, and to see, perhaps, the lessons in that bad life experience. I said to him, "You more than anyone know what it's like to not be loved, to not be cared for, so therefore, how can you take that awareness and be a different person because of it?" That's an important step in transcending personal limitations and moving from externally derived definitions of success to a more internal one. By reflecting deeply and making conscious choices about how we want to be. we can reinvent ourselves. People don't think about that, but you can consciously decide that you want to be different in your life, and that you want to be a certain way, Perhaps you want to live a life that's more in the moment, that's free from fear, that's faith- based or whatever. And those conscious choices can really go a long way to moving you toward a more internally derived sense of success.

**Wright**

Well, what an interesting conversation! I really appreciate you taking this time with me today to discuss success. I have certainly learned a lot, and also you've given me a lot to think about.

**Ambrose**

Oh, well thank you. Thank you for the opportunity to share my ideas.

**Wright**

Today we have been talking to Delorese Ambrose who holds a Doctorate Degree of Education from Columbia University. She has authored two books, *Leadership, the Journey Inward* and *Healing the Downsized Organization*. And as we have found out today, a brilliant, brilliant woman who is embracing change. Thank you so much for being with me today.

## About The Author

A dynamic motivational speaker, Delorese has shared her inspiring messages on leadership, and change management in conferences and seminars internationally since 1982. Her clients include public and private organizations such as the AT&T, the Commonwealth of Pennsylvania, Marathon oil, the Oncology Nursing Society, PNC Bank Corporation, Shell Oil, University of Chicago Hospitals, and the US Treasury Department. Her mission is to help people discover the meaning in their work lives in order to create more satisfying personal and organizational results. A specialist in leadership and organizational transformation, Delorese has authored two books: *Leadership: The Journey Inward* and *Healing the Downsized Organization*. She is completing her third tentatively titled: *Fifty Ways to Heal Your Worklife.*

**Delorese Ambrose**

Ambrose Consulting & Training

5295 Highway 78, Suite D361

Stone Mountain, GA 30087

Phone: 800.322.7219

Phone: 770.469.2090

Email: Delorese@msn.com

www.ambroseconsulting.com

214

# Chapter 15

## RICHARD A. BUCK

## THE INTERVIEW

**David E. Wright (Wright)**

Today we are talking to Richard A. Buck. Rick earned a Bachelor of Science degree from Robert Morris College after serving four years in the United States Air Force. He worked for over 20 years at a family owned wholesale and retail business with responsibilities that included inventory control, customer service, purchasing, and collections. During 2000, Rick was an employee of the United States Department of Commerce, serving as a partnership specialist for the Bureau of the Census. Rick served three years on the United States Junior Chamber of Training Task Force where he both presented and authored training programs and materials used by the U.S. Junior Chamber. He is the 22nd Junior Chamber member in the world to earn the designation of International Training Fellow (I.T.F.) of the Junior Chamber International Training Institute, the 5th level and highest honor a member of the J.C.I. Training Institute can receive. He has trained people from around the world in Glasgow, Scotland

and Pusan, Korea. Today he is the Executive Director of PeopleFirst, a professional training, coaching, and facilitating company. His mission is to improve businesses by improving their people. Rick Buck, welcome to *Conversations on Success*.

**Richard A. Buck (Buck)**
Thank you, David. It is my pleasure to be able to speak with you today.

**Wright**
Rick, as Executive Director of People First, you have chosen a career that focuses on developing people into leaders. What intrigues you about helping people become better leaders?

**Buck**
Well, David, I do enjoy working with those who are leaders and those who aspire to be leaders.

Working with leaders intrigues me because there is no one "right way" to lead. I believe that becoming a skilled leader requires having many "tricks" in our leadership bag. Leaders must be capable of recognizing situations where the actions they take are not generating the desired results. Then they must have the knowledge, the courage, and the confidence to reach into their bags, select another leadership action they think will work, and implement it.

In a perfect world, when a leader had a "leading problem," he or she could reach for their copy of the *Ultimate Guide to Being a Skilled Leader*. Then, by simply looking in the index, turning to the appropriate page, and doing what was written, the leader could solve the problem.

I believe if there were such a book, certainly someone like Tom Peters, Warren Bennis, Stephen Covey, Ken Blanchard or any number of other noted leadership experts would have already written it. We would all own a copy and solving our "people" problems would be as simple as "doing what's on page 56."

But no one has written a simple "do this" guide to leading—nor will one ever exist. Each of us has different knowledge, beliefs, backgrounds, experiences, and confidence. In addition, the people we lead and the situations in which we lead them are different and ever changing. Because of this, there will never be a universal method of solving interpersonal problems and driving the performance of others.

As Executive Director of PeopleFirst, I work to provide leaders with leadership "tricks" they can use. I expose people to new skills, explain the skills, and encourage the people to use the skills to become more proficient at leading.

Whether I'm in the classroom or on stage, I strive to help the attendees realize that all leaders have challenges and that most leaders have similar challenges. I attempt to present in ways that allow the participants to consider concepts and ideas from an "I wasn't looking at it that way" perspective. I work to provide insight, inspiration, and entertainment. My desire is to encourage participants to pursue the challenges of their personal and leadership lives with new ambition, enthusiasm, and optimism.

I believe Stephen Covey said it best when he stated, "Managing is a position, but leading is a choice." I work to help leaders be aware of and consciously choose the actions they use to lead their people.

**Wright**

In your experience of working with leaders, do you believe you have identified any common challenges or dilemmas all leaders seem to have in common?

**Buck**

There are two challenges that come to mind immediately. I believe they are universal. I also believe many leaders are unfamiliar with them.

The first challenge is that a leader cannot make his or her people do their jobs. If a subordinate chooses not to perform his or her task, a leader cannot make or force them to do it.

The second challenge is that a leader cannot make his or her people care about doing their jobs. I think it is unlikely a leader can or will say anything that will make a worker suddenly be concerned about the amount or quality of the work they are doing.

To me, these two statements can be both refreshing and disconcerting. It may be refreshing to realize that, realistically, all leaders everywhere have these same challenges. No leader is exempt. At the same time, I think these premises can be troublesome because leaders might finally, woefully realize that they have no genuine power to exert that will absolutely assure their people will perform correctly or even perform at all.

Now, I have made these statements to groups many times and typically someone in the crowd will say, "Well I can make my people do their jobs. I simply tell them if they don't perform, I'll fire them." Of course, this is true. A leader can and should dismiss people if they don't perform adequately. But it is important to realize the consequences when a leader demands, "perform or be fired."

If the worker doesn't care if he or she gets fired, they won't perform and they will get released. The boss's threatening and intimidating will not have worked nor will the leader have made the worker perform.

On the other hand, if the employee doesn't want to get fired, he or she probably will improve their performance. But I think in this situation, the leader really doesn't make the worker perform as much as the worker chooses not to get fired.

Leaders who use coercion as their principle method of influence will often get compliance from their people. Intimidation can create employees who comply with the requirements of their job. It can produce workers who do what is necessary—providing minimum effort, just enough to be sure they don't get fired—and little more.

Skilled leaders know a progressive workplace needs employees who perform beyond the minimum. Skilled leaders don't use coercion. Instead, skilled leaders use their influence to create worker commitment.

What's the difference between compliance and commitment? Well, contemplate the difference in your own performance between times when you did something because you had to versus when you did something because you wanted to. What was the difference between your approaches to solving the situations? Did you prepare differently? How did you persevere in each case? How thorough were you? What was the difference between your desire to do well in the two situations? How enthusiastic were you in each case?

Workers who comply with their job requirements often offer lackluster effort. Workers who are committed are far more likely to demonstrate high performance. Workers with outstanding performance provide that superior performance voluntarily; they choose to perform well. Skilled leaders know they cannot coerce high performance from their people. They know they must employ other means of influencing their people to perform effectively.

**Wright**

I see. You identified two universal challenges confronting leaders. Do you believe there are assumptions that can be made about today's workers?

**Buck**

I think there are and I think these assumptions affect how leaders must interact with today's workers. Overall, I believe that when most people go to work, they want to do their jobs well. They want to be recognized and appreciated for their efforts, and they want to be compensated fairly for their actions. In addition, I do not believe that most people actively sit in their offices or cubicles or stroll the work floor or contemplate during their morning commute, "How can I screw up my boss's day."

So, what does this mean for leaders? While we probably all have examples of subordinates who performed maliciously at work, I think nearly all leaders would concur that most of their subordinates are not malevolent in the workplace. So if a leader believes his or her people typically want to do their jobs well, then when a subordinate doesn't perform as the leader wishes or hopes or needs them to, the leader should conclude that the reason for the worker's inadequate performance is something other than wanting to make his or her boss angry.

A leader's primary responsibility is to get the best performance from his or her people. Therefore, if a worker's efforts are not generating the required results, it's the leader's responsibility to identify what is preventing that person from successfully completing his or her job requirements and then doing or providing whatever is necessary to help them overcome it.

It makes sense to me that leaders are obligated to do this because: If all the people who report to a leader successfully complete their jobs, won't the leader be successful?

Contrarily, if none of the people who report to a leader successfully complete their jobs, how can the person be considered a good leader? Skilled leaders know they can't be successful unless the people they lead are successful. They know they must constantly be conscious of how well the people who report to them fulfill their duties. If a leader identifies gaps between what is expected of his or her people and what his or her people are actually doing, the leader knows that he or she must provide those people with whatever is necessary to help them overcome their challenges and close the gap.

**Wright**

Throughout your materials and in what you are saying today, you refer to "skilled" leaders. If you were coaching someone to become a skilled leader, what would you share with him or her as being most important to do?

**Buck**

Well, David, first and foremost I think skilled leaders must be extremely conscious of the results of their actions.

One of my favorite sayings is, "if you always do what you always did, you will always get what you always got." For leaders that means that if the actions a leader is presently taking are not generating the results they desire or must have, it is incorrect and inappropriate for the leader to believe that continuing to do what is not working will in the future eventually work.

Skilled leaders constantly monitor and review workplace results. They don't neglect to recognize when what they are doing isn't working, and when what they are doing is working they are aware of its effectiveness. When skilled leaders determine that the outcomes of their actions are insufficient, they have both the expertise and confidence to select another action from their bag of leadership tricks, to implement it, and to monitor its results.

This reviewing process requires that the leader have the ability to determine the quality of the current outcomes, have awareness and knowledge of alternative procedures, have the skill to implement new actions, and have confidence that their decisions will, in fact, yield a better course of action.

I heard Dr. Phil recently say that life is not a success-only journey. Well, neither is leading. There is no guarantee that a leader's plan B will generate the desired results either. But skilled leaders know that if plan B doesn't yield the necessary results, then they must move quickly to select and implement plan C and then maybe plans D, E, and F and so on until a strategy is implemented that does generate the required results.

**Wright**

Change is a popular topic in today's business world. What are your beliefs about change and the leader's role in corporate change?

**Buck**

I think there are two important aspects leaders must realize about change.

First of all, I think it's important for a leader to instill in his or her people the desire not only to accept change but also to initiate it. The

Star Trek series has used the statement, "Resistance is futile." We can speak similarly about change. We can deny change will happen. We can refuse to accept it. But denial and refusal will not prevent change. The ways our companies and organizations operate today will be different in the future regardless of our wishes to maintain status quo.

I think many people have learned to hear the word "change" and imply the word "bad." To me, a skilled leader works to alter the implication of change from "bad" to "opportunity." The skilled leader works to alter the connotation of change from something that happens to us to something we create. Since change is going to happen, why not make it happen in our favor? People are much more likely to embrace change they understand and initiate.

Secondly, leaders must realize that facts alone are usually not enough to prompt change. For me, the simplest example of this is people who smoke. It is unlikely that a person who smokes could be told, "Smoking is not good for you," and they would say in amazement, "Wow, thanks for telling me. I didn't know," and would then stop smoking.

Smokers make statements such as, "Nothing will happen to me." "I'll take my chances." "I haven't had a problem so far." "My grandfather smoked till he was 86." Despite knowing the facts, people who smoke persist. They choose to continue to smoke.

So what changes when a person decides to quit smoking? The facts don't change. Instead, people typically become emotionally attached to the need to change. They might say, "Something has happened to me and I don't like it." "I can't take any chances. I want to be here to see my grandchildren." "Now I do have a health problem and I don't want it to get worse." "My brother who smoked had a heart attack at age 47 and I don't want that to happen to me."

When a person decides to take action as drastic and physically challenging as quitting smoking, it is typically spurred more by emotion than fact. When a person's emotions are significantly aroused, he or she will change despite the challenges inherent in changing. The emotional connection helps sustain the efforts to change.

Skilled leaders know that using logic and facts alone to prompt change in their people will usually be inadequate. Skilled leaders know they must stimulate their people emotionally. Aroused emotions help to instigate change.

**Wright**

You have said that skilled leaders must be aware of the efforts of his or her people—of how closely workers' efforts compare to what they are supposed to be doing and accomplishing. In your opinion, how big of a problem is it for leaders who do not address poor employee performance?

**Buck**

David, I think that not addressing poor performance prevents both the worker and the leader from achieving their goals. Even more importantly, it often negatively affects worker morale. As I see it, permissiveness—when leaders don't address inadequate or inappropriate performance—is really a neglect of a leader's duty.

**Wright**

It's almost tacit approval, isn't it?

**Buck**

I think it is, David. When leaders do not address inadequate or inappropriate performance, I think it appears that one of two situations is true.

First of all, it might signify that the leader doesn't realize that the worker's performance is inadequate or inappropriate. It could also mean that the leader does know the worker's performance is inadequate or inappropriate, but chooses not to attempt to correct the behavior. Reasons for not addressing poor performance might be that the leader wants to avoid the confrontation of asking the worker why their performance is inadequate, or that the leader doesn't think that the behavior is deficient enough to warrant attempting to correct.

Overall, either of these scenarios can be upsetting for others in the workplace, and can injure the leader's credibility. It can be demoralizing to believe that your boss isn't perceptive enough to realize that one of their subordinates is not performing correctly. It can also be demoralizing to consider that if your boss knows that someone is not performing and does nothing about it that he or she isn't assertive enough, doesn't think the problem is worth correcting, and will allow non-performance to continue in the workplace.

I have a 5-year old nephew who is in kindergarten. Recently my wife asked him, "Who's the worst student in your class?" Without hesitation my nephew, David, replied, "Sean. He's always getting into trouble." My nephew knew immediately who the worst student was.

Just as clearly, I believe coworkers know who is not performing at work. If coworkers know the performance habits of each other, shouldn't the leader also know?

A skilled leader constantly takes action to improve the performance of his or her people. They know who performs effectively—and who does not. Skilled leaders thank and encourage outstanding performers. Just as importantly, skilled leaders assist and encourage workers who need help.

## Wright

In one of your essays, you offer an explanation of how skilled leaders view their responsibilities. Will you share that view with us today?

## Buck

I think that some leaders see the output of their department, office, division, or company as a series of steps or actions that must be fulfilled. As these leaders monitor the progress of the organization's tasks, they ensure that all the steps and processes are completed correctly so that the output or the result looks like it should.

Conversely, a skilled leader approaches the achievement of the organization's output not just by considering the tasks, but also by considering the people who will accomplish those tasks. Skilled leaders monitor the activity of every person, insuring that each has the necessary information, resources, authority, support, incentives, feedback, training, and encouragement so that every person can successfully complete his or her assigned tasks.

In the first example, the leader focuses on the task. In the second, the focus is on the person. In both cases the tasks are completed, but the difference between the two is substantial.

I believe that skilled leaders are conscious of the concept that "work is done by people" rather than work being a "series of steps." In fact, I believe it is one of the factors that make skilled leaders skilled. Skilled leaders know they are responsible for improving and maintaining the performance of their people and for ensuring that their people have the skills, support, and encouragement to do their jobs correctly. Skilled leaders focus on people—and the results of their people—rather than the completion of tasks.

I was at a seminar where Stephen Covey asked the participants to write three characteristics that made their business different from their competitors. When the group finished, Dr. Covey asked if anyone had written "their people" as one of their differences. Less than one percent of the participants answered that way.

Dr. Covey explained that regardless of what business we are in, the equipment, procedures, techniques, and even the products we produce can all be duplicated. He said people, what is now being called human capital, are the only true means of differentiating our businesses from our competitors.

Companies must recognize and respect the uniqueness of their workforces and must work diligently to nurture, cultivate, develop, and support their people.

Companies can do this in a number of ways:

- Provide opportunities for workers to fully utilize their skills.
- Provide opportunities for workers to grow by assuming new tasks and roles and by learning new skills.
- Ask workers for suggestions and then act on them.
- Authorize and empower workers to solve problems immediately and independently.
- Encourage and reward creativity.
- Encourage and reward risk-taking.
- Encourage and reward continuous improvement.
- Reward and appreciate workers' efforts daily.

The individual and collective knowledge, skills, and experience of the workers at any company are unique and cannot be duplicated. Because of these distinctive and exclusive factors, leaders must capitalize on the advantages their people provide. Skilled leaders realize their people are a competitive advantage. They know their people are how the company will achieve its goals.

**Wright**

You explained earlier that a leader could not make his or her people do their jobs nor make them care about doing their jobs. You said that the best a leader could do is to influence his or her people to act. Will you share what you mean by this?

**Buck**

Well, David, we all hope that those who work for us will do their jobs correctly, conscientiously, effectively, and with a minimum of supervision. Yet despite our wishes, sometimes our employees may perform other than expected. The first letters of the words Perform Other Than Expected form the acronym POTE. I believe there are two types of POTE.

First of all people can perform beyond expectations. This is good or acceptable POTE. In this case, a leader can endorse these employees' efforts by showing them appreciation, giving them awards, and recognizing them for their efforts. By doing those things, a leader will reinforce good behavior and encourage successful employees to continue performing proficiently.

Contrarily, people can perform below what is anticipated or expected. This is bad or unacceptable POTE. Certainly, when subordinates perform below what is expected of them, their leader must intervene.

**Wright**

You provided me with a list of things you believe a leader can provide his or her people to influence their behavior. Would you comment briefly on each point?

**Buck**

The first is purpose. I think workers who merely come to work each day will not perform as well as workers who know the purpose of their daily activities. People work better when they know the answers to questions like, "How do my tasks help our department, office, or division accomplish our goals? What are our goals? How does what I do help the company succeed? How does what I do help fulfill the organization's mission statement? If I perform poorly, how do my actions affect others?"

Answers to these questions help workers realize how their actions contribute to the success of the organization. It helps workers to see how what they do is meaningful to the organization. Leaders must ensure their people know why they are being asked to do what they are being asked to do. Leaders must provide purpose.

**Wright**

Resources.

**Buck**

For instance, asking people to develop a four-color brochure but only providing them with stone tablets on which to do it obviously won't work. Leaders must acquire and provide the resources that will help his or her people successfully complete their tasks. Of course, all the resources people would like to have may not be available. The next best thing the leader can do is to help his or her people do their best with the resources they do have.

**Wright**

Authority.

**Buck**

Authority is official permission to act. To give authority signifies that a leader believes a worker possess the knowledge, has the experience, and has learned the discretion necessary to use the authority appropriately. This knowledge, experience, and discretion can help a worker make better decisions, enforce rules properly, and give orders correctly. Leaders must explain, demonstrate, and coach the judicious use of authority.

There is a caveat on authority. Leaders must clearly explain the scope of the authority they give. They must remind subordinates that the permission they have been given is not consent to do whatever he or she chooses. It is also imperative to remember that regardless of how much authority they give to others, leaders must realize that they, themselves, are responsible for the decisions and actions of all their people.

**Wright**

Information.

**Buck**

Perhaps you have heard about projects that failed because of what I call information sabotage—instances where someone knew that the facts or premises the group was operating with were faulty but never said anything. Pertinent information helps people make better decisions. Leaders must take time to inform and update their people with relevant data and details. Leaders must ensure their people have the best information available to make decisions and to complete tasks.

**Wright**

Support.

**Buck**

Believing that the boss is supportive of both you and your efforts at work is quite fulfilling. Providing support shows a subordinate that the leader cares and thus improves the leader's credibility. Leaders must provide support—that is, they must provide active help and encouragement to their people—in all aspects of the workplace.

**Wright**

Expectations.

**Buck**

I often ask groups, "Do your people know what you want from them or do you merely think your people know what you expect of them?" It is imperative for a leader to clearly explain how he or she expects their people to act, work with others, share new ideas, interact with customers, and handle problems. Workers want to know what is expected of them. Leaders must take time to carefully explain their expectations of workplace performance to each person in their work group.

**Wright**

Appreciation.

**Buck**

I think Ken Blanchard said it best, "Catch your people doing something right...then recognize them for it." Acknowledging people for their efforts by showing appreciation is one of the easiest and yet most powerful actions a leader can take. Simply saying, "Thank you, I appreciate what you did," makes a difference. Sincerely acknowledging people for their efforts is invaluable in prompting and maintaining exceptional performance.

**Wright**

Incentives.

**Buck**

Offering incentives provides another answer to an employee's question of "What's in it for me?" By carefully identifying incentives for his or her people, a leader can motivate them to provide greater effort and achieve greater goals. Incentives can encourage extra effort and motivation.

**Wright**

Modeling.

**Buck**

Modeling is leading by example and leaders must model the behavior they expect to receive from their people. Regardless of what a leader says, his or her people will follow what they do. Skilled leaders know that whatever they do, they make it acceptable for their people to do also.

**Wright**

Suggestions.

**Buck**

Suggestions are options or alternatives that are presented for consideration. Leaders must be knowledgeable about workers' challenges and always be prepared to offer suggestions to help workers overcome those challenges. In addition, offering suggestions can provide learning opportunities for workers if leaders present ideas in a "have you considered this?" format. Relevant suggestions by leaders can provide knowledge about how to solve problems—knowledge the worker can use in the future to solve similar problems.

**Wright**

Feedback.

**Buck**

Once a worker is told what is expected of him or her and they begin performing their tasks, the next step is for the leader to provide feedback. Feedback is a leader's opinion of the amount and quality of the employee's efforts. It allows the employee to know if he or she is in fact meeting or exceeding the leader's expectations. To me, not receiving feedback is like reading a thermometer without numbers on it to indicate the temperature. The worker knows what he or she has done, but they don't know how it compares to what the leader wanted. People want to know their leader's opinion of how well they are performing. Leaders provide that by offering timely and thorough feedback.

**Wright**

Assistance.

**Buck**

To assist is to help. Workers who receive thorough, timely, and respectful assistance from their leaders believe their leaders care about them. Leaders who furnish thorough, timely, and respectful assistance enhance their credibility with their people and enrich the worker-leader relationship and the probability that a worker's performance will improve.

**Wright**

Training.

**Buck**

Leaders must be aware of the abilities of their people and must constantly consider whether new skills or knowledge will help workers more successfully complete their jobs. Leaders must commit resources and time for learning opportunities—both formal and informal. Training is an investment in people and can provide additional skills, knowledge, and confidence that can enhance a worker's performance.

**Wright**

Encouragement.

**Buck**

Providing encouragement helps a person believe in themselves and their abilities, shows the person the leader believes in them and their abilities, and provides confidence and courage for the person to begin or persist. Providing encouragement is neither difficult nor complicated, but leaders often overlook its importance. Skilled leaders know that encouragement is key in helping people perform with hope and courage, and in inspiring a worker's will to improve.

**Wright**

Is there something unique about these 14 words?

**Buck**

Yes. Interestingly, the first letters of these 14 words form the acronym PRAISE AIMS FATE.

**Wright**

How about that!

**Buck**

How about that!

**Wright**

That's great. Do you have any final thoughts you choose to share with us?

**Buck**

Yes, David. I think the need for leaders abounds. I think that businesses and organizations—even our government—are all looking for people who are able to take charge, who will take charge, and who can motivate people to act successfully. I think that the opportunities and the rewards for skilled leaders will continue to grow.

One of the principal points I share is for leaders to realize that their primary responsibility is to get the best performance from their people. When they grasp this concept, it is much easier for them to understand that a leader cannot be successful unless the people they lead are successful—and that the leader is responsible for doing or providing whatever is necessary to help their people become and remain successful.

In *Harry Potter and the Chamber of Secrets*, author J. K. Rowling said, "It's not our abilities that show who we really are, it's our choices." Becoming a skilled leader is a choice we make, and I think it's an advantageous choice. I encourage people to choose to learn and practice the skills and to display the discipline, the persistence, and the desire to become skilled leaders. I hope they do because our world needs more of them.

**Wright**

What a great conversation, Rick. I really appreciate you talking to me today. I've learned a lot, as a matter of fact, and I have you to thank for that.

**Buck**

Thank you, David.

**Wright**

Today we have been talking to Richard A. Buck. He is the Executive Director of PeopleFirst, a training, coaching, and facilitating company, and his mission is to improve businesses by improving their people. Rick, thank you so much for being with us on *Conversations on Success.*

**Buck**

You're welcome, David. And I thank you.

Richard A. Buck, Executive Director of PeopleFirst, improves businesses by improving their people. Sharing insightful perspectives during training, coaching and motivational presentations, he provides opportunities for leaders to learn, understand and utilize new skills. The results are leaders with greater proficiency, confidence and effectiveness.

**Richard A. Buck, Executive Director**

PeopleFirst

214 Clermont Street, Suite 317

Johnstown, PA 15904-2104

Phone: 814.266.8806

Fax: 561.258.7772

Email: mail@peoplefirst.net

www.peoplefirst.net

# Chapter 16

## PAMELA ROBINSON

## THE INTERVIEW

**David Wright (Wright)**

Today we are talking to Pamela Robinson, founder and CEO of Financial Voyages, LLC., a CFO solutions company based in Atlanta, Georgia. Pamela, with her team, helps CFO's and financial executives in companies and government entities solve problems by working with their staff to develop leaders with strong financial and communications skills that add value to the organization's decision making process. Pamela has advised executives on resource allocation, process improvement and business decisions for over a decade. She has designed and delivered training presentations to groups and audiences in North America, Europe and Asia. Pamela holds an MBA in finance and international business.

**Wright**

Ms. Robinson, welcome to *Conversations on Success*.

**Pamela Robinson (Robinson)**
Thank you David, I am honored to be a contributing guest.

**Wright**
You talk passionately about defining moments that shape leaders. Can you share a defining moment that shaped or is shaping you and what the impact or outcome was?

**Robinson**
Yes, of course. First, it may be helpful to define a "defining moment" and then share an example and how it shaped me. A defining moment is a pivotal point in time that causes me to pause, reflect and ultimately make a choice. In some cases a defining moment may be subtle, while other times it is as if the world has stopped and I am left to examine my self- reflection. Defining moments are critical decision points that could lead to initiating a project, influencing a product outcome or moving strategies forward. Either way, defining moments are an introspective examination of a leaders character, leadership maturity and decision capacity.

As I look over my life and business career, I have had several defining moments but none has impacted me more than sustaining a business. When I decided to start a company, I had to weigh the pros, cons and realities. At the time, I was working as an expatriate in Central America. At 35, a single parent with a high school son, I knew that it was now or never. If I continued down a path of relying on someone else for my life's happiness, I would have regrets of not realizing my full potential. If I moved forward with the idea to launch a company, there was nothing lost, in my opinion. This critical moment caused me to pause, reflect and decide allowing me to come to terms with the fact that if I did not do this now, I would never experience the "joy" of creating something from the ground up and making a contributing difference. The outcome: No regrets and we are entering year 5 with a bright future. My company's focus is to grow next-generation financial leaders today by developing leaders with strong financial and communication skills. I view financial leaders as business owners, senior managers, program and project leaders, CFOs, financial executives and financial professionals that have direct financial responsibilities that affect the performance of the organization. These leaders define and solve the right problems through human capital intelligence and leveraged knowledge to impact the company's decisions and performance. We help clients create value by finding better ways to control costs, manage risks and lead projects from start to finish.

**Wright**

Defining moments, a great concept. I wonder, how difficult is it to recognize or is it difficult?

**Robinson**

Recognizing defining moments does not have to be difficult. I view the challenges as a learning experience to build character and improve leadership capacity. I have learned to trust the process and allow the learning to take place. Once I accepted this lesson, I came out stronger, more determined and re-energized to develop those around me and lead the company to the next level. We all experience defining moments and it is our response to these experiences that determine how we develop as leaders.

**Wright**

Your focus is to develop leaders with strong financial and communications skills to add value to the decision making process. Can you share the trends that you see and what organizations can do to become equipped in addressing these needs?

**Robinson**

Human capital capabilities is a key area of concern for private and public organizations. Organizations that optimize human capital intelligence, leverage knowledge-based networks and effectively develop leaders will be better positioned to drive change and increase their competitive value. Companies need to examine how they are structured and question whether it is the best balance and use your resources. No longer is physical location a constraint to access intrinsic knowledge and this will continue to be the trend as wireless communications replaces how and where we communicate. So while it is important for professionals to be technically proficient in their chosen field, it is just as critical to understand how the business really works and the interconnectivity of technology to people, processes and strategy. Organizations with departments that are stovepiped physically or mentally will find it difficult to drive or respond to change quickly. From a competitive advantage standpoint, this can create internal problems and negatively influence performance. Some recent reports on human capital issues include the American Society of Training and Development Public Policy Council who recently published a white paper addressing the "Human Capital Challenge" (www.astd.org); and of particular interest to our clients is the Joint Financial Management Improvement Program (JFMIP) white paper on "The Federal Financial Management Workforce of the Future" (www.jfmip.gov). The role of financial professionals is changing requiring the field to perform as business advisors and strategic partners at all levels of the enterprise. Financial professionals must meet the demand for accurate, timely and understandable information to managers and decision makers. Managers, in turn, must understand how decisions impact the other parts of the enterprise, people and the bottom line. Problem solving, negotiating and effective communications are necessary to ensure professionals are offering sound financial advice to executives, program managers and project leaders. The key is to execute a strategy internally that is going to create and sustain an inviting environment that will acquire, develop and retain high-performing professionals. Chief Financial Officers and other senior executives must incorporate their human capital requirements into their overall business strategy. This means examining how well professionals know the ins and outs of business to offer sound advice? Find out what products, reports and services really add value to those that rely on you for advice. Three approaches to transition from a transaction-based environment to a resource of business advisors include (1) Conduct a stakeholder analysis. Ask managers outside of your department, are they coming to your department because they have to, because you hold the purse strings or are they coming to you because they want to, because you're providing accurate, timely understandable analysis and advice? Which reports and advice work well, what does not provide value for them? Measure from time to time how the internal relationship is working for those that rely on you; (2) Conduct an internal self-assessment. What are your greatest strengths of financial operations in regards to balancing the individual, the team and organizational expectations? What are your strengths and technical capabilities and how well are they performed? Where do you need to improve? What opportunities are worth pursuing? How effective are your group's softer skills like communication and negotiating? and (3) Execute. Many times groups focus on getting to results too quickly without giving careful consideration of solving the right problem. Once you have clearly defined the RIGHT problem, your efforts must shift to how you and your staff will solve it and communicate the impact and results to the rest of the organization.

## Wright

Your workshops range from human capital and financial leadership, business analysis, risk management and project management. While your solutions are based on sound business principles, your delivery and implementation focus on both technical and soft skills? Why is this integrated approach essential to a company's overall performance?

## Robinson

In the past, operational performance was measured primarily by how well companies performed financially. Today, value is measured with both financial and non-financial metrics. Organizations are using balanced scorecard and dashboards to help managers and decision makers make better-informed decisions by viewing the most significant measures to help execute their strategy. This is an area in business that is evolving and you will see technology begin to serve as a vehicle to make this process of enterprise performance easier and more accessible. In regards to training solutions, people that participate in our seminars do not necessarily want to know how to do their jobs, rather they want to know how to do their jobs better or how to run their companies more effectively and how to work with others inside and outside the company. Our clients are looking for practical solutions that work and that can be implemented immediately. The key is in application and promoting innovative solutions.

## Wright

I've always been interested in risk management and it seems to be extremely important to you and our company. Could you give our readers some examples of managing risks in an organization?

## Robinson

Risk is an integral part of doing business and making choices. Naturally, after an appropriate level of insurance is secured organizations are faced with threats and opportunities against their strategies, human capital, core processes and technologies. Risk should no longer be viewed as only a threat or loss of fiscal or physical assets but managers must be able to extract possible opportunities worth pursuing (improve processes, entering new markets or redirecting their focus) as a result to risk exposure or a weak internal control. Most organizations we work with already have an internal control process but it may be disjointed from the decision process, or not in a format that may be viewed for the board or key leaders to view from an enterprise wide perspective. Adopting a methodology to address risk includes your ability to effectively identify, measure and mitigate the most relevant risks in relationship to your business objectives. We have a program that provides clients several tools, techniques for risk and management control to improve what they have in place and ensure managers and key leaders on speaking from the same sheet. Naturally, you will not be able to cover every risk exposure because the cost of doing so would exceed the benefits realized. What you want, is a systematic approach where there is a common language used by managers when addressing risk exposure so you can control cost and move towards solutions. Proactive measures are so important to control cost, risk must be discussed during staff meetings and financial reviews to become an integral part of your operations and decision making process. In addition, consistent reviews of policies, key processes, and working with auditors during management and financial audits. Ensure that you have an effective risk and management control process that provides accurate, reliable, timely and understandable data for you to make decisions before a crisis strikes.

Technology is a major investment area for us so protecting those assets and more importantly the information is critical to realizing our business objectives. Anyone that has lost information in the past has learned to regular back the information up. A few proactive measuring to this exposure is ensuring adequate funds are budgeted for replacements, upgrades, extended warranties and training and testing to determine if the measures are effective. The benefits far outweigh the costs of lost data or damaged equipment. Human capital intelligence is a core areas for most organizations. Examining hiring procedures and how you develop people once they are on board may be included in your risk and management control plan for review and discussion. As you go through a strategic review of your business objectives, during financial reviews and as part of project management, risk must be addressed to ensure the most relevant risk are addressed. Given this format, I have only touched the surface regarding strategies for managing the probability of risk. When we work with clients we help them with the process of risk planning, analysis and mitigation. Bottom line, all organizations, regardless of size and revenue, must have a process in place to adequately address the most relevant risk or accept exposing yourself to loss of assets, rework, damage to reputation, or trust. When an internal either is not in place, not used or is inadequate corrective action is necessary to et to the root of the problem so that it does not recur and you can get on with business. Depending on the risk exposures severity and frequency rating, managers and boards must decide to either avoid, reduce, retain or transfer the risk.

**Wright**

Your business solutions seem to be tied to making informed business decisions.

**Robinson**

Yes, I can't stress enough to adopt a method to ensure that you are solving the right problems.

**Wright**

You provide project management solutions, in fact you were recently featured in the *Atlanta Business Chronicle* growth strategies section on how planning is essential on management big projects. You state that projects should be viewed as investments and must yield a return, can you expound on your intent behind this statement?

**Robinson**

This goes back to solving the right problems. I believe that careful scrutiny must be given before projects are launched. I say this because projects consume resources. Recall projects that either you initiated or have been involved in and for various reasons the project was placed on indefinite hold or was not worth continuing due to change in direction or other priorities. Well, those are wasted resources because they did not produce an outcome. Projects consume resources. Consider projects you have going on right now, how well are they yielding a return to improve performance, satisfy customers in meeting business objectives. What projects should be in your portfolio that are really helping you realize your business objectives? It is important that project leaders are well versed in the financial aspect of business. When you decide to initiate a project, know where it is leading and why you are doing it and do not call everything a "project." For effectiveness, there must be a systematic approach on how you start and manage projects, how projects are controlled and how to communicate the impact of scope creep to project management steering committees.

**Wright**

You said projects consume resources several times, I wanted to get up and scream AMEN!

**Robinson**

It's true.

**Wright**

Have you been talking to my wife?

**Robinson**

Most of us have experienced unfinished or failed projects. Effective project management takes work. Is this something that you want or need to invest your resources in? What do we expect to happen as a results of placing people, time and money against this project objectives?

**Wright**

Pamela, with our *Conversations on Success* book, we're trying to encourage our readers to be better, live better and be more fulfilled by listening to the examples of our guests. Is there anything or anyone in your life that has made a difference for you and helped you to become a better person?

**Robinson**

Of course, we need each other for support and to get things done. Before I recognize the many people that have helped and continue to help me become a better person, I have to wholehearted give praise to God, whose grace amazes me everyday. There is so much spiritual growth that occurs that cannot be expressed in words, but in tears of joy and gratitude. In addition, I am surrounded by a great support system of friends, family and extended family around the world that are dear to me. You need a support system to stay focused and continue your course. It is amazing how people will come through for you. If you need help, ask. There are also times when you feel very alone and words cannot express what you are experiencing. Get away from everyone's opinion and stay true to yourself. At the end of the day, you really have to face yourself and resolve if you are living authentically. Are you using the talents that are uniquely yours to share. How are you using your energy to help someone else live better.

**Wright**

Down through the years, as you reflect on the decisions you've made, has faith been important to you?

**Robinson**

My life and company is based on faith. More importantly, my faith is accompanied by well-thought out plans and actions.

**Wright**

I have spoken, within the last couple of weeks, to one for the nations largest leadership guru's and he said something very strange to me, or startling to me at lead, you might have hear it before. We were talking about introspection and he asked me, "David, if you could do anything you wanted to do in your career, if you could choose any occupation and I could guarantee you that you would not fail, what would you choose?" Do you take that kind of introspection into your solutions into corporations?

**Robinson**

I have discovered that when I finally yield to the gifts and talents within, what you do, chooses you. I chose what I do because I said yes to what is natural and unique to me. When I help others or give back using my talents, the growth process I go through serves as a healing mechanism for the human deficiencies I have to make me a better person. There is nothing I would rather be doing at this point in my life than what I do day-to-day.

**Wright**

I have asked people for many years in management workshops about people who've helped them in their lives. One little exercise we used to do is write down the top five people in your life that have been most important to you going all the ways back to childhood. Oddly enough I found, down through the years, the answers were very similar. Out of the top five at least three of them were teachers. Do you find that to true?

**Robinson**

Yes! Besides experience, most of the lessons that I have learned have been from teachers even if they were managers or colleagues. I love learning and have always enjoyed it. I gained my love for reading from my mother. My mom is well read and has tons of insight and common sense. She provides antidotes and lessons to live by.

**Wright**

What do you think makes up a great mentor? In other words, are there characteristics that mentors seem to have in common?

**Robinson**

A strong appetite to give back and willingness to share. Mentors and coaches are needed to help people develop their full potential and unleash untapped talent.

**Wright**

What do you have planned for the next few years personally and in your company? Do you have any changes you're going to make?

**Robinson**

Increase our on-site training programs to provide real-time solutions and continue to build relationships. I am so blessed to have the opportunity to help others live and work better. I envision Financial Voyages, LLC. becoming a household name among CFO's and financial executives in developing their people into leaders with strong financial and communication skills that add value to the decision making process.

## About The Author

Pamela Robinson is founder and CEO of Financial Voyages, LLC., an Atlanta, Georgia based CFO solutions company. Pamela has designed and delivered financial leadership training presentations to audiences and groups in North America, Europe and Asia. She is a certified seminar leader, corporate coach and listed in *Who's Who in Professional Speaking*. Through training, coaching and business advisory services, TeamFV helps companies and government entities effectively control cost, manage risk and lead projects from start to finish. Pamela holds an MBA in finance and international business.

**Pamela Robinson**
Financial Voyages, LLC.
3345 River Heights Xing SE
Marietta, GA 30067
Phone: 770.541.0111
Fax: 770.541.7813
Email: pamela@teamfv.com
www.teamfv.com

# Chapter 17

## S. TRUETT CATHY

## THE INTERVIEW

**David E. Wright (Wright)**

Today we are talking to Truett Cathy. He is a real live Horatio Alger story. He grew up in a boarding house his mother operated where he learned the principles of hard work, fairness, honesty, loyalty, and respect. When he opened a small restaurant in 1946 with his brother, Ben, he put those principles to work and immediately began to experience their rewards. Twenty-one years later, Truett Cathy opened the first Chick- Fil-A restaurant, which was unique in America in two ways. It served the first boneless breast chicken sandwich, and it was the first fast food restaurant to operate in a shopping mall. Today there are more than a thousand Chick-Fil-A restaurants with more than one billion in sales annually. Truett Cathy's commitment reaches far beyond the people who work and eat in his restaurants. Through the Winshape Center Foundation funded by Chick-Fil-A, he operates foster homes for more than 21 thousand children since 1985, and has provided scholarships to college for more than 16,500 students. Truett Cathy, welcome to *Conversations on Success*.

**Truett Cathy (Cathy)**
Thank you, David. Good to talk to you.

**Wright**
The first time I was introduced to your company, I was with my wife, one of your employees walked out of a little store in the mall and offered me a sample piece of chicken on a toothpick. I thanked her for it, put it in my mouth, took a couple of steps, and turned directly into your restaurant and ate my first of many meals at Chick-Fil-A. Have you personally taken a hands-on attitude in your advertising programs down through the years?

**Cathy**
Absolutely. We pioneered fast food establishments in shopping malls. You must remember, David, that developers would not even consider fast foods in their shopping centers because they were afraid of the smoke and fumes. They thought it would be a mess. We proved our point, however, when my uncle opened a place in Greenbrier. It was a small spot, about 384 square feet. It had been occupied by a hearing aid shop. I talked to the owners of the shopping center and asked them to give us a chance. So, they allowed us to move into that little hole-in-the-wall. Shopping malls generally charge a base rent plus an overage when the sales exceed a certain number. From the beginning, we were paying ten times the base amount in rent because we were generating such high sales each month. This gave us a tremendous advantage and opened doors to contact other malls. So, that was the beginning for me. And, it has been very, very good for us. We concentrated on just going into malls for several years until developers stopped building malls as they had in the 60's. We still go into malls, however, most of our locations are freestanding. These have proved to be better for us than shopping center locations.

**Wright**
I have noticed you have changed directions. I frequent the free standing Chick-Fil-A near my home in Tennessee. In fact, my 15-year-old daughter's Scout Troup meets there.

**Cathy**
Great. I see my marketing plan is working.

**Wright**

In 1982, 18 years after you trademarked and incorporated the name Chick-Fil-A, you adopted a corporate purpose to glorify God by being a faithful steward of all that is entrusted to us, to have a positive influence on all who come in contact with Chick-Fil-A. How did your new stated purpose change your organization? Or did it?

**Cathy**

Well, David, it just enhanced it. It didn't change it. It had been our purpose anyway, but we'd never put it into print. As you said, this came about in 1982. We had just moved into a $10 million corporate headquarters. It was fully financed. Interest at that time was 20 to 21%. This was the year that all the fast foods were getting into the chicken breast sandwich business, and it caused the breast of the chicken prices to be inflated, while sales were declining. I called a meeting of what we called the Executive Committee. We were and are still a private company so, we don't have a Board of Directors to answer to. I was quite concerned about the situation because I had never had to cope with this problem before. We asked our sales department some questions, important questions, about why we are in business, why we are alive, and what is our purpose in being here? One of the Executive Committee members contributed words that we could identify. We came away after working two days with our corporate purpose: "That we might glorify God by being a faithful steward in all was entrusted to our care. Then we might have a positive influence on all the people that we would come in contact with." Well, we came back, shared this with our staff, and they said, "What else did you do?" And I said, "Well, that's it. We didn't know the solution for the pressing problems."

That following Christmas, they gave me a huge bronze plaque. Engraved on it was my corporate purpose. I'm not one who likes to put a lot of signs around, but since it was given to me by my staff I had to display it some where. So, I wondered, "Where would be an appropriate place to put it?" The staff said, "Right outside the front doorway might be a reminder to each of us why we're coming to work." I said, "Well, that might be a good idea." So we did. It meant a lot to me at that time, but it has grown to mean an awful lot because it's a constant reminder to me how I should treat those people in telephone conversations, sales people, or people that I have to call in to reprimand or ask for their resignation? I want to have a positive influence on all the people that I come in contact with. It's always a challenge for me to do that. So, we saw some miraculous things taking place shortly thereafter. That following year we had a record sales increase of 36% nationwide. We have only one incentive award for our operators. We had 250 stores that had a 40% increase in one year. The previous year, we gave them a brand new Lincoln Continental to drive for a year. I told them, "You might not like to drive Lincoln Continentals, but they look nice sitting in your driveway. You might even impress some of your neighbors or friends when they come by." That year we awarded 46 Lincoln Continentals. I liked to have bankrupted the company buying those Lincoln Continentals.

**Wright**

Forty-six out of 250 operators?

**Cathy**

Yes, that was a great percentage. So, I was only kidding about the bankruptcy. In addition, we had an invitation from Berry College, which is located 75 miles north of here to come up and speak to their business classes. In turn, I invited Dr. Gloria Chateau to come speak at our Airport Rotary Club. She shared with me that they had closed the academy. The academy is a boarding school on campus for eighth through twelfth grades. It was draining their funds about $2 million dollars a year, so the trustees took action to close it. She asked me, "Do you have any ideas on how we can use this space?" That motivated my wife and me to go up and take a look at it. To find out it was the world's largest campus with 28,000 acres of land.

This facility was located three miles away from the main campus. I said, "This ought to be in use. There was a beautiful chapel sitting there, also a library, dormitory, dining room, an administration building, and a practically new gymnasium." So I said, "I wonder if people working for Chick-Fil-A would be interested in coming here to go to College?" So, to excite the people to come here and go to school, they've offered them a $10,000.00 tuition scholarship. Five of that had to be absorbed by Barry and five by Chick-Fil-A. We were able to attract 68 wonderful students to start this program. There were 34 boys and 34 girls. This was 18 or 19 years ago. To date, we have a capacity of 125 students and they are on a $32,000.00 scholarship.

**Wright**

Goodness!

**Cathy**

So expanding on this, we started a Boys and Girls Camp. Last summer we had 1900 boys and girls to attend a two-week camp experience. There we built two foster homes and had the foster parents lined up. We tried to attract children that did not having any serious behavior problems, but were just victims of circumstances. Today we have 14 foster homes and 135 children. I play the role of adopted Grandpa for them. I introduce them as my grandchildren by choice. I chose them and they chose me.

I tell them they don't have to call me "Grandpa", but those who do get more. This motivates them to call me Grandpa. It's a real thrill to visit these homes and have them all come out shouting, "Grandpa's here! Grandpa's here!" and get a hug and kiss on the cheek. Those are the things that you can't buy with dollars and cents. The children give me a lot of joy and satisfaction.

**Wright**

There are many great companies in the United States that are ethical, honest, and fair in their dealings with their employees as well as their clients and customers. However, I don't remember the recognition of God in their mission statement or corporate statement. Did you have any argument or discussion from your Board or your committee as you crafted the statement of purpose?

**Cathy**

No, not at all. We don't have a board or stockholders, so I didn't have that to overcome. We had the support of all our staff people as well as our unit operators. This has meant a lot to me. You may be aware that we're closed on Sunday. This has proved to be very significant. When I first started in shopping malls, they were closed on Sunday as well. I had no trouble in the beginning. Today, shopping center developers know that if we go into a mall we will be closed on Sunday. We don't debate the issue. It is important that we stand firm on our convictions. We try to please everybody, but you can't do that.

**Wright**

That's right. Your menu has only had one major change in the last six years, and your marketing strategy steers clear of discounting and limited-time offers. What are the most important success factors that drive your sales?

**Cathy**

We are consistent in our quality of our food and our service. We have an ability to build business on bad coffee as long as you're consistent about it. But don't serve good coffee in a bad cup. That confuses everybody. If you would change the brand of coffee you serve, people would say, "What's wrong with the coffee this morning?" We would say, "Well, this is a better brand, and it's a little high, but it's better." It is very important in business to live up to the customers expectations and build customer loyalty. I have been in business 57 years. We find people coming into my original restaurant with walkers and canes, struggling with that challenge to get up out of bed and get to our house to have breakfast or a cup of coffee. Customer loyalty has carried us through.

**Wright**

In a recent press release from your company, my interest was drawn to three simple rules that were important to you and to your success. They were: Listen to the customer, focus on getting better before you try to get bigger, and emphasize on quality. Could you explain to our readers what you mean by get better before you get bigger?

**Cathy**

You can always improve what you are doing, not only the quality of your food, but the performance of the employees. We have seen from one of our seminars that courtesy is very cheap, but pays great dividends. People will go out of their way to do business with you as long as they are treated kindly, greeted with a bunch of smiling faces, and served with spirit. This is a divine business we have meeting people's physical needs, emotional needs and sometimes spiritual needs. A lot of times, people go out to eat when they are not even hungry. People go for the experience. We want to make that a good experience for them. I think people we have working for us at Chick-Fil-A realize that they are somebody special. We have 1,094 units. They are very dedicated to the task. I tell them, "If you want to really enjoy your work, work hard and have the satisfaction of knowing that you did the job your very best." I say, "You can make a living by working, and you do that if you're putting your heart and soul into what you're doing." I'm only 82. People say, "When are you going to retire?" And I say, "Retire. Why would I retire from something I enjoy doing?" I think a lot of people get shortchanged because they don't perform at the level that they could be. I think people cheat themselves when they do something less than what they are capable of doing.

**Wright**

The National Restaurant Association named your company Employer of Choice in the Quick Service Restaurant Category in 2002. You must have been proud of that honor. What are some of the things your company does to encourage your employees?

**Cathy**

We have an unbelievably low turnover in our staff and management team. The turnover rate is only 4%. This is unheard of in most any business. Of course the part-time temporary people have a higher turnover, because the majority of them are just working to supplement the income or are going to school, and their career has not yet been mapped out. We have created a great deal of leadership from people who have never worked anywhere except Chick-Fil-A. I recently received a call from one of our operators who wanted to remind me that he was celebrating his 30th year with Chick-Fil-A. He had never had any other job. We have people on our Executive Committee that have been with Chick-Fil-A at least 20 years. I think that loyalty among employees as well as customers helps to make our job much easier.

**Wright**

Right. Living out your faith, your company is known for its philanthropies. Your main philanthropic endeavor is Winshape Center. Can you tell our readers a little about Winshape Center?

**Cathy**

We established a relationship with Barry College that became the Winshape Center. This came about in 1983. The goal it to shape individuals into winners. I think we all want to be winners. We are working on another program that we will be announcing sometime shortly. We're calling it the Winshape Summit. This facility will incorporate ministry.

**Wright**

In the very beginning, Barry College, or the Barry School was about to fold up, by increasing the part of it that was three miles away, you've not only saved the college, but also opened up your own education foundation?

## Cathy

Right. I don't think Barry College is in jeopardy because they have 28,000 acres of land, and it captured the support back in 1920 from people like Henry Ford, Andrew Carnegie, and Theodore Roosevelt. It wasn't in financial jeopardy; it was straining their resources, and they said it was just not practical to operate a Boarding School for eighth through the twelfth grade.

## Wright

I see. You get involved in golf too, don't you? Haven't you added a Peach Bowl?

## Cathy

Well, Chick-Fil-A does. People ask me, "Do you play golf?" I say, "Only with Nancy Lopez." With trick photography, Ford Motor Company had a commercial made with Nancy and me playing golf together, but I'm not a golfer. I used to play when I was a teenager, but as I got older, I found that my golf score didn't improve. It got worse. I just have more important things to do than play golf. We sponsor the Atlanta Professional Golf Tournament annually, here in the Atlanta area, and also the Peach Bowl, which is an annual event. Our marketing department has been fantastic in promoting both programs and both are very recognizable now. We have a lot of participation. In the professional golf tournament, 94% of the top lady golfers play.

## Wright

I wish I had talked to you before the Peach Bowl. I'm an alumni of the University of Tennessee. And we sure could have used some help against Maryland last year.

## Cathy

It's been an exciting time for us, and you never know who's going to be the winner.

## Wright

You know, most of us can look back on our lives and highlight those persons who have made a positive impact on us and perhaps changed our lives. Who has helped you become the person you are and perhaps been a mentor to you?

**Cathy**

Well, my mother was the breadwinner in our family. We were brought up in the deep depression. I expect you don't remember that yourself.

**Wright**

I'm Sixty-four, so it happened right before me.

**Cathy**

Sixty-four. It was necessary for our family to move to Atlanta to try to make a living. My mother rented a house and she took in boarders. Young people say, "What's a boarder? Is that a boarding house? Is that like a condominium or an apartment, where they serve you breakfast in bed?" I say, "Not exactly." It was necessary that we furnish them a bed and two meals a day. It was then that I learned how to shuck corn, shell peas, wash dirty dishes, set the table, and go shopping. Back then you could buy six cokes for a quarter. I realized then that if I ever wanted to have anything, I'd have to work for it. So, I thought I could buy cokes six for a quarter, pedal around to my neighbors for a nickel apiece and recognize a five-cent profit. When I sold out, I went back and got six more, and six more. Finally, I was able to set a little stand up in the front yard, flag down the coke truck and buy a full case of Coca Colas for 80 cents. If you have a calculator, David, you put in 24 and multiply it by five, that's 80 cents. But, I made a profit of 40 cents. To me that was big business.

The first thing I bought of any consequence was a bicycle that I paid four dollars for. It didn't have any fenders on it, but it had round wheels and a good frame. I've never bought anything in my life that I appreciated more than that bicycle because, I earned the money and bought it myself.

**Wright**

Your mother must have had some impact on you.

**Cathy**

She did. She got all of us kids registered for Sunday school and Church. I was brought up that Sunday was an important day. One of the factors when we opened up our first restaurant was that we were closed on Sunday. We have followed that pattern for the last 57 years. It had been the best business decision I ever made. It had helped to attract people that appreciate every Sunday off. Our competition cannot offer that. Fast foods are very busy on Sundays.

**Wright**

You know, you speak very fondly of your operators, your staff and your team members. What do you look for when you recruit people for your team?

**Cathy**

We look at a persons character first. We can teach them to make coleslaw and cook Chick-Fil-A, but we can't change their character. It is very important that they have a lot of the ingredients that we are looking for. Most all of our people, particularly the unit operators, are about 30 years old, with a wife and a couple of kids. They have a very good job. Two things are important in business: finances and management. Fortunately for me, I had the ability to borrow the money that I needed to grow at the pace I wanted to grow. So, we look at a person's talents' and abilities. The only cash requirement on their part is $5,000.00, which is refundable should they ever sever the relationship with Chick-Fil-A. They have no capital risk involved. We treat them as independent business people, and they operate under their name. This has been a very healthy way to manage people, and they have to be totally dedicated. They have to divorce themselves from other business interests to come aboard with Chick-Fil-A. We take it as a total commitment.

**Wright**

I know a lot of other franchises sell their franchises based on money. You know it cost $150 to $200 thousand, whatever, and money is not always a respecter of character. So I would say you've made a character decision there. Someone told me at one time that there was a financing plan, where you could pay as little as $5,000.00 and get in on the ground floor and perhaps participate in company net profits. Do you still do that?

**Cathy**

Yes sir. We still do that. It's working well. Every formula has flaws, but for me it's working well. It works well if you can attract the people that are compatible with you, that will deal with you honestly, and get excited about their business. So, we have been able to capture that market of individuals that have a brilliant desire to be a winner, achiever, and willing to pay a price for it. And when I say a price, it doesn't mean that they have to sacrifice everything to be successful in this business. I believe you can be successful in managing your own life as well as a business life at the same time. That's the reason we're so careful about selecting the right people. We can't expect them to manage one of our businesses if they can't manage their own life.

**Wright**

I appreciate you sending our office the copy of your book *Eat More Chicken / Inspire More People: Doing Business the Chick-Fil-A Way*. It was very interesting reading. I would suggest everyone read it. Somewhere near the middle of the book, you started talking about individual people. There was a fellow that worked for you at the first restaurant, which was called Dwarf House, his name was Jesse Reid. He was a black teenager. At one point in time when he started college, he suggested that you hire his cousin, Eddie White, as his replacement. You talked very fondly about Eddie coming to work for you. Do you remember him?

**Cathy**

Yes sir.

**Wright**

Could you tell us a little bit about his story?

**Cathy**

It's a great story. I think he came to work when he was 12. At that time they weren't very strict on labor laws. But Eddie was one of those kinds of guys that put his heart and soul in his business. All the waitresses and everybody would take advantage of it, because if you asked Eddie to do something, he was always willing to do it. He grew up with us. One of his goals was to graduate from college and be a medical missionary someday. He did finished high school and was prepared to go to college, but his father required him to get a full time job so he could help support the rest of the family members that didn't go to school. I went with him to talk to his father about letting him keep on working and go to college, rather than quitting getting a full time job. He agreed as long as Eddie would give half of his income toward the support of the family. That was no problem for Eddie. I was willing to help him in any way that I could. I supported him in quite a few ways. He used to like to tell the story about going to the junior/senior prom and I let him borrow my car. That has stuck in his mind. He became a schoolteacher and eventually elevated up in our county to Assistant School Superintendent. He has his own family and grandchildren now. He had retired from the school system, but he's called on when they have a problem in a school. He goes in and serves as backup for a principal and he gets it straightened out. He stays pretty busy associating in the different schools that are having problems. He's been a real outstanding citizen and a great contributor to the educational system here in Georgia. He is a real dynamic individual. I take pride in having as a friend.

**Wright**

He goes all the way back to when he was twelve years old as your friend?

**Cathy**

Right.

**Wright**

What a great success story. As you consider the decisions that you've made down through your life, has your faith played an important role?

**Cathy**

It has indeed because sometimes in business the problems get so severe they are out of your hand. You have to rely upon the divine guidance for the direction that you are going to travel. I've had the support of my family, my wife and my children. My children were brought up to go to Sunday school and Church, as I was. My wife is a very dynamic, practicing Christian and has been supportive all through the years. We've been married 56 years now. I have 12 natural grandchildren and so far I haven't been disappointed in any of them. It's been a chain reaction for us. People tell me it took determination. They say, "It shows in your grandchildren how good of a father you were." I say, "Oh don't tell me that. I thought I did pretty well on my three children. Now I have to wait to see how my 12 grandchildren turn out to see how well I really did.

**Wright**

I'm always interested in people who have strong faith, especially when the problems come.

**Cathy**

Yes.

**Wright**

I remember reading in your book, the one I eluded to a few minutes ago, *Eat More Chicken/Inspire More People.* I remember reading a story in there about a fire that you had in the middle 60's. You reopened two or three days later. Could you tell us about that story?

**Cathy**

I've had two fires. I've always thought of myself as a two-restaurant operator. I opened up the second one back in 1951. Ten years later, I wished I just had one restaurant to concentrate on rather than dividing my time between the two. The good Lord took care of that for me. One of my restaurants burned to the ground. Then, I just had one left to look after. That gave me an opportunity to develop Chick-Fil-A. But, getting back to the fire that we had in my original restaurant. It happened on a Saturday afternoon. The deep-fat fryer caught fire. My experience told me to get back in business as quickly as possible. I remember one of the employees wanted to know how she could go about getting unemployment while we were under construction. I said, "We are going to be open Monday morning." She said, "No way." The place had to be re-wired, repainted, and the ceiling had fallen out. All repairs were done between 4:00 on Saturday afternoon and 5:00 Monday morning. The building was still smoking, but we were back in business. People came in Monday morning and said, "Oh, you painted the place." I had the support of all my employees, plus friends and neighbors who came and helped clean up and repair. It was a miracle in itself that we were able to pull that off in such a short time. But it proves you can do anything when you make up your mind that's what you're going to do. We had something like 50 people helping us out. We pulled off a miracle getting opened back up in such a short time.

**Wright**

You know, Mr. Cathy, it's reported that your "closed on Sunday" policy cost you $100 million in sales each year. Someone asked me what I had planned today, I said, "Well, I'm going to talk to Truett Cathy, the president and founder of Chick-Fil-A." And they said, "Oh that's the man that closes on Sunday." I said, "Yeah, and it costs him $100 million." They said, "Well, at first I though he was a nice man. Now I know just how nice he is." In addition, your philanthropic work and high morals is more evidence to your commitment in helping others and deep faith in God. What do you think the United States would look like if more businesses used God-driven principles to drive their companies?

**Cathy**

I had the opportunity to testify in Washington a few months ago. I said, "You know, I see no opposition to biblical principles and good business practice, because biblical principles work. There is a lot written in the Bible about how to please the customer, please the employees, how the employees should respond to the employer; how to treat customers with kindness and a serving spirit, and do unto others as you would have them do unto you. All these principles are basic. In my testimony in Washington, they were having an investigation on business ethics. My statement to them was that there's no such thing as business ethics. It's personal ethics. A business in itself does not fail nor does it succeed. People ask me, "Do you have to be Christian to work at Chick-Fil-A?" And I said, "No, not at all. That's a personal relationship that you have with the Lord, but we ask you to respect the people that you work for."

It's like the guy that was giving testimony that he was a graduate from the Naval Academy, and said throughout the course of the Navy he was always taught that if you have a sinking ship, the captain is the last one to leave. I feel the same way about a CEO in a business. If you see trouble, it's not the time for them to cash in the chips and leave the burdens to somebody else. Things like this are damaging to the whole nation. The economy has been depressed because of the conduct and lack of competence that we've had in our business leaders. People ask me, "Why don't you go public?" I say, "Well, number one, I'm afraid I'll lose my job, and secondly, if I had someone buy stock in my company, I would have to give it to them to make sure that their investment was safe and they were paid proper dividends." In the beginning everything I had depended on the success of Chick-Fil-A. Being in business as long as I have, I have established a relationship with banks where I could borrow the money I needed or wanted to grow at the pace I wanted to grow. I still go back to the importance of establishing a good name for yourself, and protecting your name. I testified in Washington that I use my theme line after my name with Proverbs 22:1. A good name is rather to be chosen than great riches. The longer I live, the more I realize the importance of maintaining a good name and a good reputation. Personal name as well as your business name. It's important that we do things right each and every time, not just sometimes.

**Wright**

What a great conversation! I really want to thank you for taking this much time. I know how busy you are, and I really appreciate the time that you have spent with me here today.

**Cathy**

Thank you.

**Wright**

And I would like to close our conversation out by reading something that was written about you, if you don't mind. These words were written by Jeanette, a lady that you have been married to for more than 50 years.

She says, "Two words come to mind when describing Truett. Consistency and generosity. Whether he is at home or at the office at Chick-Fil-A restaurants, at a formal event, or on vacation, Truett is genuine through and through. He never puts up a front for anybody, and he is always looking for an opportunity to help someone else, especially children. Whenever he sees a hurting child, he reaches out putting their needs before his needs, even if it means rearranging his own plans." What a great thing for your wife to say!

**Cathy**

Well, I appreciate that.

**Wright**

She must be a fine lady.

**Cathy**

Well, she has to be, David. She has to be a fine one to put up with me. I know that she has made sacrifices. I've tried to make it up to her in many ways. My first restaurant was called the Dwarf Grill and she used to dress up the kids when they were three or four years old like little dwarfs, and they would have this little jingle that they would sing to the customers when their daddy had to work late. I have a lot of contact with my family. We have a family that will support you in what you're doing and will pray together. We really don't have any problems that doesn't have a solution to it.

**Wright**

You are indeed a fortunate man, and I really do appreciate you taking this time with me.

**Cathy**

Well, it was my pleasure.

## About the Author

S. Truett Cathy, founder and Chairman of Chick-fil-A, Inc., is a remarkable individual and highly successful businessman. With more than 1,000 restaurants in 36 states, and with annual sales of over $1 billion, S. Truett Cathy has taken Chick-fil-A from it's humble beginnings in Greenbriar Shopping Center in Atlanta, to the top of the fast food industry.

**S. Truett Cathy**

Chick-fil-A

5200 Buffington Road

Atlanta, GA 30349-2998

404.765.8132

# Chapter 18

## DR. LARRY DUGAN

## THE INTERVIEW

**David E. Wright (Wright)**

Today we are talking to Larry Dugan. Larry Dugan, Ph.D., is a licensed psychologist in the state of Michigan who has been in practice for 30 years. Dr. Dugan has held faculty positions at the University of Michigan, Eastern Michigan University, and Grand Valley State University. He is a Diplomate of the American Board of Psychological Examiners, The American College of Forensic Examiners, and The American Board of Disability Analysts and a member of The American Psychological Association. He is a motivational speaker, a member of the National Speakers Association and the International Speakers Network. In addition, he has been awarded a Silver Cup as a Distinguished Poet by the International Society of Poets.

In 1970, while a graduate student, Larry directed the research arm of the Leadership Development Program at the University of Michigan. Between 1970 and 1972 he was a guest lecturer at George Washington University, teaching problem solving and leadership to officers assigned to the Pentagon. Between 1973 and 1977, he led a

Mobile Consulting Team from the University of Michigan through a six-state area, providing training and technical support to training centers and non-profit organizations. After graduating from the University of Michigan, Larry established himself in West Michigan and has served companies including McGraw-Hill (Electronic Information Division), Haworth, and the Institute for Business Design as well as numerous small businesses. He serves as a consultant to local industry and labor organizations in leadership training and selection.

Over the past twenty years, Larry has established himself as a dynamic and memorable speaker on the subjects of Leadership Characteristics, Stress Management, Creativity and Team-Building. His first book, *The Seven Principles of Effective Workplaces: A Handbook for Management and Labor*, will be available in the fall of 2003 in e-book format. His second book, entitled, *3—2—1 Lead!* is scheduled for release in December 2003. Welcome, Dr. Dugan.

**Larry Dugan (Dugan)**
Thank you for your kind introduction.

**Wright**
You're welcome. Tell me, why are there so many books written about Success?

**Dugan**
Because people buy them.

**Wright**
Okay, why do so many people buy books about Success?

**Dugan**
To become more successful themselves.

**Wright**
You know, it's funny you say that. I have been reading leadership books and books on success now since starting back around 1969. I have found that when I visit my friends, those who are successful, there are more success books on their bookshelves than are on the people who are not so successful. So, does success breed success?

**Dugan**

Absolutely. Success breeds Success. Visit a great chef; you will see hundreds of books about food and cooking. Visit a personal trainer; it's books on physiology and exercise. Visit successful people, you will see books on Success. Successful people *work* to enhance Success. Success is a passion. They read about Success. They talk about Success. They study Success to learn more about it. Having success books around reminds them of their commitment to succeed.

Last week I visited a client who is the president of a manufacturing company. On the bookshelf in his office were ten books about manufacturing and twenty-two books about Success. That told me something. He knew his true business was Success. Manufacturing is only the means he used to achieve that end.

**Wright**

So, how do we start to talk about Success?

**Dugan**

By defining Success—which may not be as easy as you think. Supreme Court Justice Potter Stewart once stated, "I may not be able to define pornography, but I know it when I see it." Each of us thinks we know Success *when we see it*. You and I may speak about Success, as though we both have the same definition in mind when, in actuality, each of us may have a different definition in mind. In many ways, we are akin to the blind men trying to describe an elephant. One of them puts his hand on the massive body and declares, "Indeed, the elephant is very much like a wall." A second one wraps his arms around the leg of the elephant and affirms, "Ridiculous, the elephant is not like a wall at all. To me it appears more like a tree." The third blind man grasps the trunk of the elephant in his hand and says, "Oh, my brothers, for you I have no hope. This elephant is not a wall or a tree, it's more like a rope."

According to the dictionary, the word "success" derives from the Latin word *succedere* meaning "to come out from under." This leads to defining Success as getting away from a burden, which I do not find very appealing. I would much rather emphasize a more positive element of Success.

**Wright**

I was raised up with the definition of success from a company down in Texas starting back in the mid 70's. That definition was

"Success is a realization of your own personal, worthwhile, predetermined goal." I worked with that for a long, long time.

**Dugan**

That approach leads to defining Success as "achieving the desired result." That is too broad a definition for my taste. Besides, it omits what I consider to be *the* critical component of success.

**Wright**

So how do *you* define Success?

**Dugan**

My definition of Success is: **Success is the internalized experience of enjoying one's state in life**.

**Wright**

It's funny you should say that. As I told you, the definition I learned was "Success is a realization of your own personal, worthwhile, predetermined goal." Nothing in that definition said anything about being happy or enjoyment. No matter how long I worked with that definition, I didn't feel very good. So, goal setting got to be a task that I mostly failed at.

**Dugan**

I disagree. You didn't fail. Your definition was inaccurate. Your experience proves the point I make. Success demands more than goal setting and attaining. Let me take it one step further.

**Wright**

Okay.

**Dugan**

To help us narrow in on a definition of success, let's start by comparing different groups of people: Zig Ziglar, Tony Robbins, Tiger Woods, Michael Jordan, Muhammad Ali, B.B. King, Johnny Carson and Jay Leno. Most Americans accept that these individuals are successful.

What about Mike Tyson, Robert Blake, O.J. Simpson, Martha Stewart and the executives from Enron, Arthur Andersen, Global Crossings and WorldCom? Are they in the same category as the people in the first group? Are they successful? How about Marilyn Monroe, Freddie Prinze, Karen Carpenter and Richard Cory? How do they compare to the people in the first group? Were they successful?

Not to me. Even though both groups of people are public figures and may have lots of money, I assert that those in the first group are successful and those in the second group are not.

What about people who are not household names? Consider the hundreds of thousands of business people, performing artists, athletes, schoolteachers, medical personnel, public safety officers, government workers and people in the forty thousand other careers who are lesser known? Are they successful?

If the answer is yes, who determines whether they are successful? What do they have in common with Zig Ziglar and the people in the first group and what sets them apart from Robert Blake, O.J. Simpson, Marilyn Monroe and those in the second group? How do we establish criteria that include all successful people and exclude those who only appear successful? To do so we must identify the *core* elements that constitute Success and then determine whether people do or do not possess those core elements. When we define Success as *"the internalized experience of enjoying one's state in life"*, we emphasize the core elements that are definable and observable.

One of the most successful people I know is my brother-in-law Vincent <u>Gagliardi</u>. To be more precise, two of the most successful people I know are Vinny and his wife Susan. Vinny was a school counselor for the New Haven Public Schools and Susan a school nurse. They live directly across the street from the New Haven airport in a 1400 square foot home. They raised six children in that home. For most of the years I knew them Susan and Vinny didn't have many material things—and never seemed to notice. Despite their struggles, they never missed a family function, even when it meant piling the kids into a used, beat-up old Plymouth station wagon and driving 700 miles. I have never met people with more joy. I have never met people more respected and accepted. Susan and Vinny—and their children—are *the defining examples* of Success. They clarify why we need to define Success in such a manner as to discern mere tangential aspects of Success from core elements of Success. **Success is the internalized experience of enjoying one's state in life.**

Let's analyze this definition. First, when I say internalized, I mean that success is something *we* literally *make* our own. As you know, the definition of character is what somebody does when no one is watching. Well, that means that a person has *internalized* certain values—he or she has made those values his or her own—no matter what anyone else in the world thinks. So when I state that Success is an internalized experience, I mean Success is not a value or experience someone else defines for us. Each of us decides what Success is—for ourselves. It follows that we have to let others decide what Success is for them.

When Success is internalized, it dictates action. In more common parlance, "You can 'talk the talk' but to be successful you have to 'walk the walk'!" Successful people live in accordance with whatever definition of Success they have created. I reiterate. This implies that we will always see certain behaviors in truly successful behavior and never see other behaviors.

Second, Success is an experience. To paraphrase Gertrude Stein, experience is experience is experience. Right now I could describe a warm chocolate cookie fresh out of the oven. I could speak of how warm the dough was, how the semi-sweet morsels melted into warm dough, how the combination of flavors brought me exquisite pleasure and how it felt to wash it down with icy cold milk. No matter how good my description, it would in no way approach the experience of you biting into that cookie and drinking milk with it. Success, by definition, must be experienced.

Next, we have "enjoying." Notice that this word comes in the exact middle of the definition—the internalized experience of one's state in life. Joy, to me, is the distinguishing feature of true success. Look at the groups of people I cited above. The difference between a Michael Jordan and an O J Simpson, between a Muhammad Ali and a Mike Tyson, between any other pairs of people you want to create from the above list or from your own, is the degree of enjoyment that each successful person manifested as compared to his counterpart.

How do we measure someone else's joy? People who are enjoying life do not harm other people. People who have joy do not sexually assault other people. People who enjoy life do not need to be greedy or inflate the value of merchandise in order to line their own pockets. They do not need to use drugs or alcohol to excess, they do not need to put others down and they do not need to *act* as though they are superior. Joy is the quality that separates those who *are* truly successful from those who only *seem* successful. The final part of the definition is "with one's state in life."

Life changes. As Heraclitus expressed it, "We never step into the same stream." Our definition must reflect the reality that life changes, situations change and people change. People can feel successful at one era and not another. Some people feel successful at thirty-five and not at forty-five or vice versa. This implies that success is an evolutionary process, *not only capable of constantly changing, but—by the very nature of its' being—constantly changing.*

Think about Paul Newman, Michael Jordan, Rosey Grier and Alex Karras. They evolved into success in a number of careers. Gil Morgan was a successful ophthalmologist who became a pro golfer. I have a friend who ran a successful business until he was in his later 40's. Then he became a priest. The experience of enjoyment must be with one's state in life—and states in life are subject to change.

So, as you and I speak about Success—and those examples of what I consider to be unsuccessful people—understand my definition: **Success is the internalized experience of enjoying one's state in life.**

By the way, I use an upper case S in this chapter—to signify that we are working from a very specific definition of Success.

**Wright**

Let me make sure I understand you. You consider enjoying life as the prime determinant of Success?

**Dugan**

No. I consider enjoying life the *prime result* of Success, not as *the determinant* of Success. There's a scriptural phrase that states, "By their fruit you will know them". So it is with Success. Successful people enjoy life. Therefore, when people are successful, we will see joy. More often, we work backwards; that is to say, we see the fruits of the success and infer the success. When we see joyful people, we know they are successful. That is how we discern those who *are* successful from those who merely *appear* successful. Those in the second category lack joy. How do we know they lack joy? They tell us by how they behave. Successful people do not engage in certain behaviors.

**Wright**

But they may consider themselves successful.

**Dugan**

They may consider themselves successful. Others may tell them they are successful. Their behavior states otherwise. Enjoying life means different things to different people. For some people enjoying life may mean being in a laboratory twenty hours a day, studying life forms under a microscope; for others, being on the golf course; for others, speaking in front of an audience brings joy, while for others gardening is joyful. Joy is the result of Success. Whatever that person does, the joy reflects his Success. If we see the joy, we can infer the Success.

The *determinants* of Success, on the other hand, lay within us.

## Wright

You make the distinction between being successful and appearing successful. I have looked at some people down through my life and thought, "Boy, if you only liked yourself as much as I like you." I don't understand why people can put themselves down so much. It is difficult to understand why people don't feel the success that they have. When I think of someone like Marilyn Monroe, I say to myself, "If I looked like that, with all that success, I'd be happy." What you are telling me is that she appeared successful but was not truly successful.

## Dugan

Correct. However successful she appeared, she did not show joy. Whether a person is rich and famous or of very modest means and unknown except to a few, this definition of Success reflects reality. Think about the individuals who appear successful but whose behavior leads me to question whether they felt truly successful. In accepting this distinction, we accept that *certain behaviors are inconsistent with joy*, that is to say, joyful people will not engage in certain behaviors. And on the more positive and constructive side, we always—and I rarely use that word—find certain behaviors inextricably intertwined with joy. So as you and I discuss Success, we can identify the behaviors that signal joy and those that indicate the lack of joy.

## Wright

So now tell us what—in your opinion—are the determinants of success? You said, and I quote, "The determinants of Success, on the other hand, lay within us." Given your definition of Success, **"The internalized experience of enjoyment with one's state in life."** what are the determinants of Success?

## Dugan

I thought you'd never ask.

**Wright**

We had to lay the groundwork, didn't we?

**Dugan**

Indubitably. I am going to reemphasize that my conceptualization of Success is but one of many available. John Wooden has listed fifteen characteristics of Success and Dr. Wayne Dyer has his ten principles? I am a little more simple-minded so I only have five principles.

**Wright**

Five is easier to remember than fifteen.

**Dugan**

I always tell people to keep it simple so I try to follow my own counsel.

**Wright**

So tell me about your five determinants.

**Dugan**

The five determinants I have discovered in every successful person are five action habits that direct how successfully people behave. They are evident before those people achieve recognition—if they ever do achieve recognition—and they continue to *exist following* the achieving of recognition. Successful people who do not achieve fame show the same traits.

These five traits are constant. They will be evident in every person who is truly successful. They will not be present in those who only appear successful. I refer to them as the Keys to Success since they are actions in the control of the individual. Taking these steps will inevitable lead to success. Hence, each is stated as a one-word command.

### Key #1: Appreciate.

Watch the Oscars. Watch the Golden Globes. Listen as award winner after award winner stands in front of seventy million or more people and gives accolades to others—sometimes having to be stopped because they are speaking too long and mentioning too many people.

Why do they do that? It is their achievement that led to the award? Or is it theirs alone? Why do they do that? Because they realize that though they are being recognized, there are 50 to 500 other people involved in their success. These individuals know their success is a result of teamwork and they are not achieving their success alone. What does that tell us? They Appreciate. The successful souls I have known, heard of, or read about *Appreciate*. They appreciate their talents. They appreciate opportunities given them. They appreciate the people they meet along their path. They appreciate the recognition that evolves from their talents. They appreciate those who appreciate them. They acknowledge their talents not as "entitlements" but as gifts that bring with them a responsibility. They view themselves not as set above others but as needing to relate to others. They appreciate and acknowledge the role of mentors in their lives, be those mentors family members, teachers, coaches or current gurus.

To me appreciate *implies true humility* balanced by healthy pride. Successful people have healthy pride in what they can do and humility in recognizing that they started off blessed with gifts. Appreciate signifies that they utilized their gifts and worked at enhancing them. Appreciate implies putting oneself in perspective. The very notion of being appreciative has to do with the core relation one has with oneself. It is narcissistic to be unappreciative. It is self indulgent to say, "I'm entitled to this. I deserve this." Such a stance *denies reality*. When people are truly successful they recognize all those who contributed to their Success. Successful people appreciate. And they verbalize that appreciation every day. Just as there are certain behaviors consistent with the command Appreciate, there are other behaviors inconsistent with being appreciative. Feeling entitled, expecting special favors or waivers and feeling superior to others all are inconsistent with being appreciative. Abusing others (in any fashion), insulting others, or cheating others (either of money or of the recognition that is their due) are inconsistent with being appreciative. Any behavior that signals that a person does not appreciate tells me that that person is not truly successful.

One recent example regarding appreciation is David Letterman—before surgery and after surgery. Prior to surgery—by reports from others and his own admission—Letterman comported himself in a certain manner. Following surgery, he changed. During one show, he introduced the entire medical team who had taken care of him, singling out a particular nurse. By report, on another occasion he was even thanking the guy who swept the floors, realizing that someone made it his business to keep the floors clean for him. From merely appearing successful, Dave Letterman moved to being successful.

## Key #2: Encourage

Encourage. So often we hear that one of the keys to being success-ful is being positive. To me, Encourage takes it further than just be-ing positive. Encourage means "to give heart to." Encourage implies that we take our enthusiasm and energy and give it to others. En-courage signifies that we have more than self-interest at heart.

Successful people encourage others. They encourage others to pur-sue Success. They encourage others to be their best. They encourage others in every conceivable manner. John Wooden summarizes it best. Look at everyone as having unlimited potential, then encourage them to fulfill that potential. Make it *your job* to bring out the genius in everyone you encounter. Tell others to pursue their dreams. Tell them they will be successful.

Just as successful people do not start Appreciating what they have and how others have helped them after they achieving recognition, successful people are positive and encourage others regardless of their own status. Encouraging others demands that we have passion for what we do. Encouraging others demands being positive. Encour-aging others is a natural extension of our Appreciation for those who have encouraged and worked with us.

What do we not see in successful people? Successful people do not need to be negative. They NEVER EVER need to put other people down. The opposite, therefore, is true. A person who denigrates the efforts, talents or attributes of another will never be truly success-ful—by the very essence of the definition of Success. Successful people encourage others. Johnny Carson was noted for having helped over 250 people get started in show business, including Roseanne and Steve Martin.

## Key #3: Initiate

In his book, *The Seven Habits of Highly Effective People*, Steven Covey makes the first habit of success "Be Proactive." I like Covey's word "proactive"—even though it's not a word found in the dictionary; maybe I like it *because* it's not in the dictionary. However, to me, be-ing proactive—or initiate—ranks third. Taking action without being appreciative and without encouraging others can lead to becoming self-indulgent. Appreciating and Encouraging—as internal habits—precede taking action.

By the same token, Appreciating and Encouraging others are meaningless without Initiating. Successful people Initiate. They take the first step. When I think of the command to Initiate, I think of the Nike commercial and smile. Three words say it all. *Just do it.*

Successful people Initiate—often. They do what needs to get done. They act to change their world. In Bob Nelson's book, *Please, Don't Just Do What I Ask, Do What Needs To Get Done,* he tells employers to tell employees: Initiate.

Initiating implies *taking responsibility.* When we initiate, we assert, "I take responsibility for what I do, I take responsibility for changing what is around me." Responsibility is the central pillar of Success. If we do not take action, how can we succeed? How can we take action unless we place on ourselves the responsibility for changing ourselves and the world around us?

There is a corollary here as well. Because successful people take responsibility, they do not complain, whine or rationalize. Successful people may allow themselves a human moment of doubting or a brief pity party. Then they regroup and act. Because successful people take responsibility, they do not blame others or God or life circumstance for whatever befalls them. Successful people look in the mirror when they want to point the finger somewhere.

**Key #4: Overcome**

Successful people Overcome. They Overcome barriers and obstacles. They Overcome closed thinking. They Overcome objections from those who say it can't be done—or that they are not the one to do it. They Overcome their own fears, such as being ridiculed or losing a reputation. They Overcome the temptation to blame luck or fate when they do not succeed. They Overcome the temptation to remain humble once they have achieved their goals. Successful people Overcome.

Success demands that people overcome every obstacle they face. All too often just as one obstacle is out of the way, another materializes. Whoever said "Obstacles are those grotesque things we see when we take our eyes off our goals" knew of what he was speaking.

Successful people Overcome. They persevere. They persist. Edison once remarked that he had never failed or had a failed experiment. Instead, he drolly remarked, he had had one thousand twenty nine successful experiments in determining what did not make for a workable light bulb. Temporary setbacks disturb successful people only for a little while. Then they work harder to Overcome.

Theodore Geusel (better known as Doctor Seuss) had had his first manuscript rejected thirty-seven times when he let a neighbor—who happened to be the spouse of an editor—read the manuscript. The rest is history. What would have happened if he had not persisted?

Successful people Overcome. They overcome everything—including that despicable inner voice that tries to tell them they will not overcome. The act of overcoming every obstacle is a measure of belief in oneself and one's ideas that reflect the determination needed to be successful.

What is the opposite of overcoming? Quitting. Blaming others for failure. Seeking security. Creating mindless rules for others to follow. Discouraging others.

**Key #5: Understand**

Successful people Understand. They Understand their business at the deepest levels. They Understand that they have to keep increasing their Understanding. They Understand themselves. Dr. Phil says:" Either you get it or you don't". Strategy: Be one of those who gets it. My way of saying that is: Understand. Understand *everything*. When successful people do not understand everything, they work harder so they will.

Successful people strive to understand every aspect of their businesses at the deepest levels. They are not satisfied with pat answers or pat approaches. They drive themselves to know new developments. They want the latest knowledge whether it has to do with machinery or flowers or new styles. They continue to expand not just their knowledge, but also their understanding of how that knowledge relates to other knowledge. They strive to create new knowledge, new techniques, and new ideas. Why? To become better. Successful people are never satisfied. They do not seek to sit back content with the status quo.

Above and beyond understanding their business and the marketplace, successful people strive to understand themselves. They want to know what makes them tick. They are as inquisitive about themselves as they are about their business. They follow the prescription at the Delphic Oracle (c. 650 BC) *Know Thyself*. To this end successful people pursue psychological evaluations, personal coaching and group engagement.

The opposite of understanding is ignorance. Those who do not understand seek only the profit motive and *their* betterment, not the betterment of their businesses and their employees. Those who do not understand fail to contribute to their communities, their organizations or their professions. Those who do not understand are intolerant and judgmental. They justify their behaviors in a flurry of words and numbers.

**To summarize:**

Success is the internalized experience of enjoying one's state in life.

Joy is the direct result of true Success. The five personal attributes that determine success are action-based behaviors: Appreciate—Encourage—Initiate—Overcome—Understand. Those are in evidence prior to and follow whatever recognition Success brings. What is more important: *We control how much we exercise these attributes*, and thus how much Success we experience.

**Wright**

Wow. What great concepts and what a great summary. We have reached the end of our time. It seems to me that to Appreciate, to be Encouraging, to Initiate, to Overcome and to Understand, just doing those five things would improve anyone's life, Success notwithstanding. What a great model, Larry!

**Dugan**

Thank you.

**Wright**

I appreciate the time you have spent with me today and I look forward to doing it again.

**Dugan**

Thank you. I do, as well.

**Wright**

Today we have been talking to Larry Dugan, Ph.D. He is a licensed psychologist, and lives in the state of Michigan. He's been in practice for 30 years, and as we have found out today, knows much about his subject. Thank you so much, Larry for being with me.

**Dugan**

You are most welcome.

## About The Author

Larry describes himself as "Passion and Personality with a Ph.D." As Director of Precision Personality Plus, he helps organizations save money by selecting and retaining high quality employees. His consulting emphasizes Developing Leadership at all levels, Team Building and Effective Work Environments. In all his work, Larry emphasizes Positive Success Thinking. ***Since 85% of all workplace problems result from personality problems,*** Larry works with companies to find the precise traits needed for each key position.

**Dr. Larry Dugan**
Personality & Passion With A Ph.D.
3934 Cascade Road, Suite B
Grand Rapids, MI 49546-4128
Phone: 616.954.0558
Fax: 616.954.2878
Email: Duganize@aol.com